FALLING THROUGH THE EARTH

Danielle Trussoni grew up and lives in LaCrosse,
Wisconsin, and is a graduate of the University
of Wisconsin and the Iowa Writers' Workshop.

Danielle Trussoni

FALLING THROUGH THE EARTH

A Memoir

PICADOR

First published 2006 by Henry Holt and Company, LLC
New York, New York

First published in Great Britain 2006 by Picador

First published in paperback 2007 by Picador
an imprint of Pan Macmillan Ltd
Pan Macmillan, 20 New Wharf Road, London N1 9RR
Basingstoke and Oxford
Associated companies throughout the world
www.panmacmillan.com

ISBN 978-0-330-44365-4

9 8 7 6 5 4 3 2 1

A CIP catalogue record for this book is available from
the British Library.

Typeset by Intype London Ltd
Printed and bound in Great Britain by
Mackays of Chatham plc, Chatham, Kent

Visit www.panmacmillan.com to read more about all our books
and to buy them. You will also find features, author interviews and
news of any author events, and you can sign up for e-newsletters
so that you're always first to hear about our new releases.

For you, Dad
With love, respect, and all that
emotional hogwash

Presently she began again. "I wonder if I shall fall right *through* the earth! How funny it'll seem to come out among the people who walk with their heads downwards!"

—*Alice's Adventures Under Ground*
Lewis Carroll

note to the reader

Although some of my father's Vietnam stories were told to me in passing, years ago, many of them were also recorded in taped interviews that I conducted with him. I have reproduced these stories as accurately as possible. In order to spare the feelings of acquaintances, I have changed the names and physical characteristics of minor characters. The names of major characters have not been changed.

Tom Mangold and John Penycate's *The Tunnels of Cu Chi* provided much of the background information about the tunnels and tunnel rats.

FALLING THROUGH THE EARTH

prologue

The guide knelt before the tunnel entrance. Old, energetic, and clearly happy with his job, he smiled as he listed
the booby traps he had planted to kill American soldiers: the
punji sticks and scorpions rigged into bamboo cages, the
explosives packed in Coke cans. The Vietcong, he said,
made weapons from whatever they could find, old C-ration
tins or beer bottles. Matériel was never a problem. The
Americans left a lot of trash behind.

Hundreds of entrances survived the war. This one—much
wider than the wartime tunnels—had probably been expanded to accommodate Western-sized tourists. The guide
motioned for us to kneel next to him, above the gaping hole
in the earth. We formed a semicircle, knees upon the hot
sun-baked clay, watching him lower himself into the ground,
demonstrating various styles of entry. He went in feet first,
then headfirst, grinning all the while. I got the feeling he
would have come to that patch of jungle even if tourists did
not. Maybe the tunnels were a kind of haven, a place to
retire to. A Vietcong's own private Florida.

My father volunteered to be a tunnel rat in 1968. The

job consisted of crawling through webs of tunnels and rooms searching for men like my tour guide, Vietnamese guerrillas hiding out underground. Tunnel exploration was considered one of the most dangerous assignments in Vietnam. The distinction set my father apart from his platoon, bumping him into the Hazardous Duty pay grade and increasing his chances of dying tenfold. Tunneling was a suicide mission, but he chose it. He saw men die underground, and yet he kept going down. It takes that kind of person—two parts stubborn, one part insane—to fight in a tunnel. Dad fit the bill. Only a man determined to see the worst that war had to offer—and to beat it—would volunteer to be a tunnel rat.

Tunneling, my father always said, was the scariest thing on earth. As I stood above the entrance, I knew he was right. I used to think Dad was all balls and no brains, a man caught up in being a cowboy. But perhaps his attraction to the tunnels was more than bravado. Maybe my father looked into the tunnels and saw what I did: a mystery, a test, a challenge hard to walk away from. Perhaps the tunnels called to him with the same rich voice I heard thirty years later, dangerous and seductive. I crouched before the entrance. A jittery adrenaline-rich sensation filled my stomach, and I knew I wanted to go down. I wanted to feel the fear, the heat, the thrill of making it through. At heart, I was my father's daughter.

I followed the guide into the tunnel. A pool of sunlight fell from the entrance shaft and expanded around me, becoming darker by degrees. The tunnel was just as I imagined it would be, a shock of darkness that gave way to a narrow communication shaft. The old man crawled ahead but turned back when he realized that I was not close behind. In the weak light I saw his face, inches from mine. As our eyes locked, I imagined a knife in his hand, its cool blade brushing my neck. *Follow me*, he gestured, and crawled off again, ahead. I let my eyes adjust to the dark and pushed forward.

As I crawled deeper, the tunnel narrowed. The heat thickened; the air thinned. My T-shirt clung to my skin. Deeper, deeper we went. I paused, to scratch a wall with my fingernails, a sensation that sent shivers up my spine, a spidery prickle that asked, *What in the hell are you doing here?* I breathed, slowly. Suddenly, I was alone. Where had the man gone? I saw nothing but dark in front of me, nothing but dark behind. I moved my hand, my knee, my other hand, my other knee, forward, going deeper and deeper.

one

Winter of '85, and we were on the run.

Dad veered the truck into an alley, cut across a parking lot, and merged with traffic running alongside the frozen Mississippi. "Cops don't come down this road," he said, checking the rearview mirror. "If they're here, it's because they followed us." My father was prone to paranoia, but the police were real. We'd been picked up twice for drunk driving that year. After the last arrest, he'd lost his license. We tried to keep a low profile, but the cops knew our truck and where we lived—*Those sons-of-bitches got nothing to do but bother hardworking taxpayers*. Faster, faster we drove. If they caught us again, Dad would go to jail.

Streets expanded before us, eerie and lonesome. Salt and steel-link tire chains had beaten the snow thin. Pawnshops and motels and tattoo parlors fell away as we passed. I unrolled my window. The city was cold and sharp-angled, as if emerging from a block of ice. I couldn't help but wish for spring. If it were warm, we could escape on a riverboat. We could float past Illinois and Missouri, down south to Louisiana. But it was deep winter, the river frozen, and the only hope for a quick getaway was the ironwork bridge that scaled out to Minnesota. I stared at it as we drove past, my vision ribboning its girders. Dad looked over his shoulder, listening for sirens.

My father was running from the police, from his first ex-wife, his creditors, and his dreams. He was running from his second ex-wife (my mother), his illegitimate children, and his past. He was running from himself, and I was right there with him, an eleven-year-old accomplice to his evenings of escape. I had been at his side for the last year, since my mother divorced us. Mom kept the house and my younger sister and brother; Dad kept me. No matter how far or fast we ran, I was there. I was all he had left.

We slowed down before Roscoe's, Dad's favorite bar, and parked near a set of rusty snow-packed railroad tracks. The lot was dim, as if seen through a starlight scope. Bleak electrocuted trees tangled before the buildings' brick façades. A blue boxcar had been abandoned mid-line, a pretty stranded Christmas present, but it wouldn't be long before an engine hooked it and trolled the freight to a warehouse beyond the city limits. Wisconsin winters were fierce. Nothing was left in the cold for long.

Dad locked his truck and walked ahead. Like most tunnel rats, he was a small man—only five feet eight inches and a hundred and fifty pounds—but quick. Impatient by nature, he always moved fast. I tried to match his pace, jogging to keep up. A neon beer sign blinked, sending chills of pink over his face. As he turned his head to light a cigarette, I saw myself in his olive skin, the hint of haughtiness in his profile. His eyes were deep brown, his face thin. He had lost his hair in his twenties, just after returning from Vietnam, a premature baldness that was beginning to look natural only now, as he neared forty. The empty nickel-hard sky bowled overhead, framing my father in a background of gray. He looked at me, his smile boyish, and pulled the door to Roscoe's open. "After you, Danielle-my-belle."

Roscoe's Vogue Bar was a mouthful, an unchewable four syllables. Everyone who was anyone called my father's favorite tavern Roscoe's or The Vogue. I called it Roscoe's. Rigid in this preference, I made fun of those regulars who called it The Vogue, finding it hilarious, with a preteen's sense of ruthless snobbery, that the worst-dressed women in America hung out at a place named after a slick fashion magazine. When I felt contentious (which, at eleven, was all the time), I told the women parked on their bar stools that they were looking *very Vogue*. That afternoon I said, "Barb, those Wranglers are great. Very Vogue." Barb tipped her beer my way and said, "You look beautiful too, smart-ass."

And she was right: I looked fantastic. My father had picked me up from school, and I hadn't had time to change. My uniform was a starched navy-blue skirt, white cotton blouse, and a stiff-necked navy-blue blazer, an ensemble I hated. I'd dressed it up with red knee socks and Doc Martens. I'd smeared on glittery eye shadow and purple lip gloss. My ears had been pierced five times; I'd written lyrics from my favorite songs (by semi-obscure and hundred-percent-depressing British bands) on my arms with red ink. I told myself that I was a post-punk rebel ready to take on the world, and it was true: I was ready to have a go at everyone, single-handedly. If it weren't for my name, people might have thought that Catholic school had done strange things to me. As it was, everyone in town knew I was Dan Trussoni's girl. This pedigree explained a lot.

During happy hour, Roscoe's was crowded. Drinks were cheap and the jukebox plugged with quarters. The way I remember it, Roscoe's was always the same—the barroom was packed (Dad and I had to squeeze onto our stools), the music played too loud, and I was forever a child, quick on my feet and dull to the truth that my father, with all his speed, could never outrun the past.

Dad ordered a round of drinks—brandy and Coke for him, a cherry Coke for me. He stubbed out his cigarette in a black plastic ashtray and lit another. My father had spent most of his adult life (aside from his tour in Vietnam) laying bricks, and his hands proved it; they were tumescent and covered with scars. The knuckles were cracked, as if cement had dried in the creases of his skin, splitting it. Dad worked harder than anyone else I knew—twelve-hour days in the summer, sometimes fourteen. When I was little, I would wait for him to come home from work and run down the driveway, meeting his truck at a gallop. I was his tag-along daughter, his dark-haired namesake, the shadow girl chasing after him wanting love, love, love. He would throw his toolbox in the garage, slap me on the back, and hit the shower. I would lean my head against the bathroom door, pressing my ear to the wood. He had not showered yet that day, and as we sat at the bar I wanted to take a toothpick from the dispenser and pry the pieces of coagulated concrete from his cuticles. I wanted to free his fingerprints of dirt.

I watched him, assessing his mood. When Dad was in high spirits, he was the most charismatic guy in the place. His buddies would walk by, shake his hand, tell him a joke, and ask how business was going. Drinks would arrive, bought by women we'd never met before. He filled the room with his presence, wherever he went. But if my father was stuck thinking of my mother, he would be surly. He met my mother the year he came back from Vietnam, when he was wild and haunted. Maybe she liked that about him— how much he needed her. I've seen pictures of my parents taken the year I was born; they were holding hands and kissing, so in love it appeared nothing in the world could stop them. After Mom left, Dad became unrecognizable. He spent all his time at the bar, drinking from early afternoon until late in the night. When Dad got drunk, memories of Vietnam crept back on him. I never knew what had hurt him more, the war or my mother.

The drinks arrived as the jukebox came to life. Patsy Cline's soft voice filled the bar with sound. A row of taxidermy hung above the jukebox: a deer head, a beaver, and a sorry-looking turkey. My father sipped his brandy and Coke in silence, his gaze fixed on the turkey. After the second round, he squinted slightly, scanned the perimeter of the bar, tipping his Stetson to anyone who met his eye. Sometime between the third and fourth drink, he loosened up and began to talk. Not to me, exactly, although I was the only one listening. Dad didn't need me. He always went back to the war alone.

"Have I told you about the Vietcong prostitute and her mother?"

"No, Pop," I said, although I knew that he had.

"We were close to Cambodia, near the Black Virgin Mountain. We walked all day through the jungle, set up a perimeter, and the village girls hung around the concertina, watching as we dug in for the night. Smart little things, those girls were. They'd finish their work and then tell us they were giving the money to the Vietcong. We didn't care, though. They snuck around the concertina and into the perimeter all the time. This one slipped right into camp, slid under my poncho, and started doing her business. Usually, I would've just let her go about it, but I didn't have any cash, not even script, so I pushed her back. I said, *No money*. Them Vietnamese girls didn't know how to talk, but they knew the word *money* all right. The girl said, *No money, this love*, and went right on with what she was doing, which was fine by me. Who am I to argue with a free meal?"

"Not you," I said. By twelve, I thought I had seen and heard it all from Dad.

"*No money, this love*, the girl says, and that was that. It was near morning when we were done. She gets up to go and I see, by the perimeter, an old lady standing by. The girl's mother had been watching us, I guess. I feel creepy all of a sudden, like maybe I shouldn't be screwing her daughter for free. Sure enough, the girl starts asking for her money, making a big to-do. They'd probably planned it this way, because the old one starts in too, screeching like a duck about *money, money, money*. I didn't have a cent on me, so I took that girl and tossed her clear over the concertina, to her mama. The old lady got mad at that. She screamed louder, so I got my M-16 and pointed it right smack between her eyes. That shut her up quick. *This one is for love*, I said. *This one's for love.*"

Dad told a lot of war stories, but there were a few he always returned to. When he'd had too much to drink, he would start complaining about the police, or the price of gas, and suddenly he would plummet into the jungles of Vietnam. A shadow would fall over his face, obscuring him from me, and I knew he had disappeared into the past. If I reached for his hand, it was rough and cold. He was no longer there.

When Dad spoke, the bar became quiet. Vines slithered up the bar stools; tunnels opened at our feet. And Tommy Goodman, my father's tunnel-rat friend, a man I had learned to imagine from Dad's war stories, pulled up a seat next to us and rested his head on the glossy surface of the bar. *Glad you could make it*, I imagined myself saying. But Goodman and my father never paid attention to me. Before I knew it, they would be gone, two boys headed out to the war. I trailed behind, mopping up blood with cocktail napkins.

two

My sister was the raccoon girl. The half-moons below her eyes had gone black and green. The lids were purple and swollen, the veins reticulated like the petal of an iris. Kelly bruised easily—she had blond hair, blue eyes, and a china-plate complexion so different from my dark hair and eyes that people thought it astonishing we had the same parents. But Kell-belle was no wimp. Her black-and-blue eyes may have looked terrible, but she didn't complain. Still, Mom wouldn't take her to the grocery store with us. People might have thought we beat her silly.

Kelly had got banged up when she ran headfirst into the edge of the oak table in the dining room. We were playing tag and she tripped. Truthfully, I egged her on, teasing her, calling her names. *Come on, Kelly-belly! Come on, slowpoke!* I chased her through the living room and made her run fast and blind. She collapsed on the carpet, wailing. But this didn't hurt her spirit. Although her disposition was sweet and unassertive, she never gave up. Even as she ran down the driveway on her short too-white legs, her blond hair bouncing in its ponytail, she was determined to get me.

14

"Wait up, Nell! Wait! Wait!" she screamed.

When she saw I would not slow for her, that I'd ride our pink and yellow banana-seat bicycle all the way down the road, ringing the bell and skidding the training wheels on the gravel, she sat on the pavement, put her thumb in her mouth, and cried. I looked over my shoulder. There she sat, my roly-poly younger sister, raccoon eyes full of tears.

"Nell!" she whined, as I rode in a circle around her. "Come on. My turn. Don't be a bike hog."

I weighed my options. I could take the bike for another lap around the cul-de-sac or down the road past the snake pit. Kelly (who always knew what I was thinking) crossed her arms over her chest and jutted out her bottom lip, pouting.

Just then, Mom walked down the driveway to our red aluminum mailbox, wearing frayed jean shorts, a terry-cloth halter top, and wood-soled Dr. Scholl's sandals. She had woven her long black hair in a braid that fell down her back. Kelly and I stopped fighting, just to watch her. With her big dark eyes and tiny ballerina's body, she always looked younger than she was. It was something of a mystery, how she did it. When my grade school teacher, Mrs. Connery, asked how my mother—who at twenty-six looked all of sixteen—stayed so young, I rolled my eyes and replied (with TV-indoctrinated savvy), "Because she uses Oil of Olay!"

Mom sifted through the mail, separating bills from coupons. She managed the household as if it were a business. "Better watch that lip," she said to Kelly, whose bottom lip nearly touched her chin, "or a bird is going to poop on it."

Kelly sucked her lip under her teeth and looked into the sky, checking for birds.

Dad had been working on his truck in the driveway all afternoon. On weekends, he was awake and busy by six in the morning. By lunch, he had mowed the lawn, cleaned out the garage, and was well on his way to replacing a fan belt. A six-pack of beer sat on ice in a cooler, and the radio was turned loud on Elvis. Smokey, our collie, slept in the Ford's shadow. Dad never sat around shooting the shit on the weekends—there was always too much work to be done.

Mom flicked the radio off as she walked past. "Shhh," she said, giving him the exasperated *you-better-watch-yourself* look she gave us when we messed up. Dad was making too much noise. Matt, my baby brother, was in the house taking his nap.

Kelly was five, I was six—both of us too old for naps. Although we played at hurting each other, we were both as happy as we would ever be, cocooned in the world our parents had made us. We were too young to imagine our lives any different than they were on that lazy summer Sunday in 1980. We had no idea what was happening between our parents.

In a picture taken on their wedding day, my mother and father stood on the church steps in a faraway world. The colors of the photograph were slightly off and, in the way that Technicolor shades old movies, the two of them had a haunting, almost fairy-tale tint. He was wearing a blue-green suit with funny lapels and a red shirt, and his arm seemed protective around my mother's shoulders. Her dress was white, sleeveless, gathered at the bodice, creating an opales-

cent china-cup setting for her neck and shoulders. My
mother's cheekbones and forehead, the fine bones of her
face, were washed in light, and her black hair was tucked
behind her ears, flipping at the shoulders. She was grim-
acing, and my father was smiling, a hint of play in his eyes.
It was as if he'd just told a dirty joke, and she was trying not
to laugh. But anyone could see it wouldn't take much for
Dad to win her over. He looked, at that moment, as if he
could have charmed the pants off any woman in the world.

My mother once said the day had started as a rainy-gray,
lead-colored morning but changed just before the ceremony
into a golden, matrimony-perfect afternoon that seemed to
hold within it all the omens of a perfect future. Clear blue
stretched to the horizon. Sunlight slid off the waxy side
of maple leaves. If a marriage's future can be foretold by
an unending blue sky, then my parents should have been
together for eternity. They should have had an American
Dream life, a Washing-the-Car-Every-Sunday life. Nobody
could have imagined that things would turn out the way
they did.

"Gimme that bike!" Kelly said, making a grab for the
handlebars.

I braked, sending up a cloud of dust. "You'll have to wait
your turn, Raccoon Eyes."

"I'm not a raccoon!"

"Yes you are!"

"No I'm not!"

"Go look in the mirror."

Kelly thought this over, biting her fingernail. "You're so
mean."

17

I swerved the bike around her and pedaled away, thinking of something Dad liked to say: *I'm not mean, just honest.*

Dad mostly ignored us, unless we were causing trouble. Even then—especially then—he would look us over with half-concealed pride before telling us to behave. He'd warned us earlier about fighting over the bike, and when he closed the hood of the truck and walked down the driveway, to straighten things out, I knew we were in for it. Dad was wearing the usual—jeans kept on with a rawhide cowboy belt, and no shirt or shoes. The sun had browned his skin everywhere except for a few pale splotches on his back, where he got ripped up in the war, and a foot-long scar on his belly, a cross-hatched centipede of a scar from his ulcer operation. The scars stood out against his bronze skin, pink.

I parked the bike near Kelly and slid off. "Your turn," I said, shoving the handlebars at her. But Dad wasn't buying it. "Follow me, girls," he said, his jaw hard. He took the bicycle by the handlebars, picked it up with one hand, and carried it to the garage.

We stood around Dad, watching him dig through his toolbox for a monkey wrench. "I saw you riding, Danielle," he said. "You're pretty good."

He loosened his belt—unhinging the big brass buckle and slipping the tooth a notch—and crouched before the bike. The training wheels fell away with a few twists of the wrench. "Here," he said, turning the bike over to me. "Take her for a ride." Kelly's eyes sparkled as she met my gaze. She knew—as I steered the bike out to the driveway, holding the handles steady—she was going to see her big sister fall.

Although I was scared, I would never let Dad know it. I

was working hard to impress him with my big-girl behavior.
A couple of years before, I had blown my standing with him
by wetting my pants. Not once or twice but over and over
again. One minute, I was jumping rope or playing hop-
scotch, and the next I was standing in a puddle. Every time
this happened, I felt a searing sensation in my groin and an
overwhelming sense of embarrassment. When I went to my
mother, she would change my play clothes, confused by my
regression. As it turned out, I needed surgery to correct a
defect in my urinary tract, but we did not discover this for
many months. Dad would not allow me to see a doctor.
Every time I had an accident, he looked me over, angry and
disgusted. Dad believed in the power of complete and total
denial: Pretend what ails you does not exist, and it will
disappear. When my mother tried to tell him I might have a
physical problem, he snapped back, "The only problem with
her is laziness," a vice he set out to correct. "What in the
hell is wrong with you?" he asked me, his voice condescend-
ing, full of contempt. If I told him I couldn't help it, he got
furious. Even after Mom took me to the clinic, and a
specialist recommended surgery, Dad didn't believe there
was really anything wrong. He cleared his throat and spat on
the sidewalk. "The problem," he said, lighting a cigarette in
the hospital parking lot, "is all in her head."

I believed him. Not long after that, when I slid over a
nail embedded in a fireman's pole in the school playground,
slicing a four-inch gouge down my inner thigh, I did not
allow myself to react. Nauseated, dizzy with pain, I stood
by the jungle gym in a haze of heat. When blood bloomed
through my corduroy pants, expanding to my knee, a

teacher noticed and carried me inside, blood dripping in our wake. I did not cry when the principal examined the wound, which gaped so wide I saw bone, and I did not cry on the doctor's table. "Look at you, not a tear," the nurse said, as she administered a local anesthetic. The needle pricked the surface of purple skin and slid in, deep. Mom had squeezed my hand, saying, "That's my big girl."

The sidewalk was hot under my bare feet, so I walked fast—the bike in my grip—to the center of the driveway. Without training wheels, the bike felt wobbly, temperamental. "Don't get too big for your britches," Dad said, as I threw my leg over the bike. He walked alongside, holding me steady, allowing me to relax a little as I went forward, slow and clumsy, the metal ridges of the pedals pinching my feet. The mailbox was just ahead, and I focused on it, pushing the pedals, one after the other. Suddenly, I was alone. Dad had stopped walking behind me. When I looked back, he was far behind, standing with his hands on his hips, watching. Kelly was jumping up and down, clapping and catcalling. "Go, Nell!" she screamed. I smiled and waved, the big sister out to conquer the world, a gesture that destroyed my balance and sent me tumbling onto the blacktop, head first.

Back at the house, Dad wiped away the blood and cleaned the wound. He never could tolerate crying and gave me a look of warning as he poured the rubbing alcohol. My knee bubbled white and fizzy. "Stop all that carrying on," he said, watching me flinch. "I don't want to hear it."

*

DURING THOSE YEARS, WE LIVED AT THE EDGE OF A THICK oak and birch forest. I have never loved a place as much as I loved that one, and perhaps this is because the land was ours, bought by my parents when I was a baby. From the back porch of our house, I could see all that we held: a triad of low brontosaurus-back hills; a field of sage-stitched prairie grass streaked with Holsteins; a garden cultivated on a hill above the ranch-style house. Every rock and every tree for as far as I could see belonged to my family.

My father had built the house himself. One of my first memories was of a barrel-bellied concrete mixer rolling over a bog of mud to pour the basement. Dad lowered a metal tube into the ground, as the mixer's abdomen spun. Gray wet concrete oozed down onto the earth floor, wrinkling open like the skin of an elephant. Once the foundation set and the wooden skeleton had been erected, we paved the road to our house. Bulldozers and graders leveled off the land; a truck dropped chunks of steaming black asphalt; and a water-heavy drum roller smashed a smooth solid pathway through the wilderness. We named it Trussoni Court and erected a sign at the end of the street, the one vertical presence in the tangle of scrub grass and overgrown black-eyed Susans.

On summer afternoons, I rode that banana-seat bicycle over the hot smooth road to our sign, reading and rereading it. Part of me thought that Trussoni Court did not refer to the street at all but to my family, that we formed a royal seat among the birch trees. My father always said the best years of his life were spent there. After the divorce, he would talk about Trussoni Court as if it had been a paradise from which we had been expelled, our own forever-lost Eden. And although I remembered the bad times along with the good, over time I found myself remembering Trussoni Court that way, too.

Kelly and I shared a bedroom. We had two single beds with matching Winnie-the-Pooh sheets and comforters. Matt slept in a crib, in a room with plush blue carpet and wallpaper pattered with trains and airplanes. Our parents' bedroom was just down the hall. It had a warm medicinal scent, like chamomile or a baby after its nap. All my childhood, I loved that smell. I craved it. There was no word for it in my six-year-old mind, but I always thought of it as Safety. My parents' bedroom was the center of the world for me, a sanctuary from the monsters of my imagination.

When everyone had fallen asleep, I would try to sneak into their bed. Although my father didn't always rest easy—he sometimes woke two or three times a night and sat at the kitchen table, smoking cigarettes—I felt protected just being close to them.

As I remember it, the walls were washed with blue shadows. If I made it to the edge of the quilt, I had made it far—past the squeaky door, over the crick in the floor. Sometimes I tripped over a shoe or stepped on our cat, Tootsie. But that morning—it was July, and maple leaves brushed against the windowpane—everything went perfectly. I touched the foot of the bed and crawled over the quilt, between my sleeping parents, twisting myself a bit (my leg against my mother's hip, my cheek on the soft hair of my father's arm) so that I fit perfectly between them.

Dad and Mom did not sleep close to each other, and as their bed was king size, there was always enough room for me. When I was sure I hadn't woken them, I became very still, listening to them breathe. My mother's breathing was soft, kittenlike, barely audible. But my father, who slept on his back with his mouth open, breathed loud and noisy. He had circus-man lungs, huge and infinitely expandable. The air gushed down his windpipe and filled his chest, where it remained for five seconds, ten seconds, before he slowly expelled it, releasing the air as if he were filling a balloon, deliberately, intentionally, with a strong, slow pressure.

I imitated him, breathing as he breathed, exhaling as he exhaled. If I held my breath too long—as I had to do, to keep his pace—dizziness brushed over my senses. When I couldn't stand it any longer and felt my lungs would explode, I held out just a little more. I played a game of chicken with my father; I followed his lead. And I wondered (as I took a breath, forfeiting) how he did it. How had my father learned to live on so little air?

ONE AFTERNOON, WHEN THE SUN WAS HIGH IN THE SKY, mom went up to the garden to pick the ripe tomatoes, a wide wicker basket in her hand. Kelly—who was never far from Mom—rustled through the stalks of chapped sweet corn, while Matt played with Dad's trowels near the potatoes. Matt was two years old and loved to play in the mud. Once, Kelly and I force-fed him mud pies, spoon by spoon. He ate what we gave him and soon became sick and bloated and green. Mom drove us to a clinic in Onalaska—the closest town to Trussoni Court—in her green El Camino.

Below the garden, I sat on a lawn chair in my polka-dot swimming suit, raising one foot heavenward in the direction of the garden, toward my mother, feeling the heat of the sun on my legs. I was so slick with sun block that I slipped down the plastic bands of the chaise, until my butt fell into the hard brown grass. Although Mom was careful to water the garden every day, she neglected the lawn. It was brittle and thorny. I pulled myself from the grass, drawing my cinnamon-brown legs to me, wary. One afternoon a bull snake had found shade under my lawn chair. I had looked down and found a three-foot-long shiny black-splotched snake twisted around my purple radio. I screamed so hard Mom thought I'd been ambushed by a badger. She dragged a metal garbage can from the garage and lassoed the snake (and my radio) inside as I ran to the back porch, safe.

Earlier that day there had been a different kind of trouble. Mom got upset after a phone call from one of her friends. She took Dad out to the back porch and said, "How can I show my face in town again, when everyone knows what you do? You messed around when I was pregnant, and now this." Dad sauntered inside—he always seemed to strut when he was defending himself—took a beer bottle from the fridge, and opened it with his back teeth. "Look here," he said, wiping the sweat from his brow with a bright red cowboy bandanna. "If you believe Mary Monti and me got something going on, then you just bought a load of horse shit."

Dad ended up leaving in his truck. Mom walked through the house, silent and furious, picking up dirty socks and stained T-shirts, throwing them in a laundry basket. She hung the wash on the line mechanically, stabbing the clothespins over the shoulders of my sundresses. Later, after lunch, she took the checkbook and an envelope of receipts from a shoebox in the closet and tallied our weekly expenses, a procedure she called "balancing the books." Punching the numbers on our calculator with pure anger, she said, "We're over on groceries, over on electricity, over on entertainment." We knew that setting our finances in order was Mom's way of making herself feel better. When she went for the shoebox and calculator, we knew well enough to keep our distance.

Mom had been mad at Dad before. Some nights she would prepare big cookbook-inspired dinners, taking out her linen napkins and laying five place settings at our octagonal kitchen table. One night, after she had spent hours making Peking duck from a Chinese cookbook, she sat us down— pouring glasses of milk and cutting Matt's food into little pieces—and waited for Dad to come home. We ate, staying very quiet, waiting for headlight shadows to wobble up the kitchen cabinets. Mom wouldn't meet our eyes when we looked at her. *Eat, eat*, she said, but she left her own food untouched and checked her wristwatch every five minutes. Leaning her shoulder against Dad's empty chair, her long black hair curling around her shoulders, she seemed to grow smaller and smaller as the time passed. My mother had never looked so defeated.

When we finished and Mom had put Matt to sleep, she picked up the phone and called Frog Point, then The Nut Bush, and then Roscoe's. She asked to speak to my father and waited, twisting the phone cord around her long thin fingers. I remember the way she tapped her foot on the yellow linoleum floor, the tiny red pom-pom on the heel of her white ankle sock bobbing. She bit her lip as she waited, her face intense, as if she were trying to hear my father's voice in the crowd. After a few minutes, she gave up and replaced the receiver. Dad wouldn't come to the phone.

At the hottest time of day, the air conditioner would kick in, filling the house with frigid air. Feeling chilled, Mom packed the checkbook and receipts back into the shoebox and decided to go out to the garden. "You kids coming?" she asked, as she grabbed a wicker basket from the porch. "Here," she said, when she saw I'd changed into my swimsuit. "Let me put some sun block on your back."

An hour or so later, I heard Dad's truck in the driveway. He walked through the garage, grabbed the Sunday paper, flicked off the rubber band, and sat on the porch swing reading, his cowboy hat tipped low over his head, shading his eyes. He buried his nose in the sports section, humming some country song. Dad had a talent for tuning out the world. If he didn't like something—losing lottery numbers or the results of a Packers game—he would simply pretend that the unfortunate event had never happened. After a fight with Mom, he would create a layer of silence around himself that nobody could break through. Mom could cry and beg and scream, her pale skin blushing red, but he never seemed to hear her. He eased into the chair, untouchable. I always thought of this as Dad pulling the plug, cutting out as if he'd blown a breaker. When I heard Dad humming, his voice willfully cheerful, I knew he had tuned us out.

Mom lifted a hand to her brow and looked over the steep

push of grass and dandelions, her white gloves stained red with the blood of burst tomatoes. As she walked down from the garden, peeling her gloves as she went, Dad must have seen her coming, but he pretended he didn't. When she came up next to him, he raised the newspaper higher over his face.

Mom's hair had loosened from its braid and clung to her damp neck. She undid the rubber band and rewove the braid, quick and efficient. "There are a lot of tomatoes that need to come in," she said. "Think you can give me a hand?"

Dad mumbled that he'd bring the tomatoes down in a minute, keeping the newspaper firmly over his face, and this drove Mom crazy; she dropped her gardening gloves on the porch's all-weather carpeting and whacked the newspaper with the back of her left hand, her wedding-band hand.

Lowering the newspaper, Dad raised his eyebrows, looking at Mom with an *I-don't-know-what-your-problem-is-lady* expression in his eyes.

Fighting tears, Mom whispered, "I know that woman. I know her family. Don't think I'm going to forget so easily." Her voice was cut with something I had never heard before: insecurity, desperation. She said, "You owe me more than this."

I slithered off the lawn chair, worked on my flip-flops, and wandered to the edge of the porch. The pain in my mother's voice shocked me into noticing things a kid normally would not: the way Mom's hands shook as she picked up my baby brother, put him in his carrier, and hoisted him on her back. The way Kelly, who had followed Mom to the porch, bit her nails. The way my father would not, under

27

any circumstance, answer my mother. It was as if he had turned to stone.

Sunlight fell over the pearly buttons of Dad's cowboy shirt as he stood, threw the newspaper on the floor, and walked into the house, leaving us on the porch.

Mom took Kelly's hand and my hand, and led us away. With my brother on her back, she walked down Trussoni Court and out onto Moose Road. We went west, into the sun. The afternoon was so hot that the blacktop was a vortex of mirages. Plateaus of sparkling silver water appeared ahead, always just ahead. We walked toward them, past the Ritters' horse farm and a field of milk cows. We passed a sign for SHUFFLEBINE'S ORCHARD: $9.99: ALL THE APPLES YOU CAN PICK! An old front-heavy Chevy truck sped by, sending up whorls of dusty air.

Kelly and I dragged our feet, exhausted, but Mom wouldn't stop for us. She did not pause to tie her muddy shoestrings, or to collect the wildflowers growing at the side of the road. My sister and I lagged behind, picking black-eyed Susans, which we tossed into the air, scattering yellow flowers upon black pavement. When Mom got too far ahead, we ran to her, grabbing at her hands, afraid to be left. I squeezed her soft fingers. I believed that if I pressed them hard enough she would stop crying. She freed her hand from my grip, wiped her eyes, and gave it back, salty and wet. Matt fell asleep on her back, sucking a strand of her hair.

"Where are we going?" Kelly asked.

"Don't know," I said. "Ask Mom."

Kelly looked up, to Mom. "Where in the heck are we going?"

28

"Crazy," Mom said.

"Where's that?"

"Onalaska."

I looked up the road, at the endless miles of blacktop. I knew if we walked another hour we would make town. If we turned back, we would eat a late dinner at the kitchen table, with Dad ignoring all of us as he picked his teeth with a toothpick and finished reading the paper. Mom would not speak to us for the rest of the evening. Nothing more would be said to Dad of his most recent affair. My mother would act as though my father had not betrayed her—again. Mom was good at pretending. She did it every day.

Kelly and I whined for home. We said, *My feet hurt! I'm huuungry!*

Mom squatted at the gravel shoulder, to adjust the baby carrier on her back. Her eyes were swollen. The ends of her shoestrings were frayed. She gave my hand a quick reassuring squeeze as we turned back, toward Trussoni Court. We had nowhere else to go but home.

PERHAPS I SENSED THAT MY MOTHER MIGHT TAKE US BY the hand and lead us away forever, because I had a hard time falling asleep that summer. I stayed in bed, watching my sister sleeping on the other side of the room. Sometimes I would raid the cupboards for potato chips and juice boxes. On the nights I felt most restless, I crept through the house. The hallway was quiet and dark, the rich pile of the carpet soft under my bare feet. I felt my way to the living room, which opened like a cave off the hall. Moonlight had cluster-bombed the walls, spattering chips of illumination over the cathedral ceilings, over my arms and legs. I tiptoed past my father's gun cabinet, filled with rifles, and opened the door that led down, to the basement.

When I found the light switch, my father's office blinked into clarity. Against one wall was an old couch where Dad crashed if Mom kicked him out of their bed. A wool blanket and a flat flannel-cased pillow retained the shape of his shoulders and head. There was a piece of plywood propped on sawhorses with invoices from a building supply company, heating bills, and paycheck stubs strewn over its surface. Behind this mess, taped to the unpainted concrete-block wall, was a photograph. I leaned close, to get a better look, and saw my father and Tommy Goodman standing side by side in the middle of a field, two tired-eyed boys with M-16s in their hands.

Next to the desk, a layer cake of cement blocks and planks rose into a wobbly homemade bookshelf where Mom had put up Mason jars of pink-fleshed tomatoes preserved with curls of basil. On the top shelf, too high for me to reach, was a box of pictures. Using a metal milk can (the antique kind my grandfather used on his farm), I climbed up, one foot on the can, one supporting my weight on the bookshelf. The box was just out of reach, but I made a grab for it. The soggy cardboard collapsed in my hands just as the milk can tipped. The box flew one way, I the other, my knee losing skin against a cement block, my elbow banging the floor. My father's war pictures snowed around me. The top of the milk can, round and metallic, rolled under the desk, a unicycle wheeling away.

I sorted through them, flipping images onto the floor (a

hooch, a Huey, an army jeep, a rice paddy) as if playing solitaire. My hand stopped on a photograph of a Vietnamese soldier, who appeared to be about fourteen years old, on a bed of elephant grass. Bullet holes peppered his chest, each one dime-sized, blood-ringed. For a long time I looked at the picture, until the image lifted from the paper and embedded itself in my memory. Who is this boy, I wondered, this body full of holes? I knew, even then, that my father had killed this person and that I was gazing upon the trophy photo of his kill, one no different for Dad than the photo in our living room of him with the twelve-point buck he'd shot the previous winter. Suddenly, I was terrified of what I saw before me. My father had killed men—his photographs told me that much. What I did not understand, as I looked at the death my father had inflicted, was why.

I began to get sleepy and the photographs went back in the box. I propped the milk can up and heard, in the can's center, a *bang roll bang clank*. When I shook it again, the sound repeated, in reverse. *Clank bang roll bang*. Tipping the can sideways, I peered into its mouth: the interior extended before me, black. I pulled out a small paper-wrapped object. As I unfolded the paper, long legs, mermaid-curved hips, and a set of pink-nippled breasts appeared. There were more pages, all from *Playboy*, all with a small italicized date at the top of the page that read *July 1968*. Folded inside, there was an old-fashioned camera, compact and heavy. I twisted a knob and a rectangular door popped open, exposing a sleek reel of film to the light.

Sure I had done something terrible, I shoved the camera back into the can. There was something else inside; I grasped a cold hard sphere and pulled it out. Small and oddly angular, weighing a pound, maybe a pound and a half, it was impossible for me to guess what it was. I moved it this way and that, like a jeweler inspecting a gem. And then, recognition: eye sockets and nose holes separated by a thin, brittle ridge, the round forehead cracked like a porcelain bowl. I rolled back onto my haunches and lifted it (held in the casement of my fingertips like a pearl in a silver setting) to my face. It was a human skull, brought home from Vietnam by my father. And although I was not old enough to question Dad's actions, and I always accepted what he said and did as the law of the land, I knew that the skull did not belong there, in our home, with us.

three

In my early twenties, when my father's photographs would not fade from my memory and I believed that a trip back would help explain the lives we had led, I bought a ticket and flew to Vietnam.

The airplane rolled to a stop mid-runway, in the unpunctuated darkness of Ho Chi Minh City's Tan Son Nhut airfield. I stepped onto pavement so smooth and black it was like a lake-sized reflection of the midnight sky. The other passengers, mostly Asian businessmen, ambled toward an industrial-drab building, pulling carry-on luggage. As we passed under the sluice of floodlights near the terminal, I saw that the tropic air had steamed the men's eyeglasses. They turned to me, opaque-eyed. I clutched my bag to my chest and followed these blind men.

The businessmen presented their passports and received their stamps. Standing at the end of the line, I was sure (suddenly, for no good reason) that the thin military-uniformed customs guy would look at my passport and turn me back. He would study my date of birth, my place of birth, and shoo me back toward the airfield, for deportation. Instead, the man flipped through my passport, looked me up and down (from long black hair to low-top Converse All-Stars), and waved me through.

After retrieving my bag, I walked into the hot, humid night. My travel agent had said I would find taxis outside the airport, but after the businessmen had left there wasn't a taxi in sight. It was two in the morning and I was stranded. There were no pay phones, no buses, nothing but a palm-lined avenue leading to Ho Chi Minh City.

I walked toward town, steering clear of puddles and potholes, the city lights fogging in the distance. After a few minutes, a beat-up Citroën pulled up beside me. The window fell, and a Vietnamese man barked at me in terse, sharp syllables. Shifting my weight against my suitcase, I gazed into the boat-big cavity of the car, contemplating the many ways this man could hurt me. He interpreted this moment of hesitation as refusal. The window ascended and the car rolled down the silent, hollow, oil-slicked road.

Less than a mile later, I waved down a taxi. The driver took me to the "tourist village," a three-block area around Dong Khoi (formerly Tu Do, which was formerly rue Catinat) shoved full of cafés, hotels, and tourists. The cafés and bars were still open and loud. I wandered through the streets until a blue neon sign appeared, blinking the word: HOTEL, HOTEL, HOTEL. I pounded the door with the heel of my hand until a half-asleep man in his twenties dressed in a Nike warm-up suit let me in, took my passport, charged me double the posted room rate, and lodged me in a moldy basement flooded with rainwater. Jet-lagged and wide awake, I didn't even attempt to sleep. Instead, I sat cross-legged in a wicker chair, staring at a rectangular window above the bed. It was barred, like a zoo cage. At daybreak, sunlight strafed the bars, a barrage of orange and yellow with flecks of pink, the colors of explosion. A set of small bare feet stopped before the window, and a child squatted and gazed in at me: ATTRACTION #1, SCARED AMERICAN TOURIST. Our eyes met. The child turned away.

My father went to Vietnam more than thirty years before me. He arrived a cocksure country boy from a family who thought war would make him a man. Although two of his older brothers were already stationed there, Dad had no expectation of where he was going and little knowledge about the war waiting for him. He had been raised to see war as a challenge, one that would teach him strength and dignity. He grew up on John Wayne and cowboys and Indians and stories of the Second World War: The fighting was always rough but worth it. My father once told me that before he had been drafted, he was neither for nor against the war—he had simply never paid attention. After his number came up, he started reading the newspaper. When he saw the kill ratio they printed—the high Vietcong body count and the ratio of Vietnamese to American deaths—he felt better. Our side was winning, or so he believed. Dad wanted nothing more than to put in his time and make it out alive, and this wish was granted. He was wounded, but he made it home. And he believed, like so many men after so many wars, that he could leave it all far, far behind.

OUTSIDE THE HOTEL, A CART SELLING *PHO* SPICED THE air with chilies. I bought a bowl and sat on the curb, nestling it between my knees. Spring onions, baby corn, and transparent noodles wove through a broth of pork fat. An old man sat next to me, slurping noodles and drinking broth. Sweat dripped over his forehead.

A rickshaw driver pedaled before me. He hiked up his worn blue jeans. "Mademoiselle?" he asked. "I will take you to see the sights?" When I climbed into the rickshaw, the chassis sank like a hammock.

We stopped before the War Remnants Museum, formerly the Museum of American War Atrocities, which was housed in the old U.S. Intelligence center, a dilapidated, squat concrete building overwhelmed by history and palm trees. Tourists snaked through a courtyard. I paid an entrance fee and joined them. Inside, there were bombastic slogans decrying the American Aggressors and lauding Communist Bravery. There were walls of photographs, black-and-white images of men mounted upon hulking machines, diminutive peasants standing below wearing conical hats and the black *ao ba ba* that Westerners usually called pajamas. There was a picture of a jeep with a chorus line of Vietnamese men roped to the bumper, each neck elongated, slightly giraffed. A happy-go-lucky GI smiled big for the camera from the driver's seat. The caption below read AMERICAN TORTURE DEVICE.

On a wall to the left of these pictures hung a large multicolored board resembling an optometrist's chart. Circles of orange, blue, purple, and white—each one with the word AGENT printed next to it—codified the chemicals deployed by American forces during the war. These substances were sprayed primarily as herbicides as part of

Operation Ranch Hand, Kennedy's attempt to expose guerrilla fighters by shucking their cover. Operation Ranch Hand dumped over nineteen million gallons of chemicals over South Vietnam, 66 percent of which was Agent Orange, a mixture of acids with a dash of dioxin—one of the most lethal poisons to the human body—thrown in. These agents were effective: The jungles shriveled, the crops died, and the drinking water became contaminated. A pervasive poison moved through the air, indiscriminate, filling peasant lungs and Vietcong lungs, filling the lungs of the U.S. military, general and grunt alike.

On a pedestal before the chart there stood a large glass vat, like something one would find in the laboratory of a mad scientist. It held the bodies of two deformed babies twisted around each other. The placard below read RESULT OF AMERICAN CHEMICAL ATTACK. The babies swam in a pretty sapphire-blue liquid; upon closer inspection, I saw that these little bodies were Siamese twins, two children woven into one. The babies had a shared head, a shared chest, a set of shared hips. One of the mouths was open and a tiny kitten tongue licked at the blue liquid. The little creature clung to itself, and I imagined this baby, with its tiny tapering fingers, all twenty of them wiggling, holding on tight as it was born. It wailed, as if to ward off the poisoned world it was entering, and then, with a look of disgust, departed.

I walked outside, to the courtyard, where a ramshackle souvenir market awaited me. There were bottles of Chinese Tiger Oil, boxes of ginseng root, hundreds of luminous globs of amber—some with ants and beetles petrified at their center. Pictures of Ho Chi Minh—Uncle Ho, as some of the postcards read—were propped on every table. I chose a piece of amber as big as my fist. There was a scorpion inside, its tail cocked to sting. An old woman gave me an inflated price; I accepted it without haggling. I held the amber to the sunlight, running my fingers over the gummy surface. Back at home, this chunk of amber would weigh down papers on my desk. Light would fall through the resin and become trapped inside, infusing the amber with warmth and illumination. The flex of the scorpion's tail would be exactly as it was when I first saw it—about to strike. I would hold it and remember the moment I bought it, thirty seconds before I came face-to-face with the man who made me wish I had not come to Vietnam.

He stood behind me, inspecting the piece of amber in my hand. I turned to him. His aviator sunglasses were gold-rimmed with a malachite-green tint to the lenses. They were bulbous and metallic and gave him the aspect of a horsefly. I could not see around them, and I was uncertain of whether he was Vietnamese or simply dark. He was long-legged, slump-shouldered, and much taller than other Vietnamese men. His jeans had a hole in the knee, his black T-shirt said IRON MAIDEN, and this led me to believe that he was an American greaser guy, the kind I might have shared a cigarette with in high school. But there was something in his stance, in the way he moved, that made me believe he was native to this city. He pulled a white baseball cap over his forehead, shading his glasses.

The sickening feeling of recognizing a stranger—the sense of déjà vu that signals True Love in romance novels—had never happened to me before. Maybe I'd never been open to the idea; I was not interested in past lives, future lives, tarot cards, or my star chart. And yet I knew I had seen this man before. I sat on a bench and tried to place him. Could he have been in the lobby of my hotel? Was he behind me at the bank as I withdrew cash with my credit card? I could not remember, but perhaps he did: The man would not stop looking at me. He stood at a metal gate, near the rickshaw driver, smoking a cigarette. There was a strange persistence in his gaze, and it was this lack of fearlessness in his stare that frightened me the most. It said, *I know you*. It said, *I have been waiting*.

NOT LONG AFTER I LEARNED TO RIDE MY BICYCLE WITHOUT training wheels, Dad brought home an olive-skinned four-teen-year-old boy with feathered hair and a face that resembled my own. Dad told Kelly and me to play in the yard with the boy, and we spent hours running into the woods and building forts in the bushes. Soon, the boy began to sleep over, in a room in the basement near my father's office. He liked the basement and would sleep all morning, refusing to come upstairs and watch cartoons. When he finally appeared, he sat next to me on the couch, eating powdered donuts until his lips were coated white. This boy was my older half-brother, Phil, my father's child from his first marriage.

Dad's first marriage had lasted only a year or two and was over by the time he went to Vietnam. According to my father, his first wife had done many things to destroy his life—she had gotten herself pregnant and then forced him to marry her. When Dad talked about her, I got the sense that women were evil creatures who lured a man into a web of trouble, keeping him there against his will. Dad believed this had happened to him—the first wife had gotten pregnant by simply wishing to be so, and he had played no part in it at all. "She only lets me see Phil so I pay the child support," he would say, scowling. "That woman has done nothing but suck me dry." And this wasn't the worst of it.

A few days after the divorce became final, the first wife drove her beat-up Ford to the local recruitment office. She knew the officer; he had been one of her brother's high school classmates. Holding Phil on her hip, bouncing him, she said, "I thought you might like to know that this boy's daddy is no longer married and is free and able to serve his country. I wrote his address, date of birth, and social security number out here for you." The recruitment officer looked over the scribbling, copied the name and the numbers, and thanked her. She got her revenge: A month later, her ex-husband was drafted into the army.

I'd heard my father bitch about his first wife, but I had never seen her until one winter afternoon at Roscoe's. One of Dad's friends said, "Hey, Danny, look what the cat dragged in." Aware that she had Dad's attention, she had tapped the snow from her stiletto boots, tossed her hair over her shoulder, and thrown her battered purse on the bar. She had probably spotted my father's truck parked out front and came in just to irritate him; she had a look of mean-spirited defiance on her face as she threw a dollar on the bar and ordered a Bud Light.

The first wife wasn't of much interest to me—she wore

the same tired expression as every small-town woman who has survived a lifetime of hard work and failed romances—but her daughter was. The girl was five years older than I, with big brown eyes and sand-colored hair, and I knew right away that this was Phil's younger sister: Rita Trussoni, the Denied Daughter. Although Rita had our family name, Dad told everyone she was not his. He said she had been conceived when he was at war, after he'd divorced her mother, and he'd only given the girl his name to cover the first wife's ass. Whenever Dad said this, my mother's face would change completely, and she would say, "Rita certainly looks a lot like Kelly," but Dad remained adamant—he refused to acknowledge the girl and did not allow her into our family. I grew up fearing the exile imposed upon Rita Trussoni. One wrong move and I'd be history. In the battle to love my father, anything could happen. I had to be careful.

I stared at the girl across the bar; she stared at me. She was both a Trussoni and not one; she was my sister and not my sister. I didn't speak to her, but I felt that we were more alike than either of us knew.

And yet, we were different. My mother was not the kind of woman who hung out in bars or tucked a pack of cigarettes in the strap of her bra. If anything, she tried to help Dad leave his hard living behind him. In the years when I was closest to my mother, when she stayed at home with us, I saw her as an infinite source of love and comfort and care. Occasionally, I would notice that she was unhappy—she would leave the room when my father spoke about Rita Trussoni, and sometimes, for no apparent reason, she locked herself in the bathroom to cry. But I did not

41

know why she did these things, and even if I had, I would not have been equipped to comfort her. It was only much later, when I knew what she had been hiding from us, that I understood her sadness.

When Matt was old enough for day care, Mom decided to go back to school. She sat at the kitchen table every evening, studying for a bachelor's degree. We were used to seeing her there, surrounded by papers. She did all the accounting for Dad's construction company, sitting up at night with receipts and payroll stubs and tax forms. Mom had always been good with money. She found ways to keep the business going when there was nothing in the bank. She knew how to refinance the house and the land. She even found ways of hiding the money she spent on us kids. When we came back from Kmart, each of us with a pair of shoes and a toy in our lap, Mom turned to the backseat and said— with a severity meant to scare us silent—*Do not tell your father about this. If he asks about the toys, tell him they came from last year's Christmas.*

I remember my mother spreading her books across the table. The house was ammonia-clean, the rugs fresh-vacuumed. She had washed her long black hair and tied it in a knot on top of her head. She opened a book, a collection of myths she had bought for her humanities class. Each night, she showed me pictures of Zeus and Demeter, of Narcissus and Echo. Smoothing the pages with her small fingers, she caressed a picture of a girl dressed in a white robe, an ear of corn in each hand. Mom said, "This girl was stolen from her mother and taken far below the earth, to Hades. Every year she travels to the underworld for three months. All the crops die when she is gone. When she comes back to the earth's surface, she brings spring."

THE RICKSHAW DRIVER HUFFED ME UP A WIDE DUSTY boulevard to Cholon. This was the Chinese district of Ho Chi Minh City, where Marguerite Duras's *The Lover*—a story filled with silk, sex, and opium—was set. Pedaling uphill, we inched past a thicket of willowy bamboo, each stalk pale as the wing of a moth, and then passed a market selling piles of rice, coffee beans, and cornmeal. Saffron-robed Buddhist monks swept the steps of a temple near the market square. As we rolled by the terrace of a restaurant, the air smelled of limes and fish sauce. I was about to ask my driver to stop, so that I could get something to eat, when he suddenly veered into an alley, a pinched tubular street not much wider than the rickshaw. He stopped pedaling and turned, curiosity in his eyes. He said, "I learned to speak English when you Americans were here."

I sat up. "You mean when the military was here?"

"Don't worry. I do not hate you Americans. Maybe it would be better here if you had won."

I must have looked confused, because my driver's expression soured. He said, "Do you understand what happened here? Do you know about the war?"

He had just pedaled me to every war museum in Ho Chi Minh City. I said, "Sure."

"What? What do you know?"

This was surely a trick question. I said, "It happened before I was born."

My driver did not like my response. He said, "Of course,

you are young. You do not know war. How could you?" He turned, mounted his gnarled ginger-root feet on the pedals, and carried me off.

I pulled the brim of my sun hat low over my brow. For some reason, I wanted to stop the rickshaw driver and tell him I knew more than he suspected. I had learned to recognize the war in the quicksand personality of my father: his mood shifts, his sneak attacks, his drinking. Through the years, I saw the war in everything bad that had happened, to him and to us. For me, the war caused Dad's sadness, his bar brawls, his treatment of my mother, and his inability to express love. It explained my parents' divorce and the alienation I felt from my family. And although I knew I could be wrong—yes, my father could have had problems without the war—it didn't matter to me at the time. I went to Vietnam knowing my father was a damaged man. The war was responsible.

Or so I believed. I remembered, growing up, how military Dad could be with us, how he valued discipline and order and obedience above all else. Pain, he always said, brought wisdom. Suffering, he thought, brought strength. My father had a story he liked to tell, about raising me. When I was little, I had done something naughty (coloring with crayons on the living room wall), and he decided to teach me a lesson. He pulled my pants down, lifted my shirt, and spanked me. Mom, who did not approve of Dad's harshness, ran to the living room and pulled me away. "Stop that, you're hurting her," she said. To which he replied (and as he told the story he would always grin, for the punch line), "Damn right I am. I *mean* to hurt her." I don't remember if the spanking hurt—physical pain never remained long in my memory. What stayed with me was the strange sensation of being pulled between my parents, the feeling that they might tear me in two, and the realization that my mother could save me from danger.

Dad loved this story. He told it with pride, as an example of his strictness and a parable of what he thought necessary to raise a child. Once, he pulled my boyfriend aside at a family event, handed him a beer, and told him his tale. "Now you know," he said, slapping my boyfriend on the back, jovial, "how to straighten her out."

Although Dad liked to tell the story of my first spanking, he never told the one about the last time he hit me. I was fourteen and, as he liked to say, "too damn mouthy for my own good." During an argument, he grabbed my arm and tried to pull me off the ground. Heavy and unmanageable, I twisted free, so he did the best he could, holding me still with one hand and whacking me with the other. When he'd finished and saw that I was not hurt in the least, he looked me up and down—assessing my stance, my posture, my ability to fight back—and said, "Maybe you're getting too old for that."

It became clear, as I grew older, that there was a strong unbreakable love between us but also a tendency toward conflict. Dad respected strength; I never wanted to let him down. When I was weak, he didn't want anything to do with me. When I was strong, he was the first to announce that I had succeeded on my own, and that I was better off that way. If I was in need (of his time, his attention, his love, his money), he would attack, giving it to me with everything he had, reducing me to ashes. Loving him was a battle. It was Operation Wheeler Wallawa, Operation Speedy Express. "I don't want to see you around here looking for a handout," he would say. After years of trying to be close to the man I loved so much as a child, I stopped going to see him at all. *We had to destroy Ben Tre in order to save it.*

BACK AT DONG KHOI, THE DRIVER HELPED ME FROM THE rickshaw and charged me the going rate. I paid him and walked into the lobby of the Dragon Hotel, which turned out to be a modern five-story building with an Internet café and a grocery filled with instant Ramen noodles and bottles of liquor. After I had made arrangements to switch rooms, I carried my backpack from the flooded basement to the top floor.

Upstairs, I opened a sliding-glass door to the terrace. Saigon—the official name for District 1, the small downtown area of Ho Chi Minh City's business district—was a tangle of power lines, Honda Dreams, and polluted air. I sat on the back of a plastic chair, resting my chin in my hand, trying to imagine the city as my father had seen it. The sun was coercive, prodding the past to melt into the present, the present to seep into the future. Past and present fell over the streets, layer over layer of time. Ho Chi Minh City and the Tay Ninh jungles became the cold barren streets of La Crosse, Wisconsin. My father was young, gung ho, and healthy; he was old, bitter, and ill. I half expected to open my eyes and find streets filled with U.S. soldiers in uniform, with White Mice, with the slinky metallic music of machine-gun fire. I half expected to find my father sitting next to me—his cowboy hat cocked sideways—ready to act as my tour guide: *Vietnam offers a fantastic array of experiences for the curious traveler! There is something for everyone in this idyllic tropical nirvana!*

Dad arrived in Vietnam in February of 1968, during the Tet offensive, landing at Ben Hoa Air Force Base, Saigon, on a gutted B-52. The bomber had originally been scheduled to land at Tan Son Nhut, but the landing strip had been overrun with Vietcong. The plane circled the airfield for over an hour, trying to land.

As I leaned back into the noise and heat of a Vietnam dusk, Dad's cigarette-raspy voice fell through my mind: *It was mid-morning when a sergeant checked me in at the runway. He ordered me to the replacement depot, and within a matter of hours I was in a helicopter going out to the war.*

He was assigned to the Twenty-fifth Infantry Division in Cu Chi, twenty miles northwest of Saigon, near the town of Tay Ninh. As the Huey maneuvered toward War Zone C, the countryside opened below. Charred land, land on the verge of disintegration, stretched from dirt roads. Flooded rice paddies and dikes broke flat burned fields.

The chopper dropped Dad in a marshy spot. Tropical heat seeped through his fatigues. The air smelled horrible, like burning sewage, and it had begun to rain. Pulling his poncho hood up, he rubbed repellent over his neck as rainwater soaked through his socks, surrounding his feet. The air seemed a solid wall of heat.

The platoon stood at the end of the field, packing up. Dad reported to Lieutenant Graves, a prematurely bald man called Pops, who sized him up wearily and reported the platoon's coordinates via radio: ten klicks west of Tay Ninh, near the Cambodian border. Pops informed the men that they would head out toward Nui Ba Den, the Black Virgin Mountain. They packed rucks, checked weapons, and stumbled out to the boonies.

They walked for hours through jungle. Eventually, the rain lightened to a fine drizzle. Fat wet centipedes, orange as rust, half an inch thick, clung to banyan trees. Cockroach-sized mosquitoes hovered between blades of elephant grass. The ground ahead and behind was muddy and pocked with puddles. My father matched strides with a man whose name patch read GOODMAN. Tommy Goodman was thin and blond, with big ears and a southern drawl. "Hey, new guy, some advice," Goodman said, by way of introduction. "Guard that poncho with your life." Dad liked him right off the bat, a reaction he rarely had. Although Dad made friends easily—his charm and easy humor always won him allies—he didn't take to many people. But for some reason he trusted Goodman.

A bomber dropped its load in the distance, beyond a flank of palms. There was an explosion. Clouds of white powder rose above the trees; confections of fibrous chemicals lifted and disintegrated above the bombs' fire. The wind blew; leaves became coated white. My father watched the chemicals sift through the air. "That's napalm?" he asked.

"White phosphorus," Goodman said. "Napalm isn't nearly so pretty."

The platoon left the jungle and humped past a village. Children ran through the gas and rain, pushing one another into the fog. They laughed and ducked behind trees. The air smelled bad near the villages. There were no sewers, nothing resembling a drainage system, and every paddy was fertilized with human waste. Urine and shit mixed with chemicals, creating a harsh gasoline smell. As they left the village, they passed an old man holding a pig by a rope. He turned and stared sullenly, following the troops with his eyes as they moved past.

ON DONG KHOI STREET, EVERYTHING WAS FOR SALE. KIDS hawked t-shirts printed with Che Gŭevara's face; old women trundled baskets of coconuts. Tour agencies advertised their services, buses that took tourists to places made famous by the war: Khe Sanh (near the former DMZ) and the Cu Chi tunnels. There was a beauty salon on a corner of Dong Khoi, near a fruit stand. Women stood before it, talking and gesturing, the thin white silk of their *ao dais* catching in the breeze. Vietnamese was all nasal tones, like the sound of a trumpet, and although I had heard the language spoken in foreign films, it was stronger and stranger in person. As the women spoke, I tried to follow the tones, knowing that each pitch corresponded to an object or feeling or action. I watched as a woman emerged from the beauty salon and walked across the street. Another woman placed a bag of jackfruit in the basket of her bicycle, mounted the seat, and peddled off, the tail of her *ao dai* fluttering past the tire's spokes. She wove through the street, between motorbikes and rickshaws, and disappeared.

I hunted through my pockets, looking for money to buy a bag of fruit, and there he was, standing in an alley, near a beauty salon filled with Western backpackers. There was nothing different about him; the ripped jeans, the heavy-metal T-shirt, the mirrored aviator sunglasses were exactly as they were hours before. Only now his presence caused an electric charge through my senses. My first reaction was to turn and run. But I didn't. I stood my ground. And I knew—when he lowered his head and pushed his sunglasses over the bridge of his nose—that this man wanted to hurt me.

"Excuse me," he said, as I walked past him. When I did not respond, he grabbed me by the arm and pulled me back, so I had no choice but to look him in the face. I saw that he was, in fact, Vietnamese, but mixed, probably half white.

"Ouch," I said, rubbing my wrist. "What do you want?"

He looked at me a moment, then released his grip.

I turned and walked through the first door I saw. The beauty salon was full. I pushed my way in and sat at the far end of the room, under an old electric fan. There were two pink marks on my wrist, where the man had grabbed me. I tried to calm myself by flipping through a Japanese fashion magazine and studying the pictures taped to the walls. Each Vietnamese model was forlorn and emaciated, her arms lithe, her cheeks chiseled. The Vietnamese women in the salon were equally thin, and although I resembled my father in stature, and was considered small in the States, in Vietnam I was bulky. My hair, however, was not so foreign; it was long and straight and dark. The beautician, an older woman with sculpted eyebrows and a mole on her cheek, waved me to her chair.

"How much for a haircut?" I asked.

"For you?" she said, looking me over. "Twenty thousand *dong*."

After agreeing to this price, I pointed to a picture on the wall of a model whose hair was only slightly shorter than my own, with the ends brushing her collarbone.

The beautician nodded—*OK, OK, OK*—and eased a plastic sheath over my shoulders. She ran her hands over my hair, smoothing it. I pointed to the picture again, to confirm that I wanted nothing more than a trim. Again, the beautician nodded—*yes, yes, yes*—but perhaps she had not understood me. Or maybe she had devised some plan of revenge for a wrong done her years before, by a different American in a different Saigon, because she glided the cool edge of the scissors at the base of my neck, far higher than the collarbone, and snipped. Six inches of hair fell across the white tiles at my feet. I gazed at myself in the mirror, too surprised to do anything, as the woman used a fine-tooth comb to collect the remaining strands of hair from my neck. She chopped them away in two quick clips, working the blade close to my neck, flipping the scissors this way and that. As she went to work around my ears, shearing an arc above them, I wanted to put my hands in the scissors' path, but it was plain that I could do nothing. It was too late; the damage had been done.

four

The echo of a gunshot sliced through the house. Although I was sprawled out in the living room watching Saturday morning cartoons, I knew Dad had gotten his deer.

My father went hunting every season. He used to take our collie Smokey with him, but Smokey died when I was six. Although it had been three years since then, Dad hadn't found a new hunting dog. He would go alone, heading out before sunrise and returning late in the day. It was still early when I heard his gunshot. From the sound of it, he wasn't far from the house. I left Kelly and Matt in front of the TV, threw on a ski jacket, and rushed into the cold windy morning.

The snow crunched under my boots. I tucked my hair into a neon-orange stocking cap and pulled it low, over my ears. An electric barbed-wire fence skirted the edge of the cleared land that we called the lawn. It had been erected by a farmer whose cattle wandered free through the winding dirt trails in search of clearings and small fields filled with grass. The fence was useful. It kept heifers from the house; it kept kids from the heifers. To find my father, I had to get past the fence.

The electric charge zapping through the wire was not high, just enough shock to singe the skin. In summer, when I wore sundresses and sandals, I often had slats of burns laddering my arms and legs. Once, a strand of my waist-length hair caught on a barb and singed, giving off a sickening stink. But as it was freezing cold, and I was mummied in clothes, I wasn't too worried about the fence. I knelt before it, gauging the space from the snow to the first wire. It looked to be about twelve inches, not enough gap for me to wiggle under. There was more room between the first wire and the second wire, almost two feet, so I decided to work myself through this opening. I pulled the sleeve of the jacket over my hand—protecting the skin from the electricity— and pushed the top wire up while, as quick as I could, I slid one leg across, arched my back, and swung under. I was almost through when a gunshot rang through the forest, making me jump. The wire guillotined, skimming my cheek. A jolt of pain burst through my teeth and into my neck.

A second shot meant that Dad had not killed the deer on the first attempt and probably had to trail it. This was confirmed when, about one hundred yards from the house, I found a thin vermilion trail of blood. Dad's footsteps and the deer's prints mingled, and I followed the prints and the blood through the narrow banks of maple trees. It was a cold clear morning in late November. Sunlight tickled the snow; wind razored around me, whistling through branches. I shoved my hands in the pockets of my jacket to keep them warm. Everything had abandoned the woods—there were no birds, no squirrels. But the sky seemed a billowing ocean of blue that gave the snow and ice a solid crystalline beauty.

This was the irony of Wisconsin winters: the liquescent sunlight was always brittle with cold; the illusion of warmth always retained an evil-tempered chill.

Dad stood over the deer, his Winchester in one hand. The animal was dead, killed with two bullets, one in the flank, the other in the chest. My father was a good shot, although he never worked on it. Some hunters practiced all year, shooting bottles off tree stumps, going to the rifle club to slam clay pigeons, but Dad never did any of this. He cleaned his gun once a year, loaded it with .270 cartridges, bought a hunting license, and got his deer. Always practical, he skinned and cleaned it himself and took the meat to a packer, who processed it into tight bundles. If my father felt pleasure in the sport, he didn't show it. He didn't invite his friends to hunt our land. He didn't brag about his kill. He went out alone. We ate venison steaks all winter.

I saw, as I crested a hill, that my father was not in hunting colors. He should have put on an orange vest, or at least an orange hat, like mine, but he was wearing jeans and his dirt-green army jacket. He appeared as washed out as the surrounding trees—dull, drab, hidden. A black stocking hat was pulled low over his brow; his scraggly brown beard covered his cheeks and chin, leaving no part of him exposed. If I hadn't seen him early that morning, as he drank a cup of coffee before leaving, I might not have recognized this man at all. He caught my eye and waved me over.

Propping the Winchester against a maple tree, he approached the deer. It was a doe, a big one. He whittled a hole into the slab of her ear and tagged her. Then he rolled her on her back, pushing the head up. With the tip of his

Bowie knife, he made an incision below the breastbone, a tiny puncture under the fur, and then dragged the knife down, cutting to the pelvis. I expected a lot of blood, and there was some, but my father didn't cut deep. As the knife slit the skin, a creamy white substance spilled off the body and into the snow.

"What's that?" I asked.

"Milk," he said. "Looks like she was nursing."

Dad cut deeper. Steam rose from the deer, as it did from my father's mouth when he explained what he was doing. "First, you cut the esophagus. You need a clean cut to break it. Once it's cut, remove it. The rest comes out easier once it's gone." He worked the knife into the deer, and cut the esophagus. It resisted and then gave. Blood spilled over the matted brown fur, over my father's hands, and into the snow, staining it. "Never cut the stomach, the bladder, or the intestines," he said. "Be careful to get them out without making a mess." Dad worked fast, removing pieces from the deer and tossing them on the ground. "Sometimes you need to get the pelvis bone out of the way, and sometimes, as with a big girl like this one, you don't."

"How do you get the pelvis bone out?" I had never wanted to kill an animal and there was little chance that I would ever take up deer hunting, but I'd always been my father's student, no matter how repulsed I was by my education.

Dad was happy that I'd asked. He showed me a small handsaw that he brought along. He brushed his finger over the comb of tiny teeth, inviting me to imagine it biting through bone.

I stepped back, to stay clear of the blood. Dad opened a cooler, a HungryMan that could hold about a dozen cans of beer. He scooped the cooler full of snow—cleaning his hands in the process—and then placed the marbled, viscous organs (heart and liver) inside. After the deer's chest cavity was clean, he packed it with snow as well, to keep the meat free of bacteria. The unnecessary pieces lay scattered around us, food for wild dogs.

We tied a rope to the deer's front legs and pulled her toward the electric fence. As we retraced our steps, a second trail of blood covered the first. Even though we were walking downhill, the deer was too heavy for me. I struggled to pull my share of the weight. My hand burned from the rope. I stopped to wrap the sleeve of my jacket under my fingers, but I was no real help, so Dad gave me the cooler and dragged the deer alone. I walked alongside, the cooler under my arm. The doe's eyes were locked open and, although I'd seen this ritual every year of my life and was not as squeamish as the other nine-year-old girls I knew, I had, after all, seen *Bambi*. "I wonder what her baby is going to do," I said. "What if it starves?"

Dad adjusted the rope on his shoulder. He was dismissive, almost contemptuous. He said, "If it's strong, it will learn to feed itself."

AFTER DAD HAD HUNG THE DOE ON A TREE, LEAVING HER to drip blood into the snow, he pulled the truck around and told my mother we were going to Roscoe's for a beer. Mom walked down the driveway, her winter boots sinking into the snow, a thick wool scarf wrapped around her neck. "I don't like her going," she said, crossing her arms over her chest. The wind was so cold, her pale cheeks froze pink. "Kelly and Matt are inside, watching TV. A bar is no place for a child."

"Nonsense," Dad said, opening the door for me, and I was on top of the world. As we backed down the driveway and pulled onto Trussoni Court, I felt lucky, chosen. Mom turned back to the house without waving goodbye.

Most of the people at happy hour came from small towns along the Mississippi River: Victory, De Soto, Romance, Genoa. Many of Roscoe's regulars were Vietnam vets, not much different from my dad. Our hometowns were reservoirs of the draft, an ever-replenishing source of soldiers. Immigrants' sons, farmers' sons, they went to war without resistance, accepting Vietnam as the price a young man paid. Nobody dodged duty and nobody signed up for community college to get out of going to boot camp, although many wished that they had.

The Trussonis came from Genoa, population 250, a town that was all stretch and no slump. Rising from a gap in the bluffs, it ventured vertically into the steeps rather than horizontally along the Mississippi River. The town center consisted of little more than a dairy cooperative, a small business district—a grocery, a café, a row of bars—and a Catholic church. A caramel-colored dirt road funneled from the church to a two-lane highway where cars rolled by, their metallic reflections foiling the Mississippi's surface. East of town, the shifting roller-coaster hills began. This was where my father was born, in a farmhouse surrounded by fields of yellow and umber and brown. Corn and wheat and potatoes.

An overblown barn rose over the farmhouse, red as a rooster's jowl. My family didn't live there any longer, but I liked to imagine how it had been fifty years ago, inhabited.

The farmhouse had been built by my great-grandfather, Giovanni Battista Trussoni, to resemble the stout mountain houses of northern Italy. Family lore has it that, in order to earn his passage to America, he hiked the steep, snowy paths of the Italian Alps into Switzerland every Friday to sell goat cheese at the Saturday market. He climbed and sold and saved. After marrying a girl from his village named Martina, he set his sights on two transatlantic fares. When he'd saved enough, he purchased tickets and a piece of land near his cousin's homestead in Wisconsin. My great-grandparents arrived in winter. Half of Campodolcino—the Alpine homeland of Genoa's founders—was already there. The snow was deep, the wind icy, but despite the freeze my great-grandfather set to work on the farmhouse immediately.

When Giovanni had almost completed his house—the windows and doors installed, the front porch painted blue—and the family was preparing to move in from the granary, he spent the last of the goat-cheese savings on materials for the terrazzo floor. He drove the horses to town and returned with a wagon loaded down with bags of cement and boxes of Italian marble chips. He installed the floor himself. First, he delineated the soon-to-be floor into sections, crisscrossing metal partitions over the dirt. Then he poured cement (small batches mixed in a trough) to fill these spaces. Next, he placed fingerprint-sized trapezoids and triangles of marble across the surface and pressed these shapes with the tips of his fingers until they became co-essential with the cement.

Giovanni instructed his children—my grandfather and his sisters—to go out and find stones, the flashiest ones they could, and he saved the corner spaces for these rocks. The children hunted all afternoon, lugged their treasures in a gunnysack to the farmhouse, and emptied their offerings. My great-aunts held out pieces of graphite and turquoise, candied rocks that looked as pretty as jewels in a store window. But my grand-father insisted upon perfectly plain stones, white and river-smoothed, that when pressed into the cement created only the slightest contrast to their blue-gray setting.

ROSCOE'S WAS MORE THAN JUST A NORTH SIDE DIVE—IT was an all-inclusive movie set. The characters of my childhood entered right, exited left, as I watched from the padded edge of the bar. At this theater, the lights flicked on and off, the scenery changed. I witnessed the magic of costume and makeup. I was on the inside, accepted by this troop of outsiders as one of their own.

My family name had currency here. The Trussonis had a reputation, one acquired over thirty years. Once, a woman working the hot-lunch line at my elementary school looked at my name (printed on my punch card) and said, "Trussoni as in the *Genoa* Trussonis?" This woman had spent time at Roscoe's where, aside from the usual gossip, she had probably heard rumors about our part in the infamous Pizza Connection, an embezzling operation that involved the Italian mafia, drug smuggling, and a Chicago pizza joint. Whether this was true or not didn't seem to matter (it was, in fact, true); the gloss of mob connections added an element of sordid allure to my family.

"Hey, Jan," Dad said to the bartender, a woman in her mid-forties with a sharp tongue and a pineapple-bomb bouffant hairdo. "Give me a brandy and Coke, and I'll roll for it."

"Ready to lose again, I see." Jan slammed the black dice box on the bar top, a *let's see what you're made of* wiggle in her walk. "You regulars are just dying to throw money my way."

Rolling for a drink was, essentially, gambling with the bar for your liquor. A straight or three of a kind won a round; asymmetric numbers inflated a drink's price to double. Winning didn't bring much, but nobody cared. The regulars were used to losing. The North Side was hard-talking, straight-shooting, and clean of hope. At Roscoe's, if you hadn't had the short end of the stick most of your life, if you hadn't been screwed over in some form or another, there was surely something wrong with you.

"Better close your eyes," Dad said, shaking the dice box.

"Why?" Jan asked, eyeing the streaks of deer blood on Dad's jeans.

"I don't want to hurt your feelings," Dad replied, shaking a two, a three, and a four, "when I get my straight."

When Dad was a winner, his good humor was uncontainable. He smiled and snapped his fingers, singing along with the Dolly Parton song playing on the jukebox. He cracked peanuts between his teeth and stomped the shells under the heel of his boot. Jan made Dad's free drink, a tumbler of Five Star brandy with a splash of Coke, for color. She slid a cherry Coke—with three cherries skewered on a plastic sword—to me and winked. "Hello there, squirt. Is your dad keeping you out of trouble?"

"You bet I am," Dad said, his spirits soaring. "My little troublemaker needs someone to keep her straight."

"More like I'm keeping *you* out of trouble," I said, smiling at my father, who winked at me.

"Speaking of trouble," Dad said, "here are the boys."

My uncles, who always showed up late and en masse, stumbled into the bar, lighting cigarettes and tucking in T-shirts—a Trussoni gang, ready for fun. They sauntered in as if the jukebox played for them alone, their blue jeans faded to gray, their sideburns and mustaches of identical bushiness, each brother just a variation on the Trussoni theme.

The Trussonis were a big family with a lot of boys. Uneducated but street-smart, poor but hardworking, sharp as a bayonet in the gut, my uncles lived their lives like they meant it. It was with this earnest spirit that they went to war: The oldest brother fought in Korea; my father and two other middle Trussoni brothers fought in Vietnam; the baby of the family—too young for Vietnam—joined the army in peacetime. Three of my uncles did not serve in the military. One of these uncles was dapper and lanky, an ex-runner who, if he'd gone to war, would have charmed the enemy into surrender. Another was gay and felt slighted that he was barred from military service. And then there was my uncle Albert, who had been banned from my consciousness when he and my father nearly killed each other over a piece of property. There were lawyers and settlements, fistfights and dramatic phone calls. I never knew who was right and who was wrong, but my father removed this uncle from my life. For my father, a fight was a complete and total act of destruction, an annihilation that could not be repaired. You were either with him or against him. I didn't know a thing about that uncle or his children, and I didn't want to.

Although there were eight boys, everyone at Roscoe's saw my uncles as a single entity: a sixteen-armed eight-mustached monster, all reach and bristle. Even I, their niece, sometimes had a difficult time telling them apart. When my attention became ever-so-slightly lax, my uncles seemed to be simply smaller or bigger versions of one another, a Russian nesting-doll progression, each uncle *matroshka* similar in shape and coloring but just slightly smaller, with a wider or thinner forehead, a different placement of a scar or a freckle. I found myself noting each of these odd distinguishing traits in order to keep my uncles distinct in my mind. Sometimes I mixed up their names, an embarrassing thing for a girl who had known them all her life. As most people saw my uncles as a gang, they didn't worry about proper names. They simply lumped them all together as "the Trussoni boys."

My grandmother knew everything about her children, all twelve. She knew their weights, their heights, their preference for dark meat or white. She knew the intricacies of her children's personalities and mediated fights with the authority and grace of a referee in a boxing ring. Once my grandmother claimed that she could identify each of her children without even seeing them; all she needed was to hear them walk. This seemed incredible, so one day after church I tested her. Each of my uncles and each of my aunts walked in turn behind my grandmother so she could guess the walker. My grandmother called out her children's names as they passed.

"Each of my children has his own way of walking," she said. "Cecelia's walk is gentle; Geraldine's walk is broken-hearted. Your daddy's walk is gutsy and full of pride. He never drags his feet, and he gets his heels off the ground quick, unlike the rest of my kids."

She finished with Bobby, the youngest boy, whose walk (she claimed) was "lucky." Years later, Bobby would justify this assessment when his heart froze in his chest and he died mid-step. As it turned out, he was at that very moment hurrying past a hospital and was revived after he had been dead for over five minutes, a feat so marvelous I had to ask him what he'd seen. He saw nothing in death, he said, nothing to reassure a religious man. And although Bobby never recovered his easy smile or his blind faith, he knew his lucky walk had saved his life.

Dad shouted their names—Gene! Dick! Bernard! John!—as my uncles crowded the bar. They took over the bar stools and swamped the pool table with quarters.

"I've got their drinks, Jan," Dad said, opening his rawhide wallet, the one that matched his belt.

"Bumps, Danny," one of my uncles said, which means *I've got the next round* in Roscoe's-speak.

"About time you're buying," another uncle said.

"Yeah, thanks, you cheap son-of-a-bitch," said another.

"Hey," the oldest uncle said. "Who do you think you are, talking about my mother like that?"

My uncles fought among themselves about something unimportant they'd seen on television or in the local newspaper. Each took a side, staked a defense, launched attacks and counterattacks. There was no such thing as neutral. At the dinner table they all screamed to be heard, jumping up, pounding silverware: *Let me make my point, damn it, just let me make my point!* They had no sense of diplomacy. They went for the throat.

It was a family tradition. Trussoni Thanksgivings were like boxing matches. There was sure to be a rumble on the front lawn of my grandparents' house and a rematch at the tavern down the street. As my aunts and cousins watched from the sidelines, I jockeyed for a better view. Everyone knew that after the fight was over we would take our paper plates and plastic utensils and walk past the table my grandmother had loaded with turkey, cranberry sauce, and cases of beer. A little blood before dinner was what aperitifs were to other families.

Hunger brought out the worst in us. There was the time Dick, who served three tours as a marine in Vietnam, beat the hell out of a delivery boy who was half an hour late with a sausage and pepperoni pizza. Uncle Dick had Elvis's black hair and a hint of Rocky Balboa in his walk. He was a lady's man, a real hard-ass. He grilled the delivery boy, drill-sergeant style. "Where were you, boy? Don't you think we're hungry here? Don't you think we deserve a little service here? What do you have to say about your lazy, stupid, pimply, pansy-ass self? I damn near drowned in the Mekong so you could have this job. We're hungry!" When the kid protested, Dick broke the boy's jaw and a few of his ribs.

The police came to our house just after the ambulance, to escort my uncle away. They called him by name and let him finish his pizza before cuffing him.

Maybe this empty-stomached belligerence had to do with my father's childhood, when there wasn't enough food to feed a family of fourteen. On lean winter evenings, my grandmother would set a bowl of potatoes—all they had— on the table and walk away, leaving the children to share their dinner. More often than not, the younger kids went to bed hungry. My father was a middle child. Sometimes he got a potato, sometimes he didn't.

"Trussoni," a man at the end of the bar—who was probably drunk and certainly suicidal—called to my father. "Looks like you've got some extra cash. How about buying *me* a drink?"

My uncles looked at this man, astonished. Money was not simply a medium of exchange for them. Freeloaders, welfare-checkers, any of those lazy-asses had no place in their lives. Dad didn't even look at this man. He stared at the TV as he said, "I buy drinks for my friends. Do you consider yourself my friend?"

"I'm your friend, buddy. I got your back."

Dad lit a cigarette and invited the man over. He was a big guy, but more fat than muscle. His flannel lumberjack shirt stretched at the buttons. He said, "I'll have a Pabst, Jan. No, wait. Make that a Heineken. I'm with the first-class members of society here."

Jan paused, waiting for my father to confirm the order. Dad nodded his assent and Jan delivered a green glass bottle and a high-necked beer glass.

My father offered the man a cigarette. He accepted one. Dad did not look at the lumberjack, but he didn't need to—he knew without looking how big, how strong, how much of a threat was his enemy.

"What makes you think I want to buy you a drink?" Dad asked, his voice steady, giving nothing away. "Why would I want to spend my hard-earned money on someone like you?"

"Shit, Trussoni," the man said, "you can afford it. I hear you get a payoff from Vietnam."

One of my uncles—who served his tour in the Central Highlands—started from his seat, his fists clenched, but my oldest uncle pressed a hand on his brother's shoulder, reseating him. My uncles knew my father had had the worst assignment in Vietnam: a III Corps grunt, an infantryman, a sitting duck for jungle guerrillas. This misfortune gave my uncles a peculiar respect for my father. He had an older-brother patina, despite being the sixth child. They knew Dad could take care of himself.

"I get a disability pension," Dad said. "A hundred bucks a month for a piece of shrapnel in the back isn't a good trade."

"Trade, my ass," the man said. "Free money is free money."

The TV zapped and sputtered, presenting the six o'clock news. Dad let the lumberjack finish his drink and bought him another.

"Let me tell you something," my father said, never looking up from his drink. "In the war, you never knew who was on your side. Friend, enemy, neutral—you never knew who you were dealing with. The Vietcong dressed just like the peasants. The villagers were playing both sides, and we damn well knew it. During the daytime, you had to let them be, although you knew they'd come back and shoot you in the ass, soon as the sun went down. Once in a while you'd catch one sneaking around with a weapon, though, and that was when you got your chance. Then you could shoot, no questions asked. One afternoon I saw this old guy riding his bicycle toward me, smiling, waving, all friendly. But I could see he had a bazooka under his arm. Close, closer he came, pedaling his bike like nobody's business. When he was real close, I lifted my rifle and shot him, square on. His bike veered off the road, into a rice paddy. My lieutenant, who was the platoon leader, got right in my face and chewed me out good. I didn't get worked up, though. I said, 'Hey, what am I supposed to do? The guy was carrying a bazooka.' I had to defend myself, didn't I? My lieutenant didn't believe me. 'He wasn't carrying no bazooka,' he said. So I took him down, to the rice paddy. Sure enough, that guy's bike had gone one way and the bazooka the other."

The lumberjack looked at Dad. "You got a point, Trussoni?" he said.

"Point is," Dad said, "you got to be careful who you're calling your friend."

Dad gave me a look of warning, so I knew to go stand by my uncles. Then, before the lumberjack had a chance to react, Dad grabbed him by the scruff of the neck and jackhammered his head into the bar. The first hit knocked the green beer bottle on its side; the second broke it. A crackling of glass spattered the bar. One, two, three times, my father slammed the head, working the glass in. Then, as

67

if nothing had happened, my father went back to his drink. He took a sip, Clint Eastwood cool, and said, "Somebody tell that guy there's no such thing as free money."

The lumberjack was bleeding all over the bar. Jan picked up the phone, her hand shaking.

"Keep the police out of this," Dad requested. "Please."

Jan rested the receiver in its cradle as my uncles carried the man out the back door to the alley, where they dumped him in a drift of snow. The lumberjack woke fifteen minutes later, his face swollen to Elephant Man proportions, the taste of Heineken still in his mouth, and wondered what the hell had happened. Inside, Jan made Dad another free drink and set it before him. "I guess that asshole don't know how to drink with the first-class members of society," she said, and she was right.

five

The Vietnamese beautician charged me forty thousand *dong* for the haircut, double our agreed-upon price. I placed a stack of bills on the counter, walked outside into the hot wet afternoon, and stood at the fruit stand on Dong Khoi, looking for the man with the aviator sunglasses. The street was crowded with bicycles and motor scooters. The fruit stand was still surrounded by women in *ao dais*, but the man was not there.

A blond girl with dreadlocks and a nose ring tapped her fingers on the counter of the Sinh Café, a tourist agency on Dong Khoi. She wore a tie-dyed T-shirt and a pair of expensive Birkenstock sandals and a cranky look on her face. Tickets for the Cu Chi Tunnels Bus Tour cost ten dollars. She presented the cashier, a Vietnamese man in his mid-twenties, with her Visa Gold card. He looked at the card, front and back, as if it had been dropped by a UFO.

"Passport?" he said.

She handed over a royal-blue folio embossed with gold.

"There is a problem," the cashier said. The name on the card and the name on the passport didn't match. When the cashier showed the girl the discrepancy, she said, "It is my father's card. I am *authorized* to use it!"

The cashier shook his head, unwilling to accept responsibility for this dubious transaction, and pointed her toward a Vietcom bank. He then turned his chestnut-shaped eyes to me and sold me a bus ticket. I paid him in currency; he was relieved. He seemed to be a few years older than I, and I couldn't help but wonder (as I had time and time again) if I had a brother or sister wandering around the streets of Ho Chi Minh City, a fellow love child of the Vietnam War.

The pack of tourists climbed aboard an ancient Soviet bus that missiled us north, past knots of rickshaws, crumbling colonial compounds, and out beyond the city. Electric-green rice paddies angled from the road like baseball diamonds. I heard my father's voice in the wind. I heard machine-gun fire and helicopters. But it was only the bus, rumbling on. We drove twenty miles north of Saigon, to the boonies, into a place my father had called War Zone Three, but that *The Tunnels of Cu Chi* (a meticulously reproduced Vietnamese pirate copy of Mangold and Penycate's original that I had bought from a market near my hotel) called the Iron Triangle.

Triangle referred to a triumvirate of cities—Cu Chi, Tay Ninh, An Loc—in which the Vietcong had maintained an unbreakable hold. The Iron Triangle couldn't be cleared of the enemy with Rome plows or chemicals (or the other weapons of mass defoliation); it couldn't be taken with tanks or napalm. And although more bombs fell on this patch of land than on any other in the history of warfare (6.2 million tons of bombs, 300 pounds for every man, woman, and child), it could not be taken with Bouncing Betties or F-105s. The enemy transformed into peasants, into ARVN (the Army of the Republic of Vietnam), into thin air. When the bombs fell, they crawled into tunnels, a web city that branched under the Americans'—under my father's—feet.

After January 30, 1968—when the Tet offensive blossomed in city after city in the South—the guerrillas in the Iron Triangle became even more evasive. While ARVN and American troops quelled the offensive, the countryside was left unattended. The months of January and February of 1968 saw a renaissance of guerrilla resistance as the Vietcong recruited more South Vietnamese peasants than they had since the war had escalated in '63. My father's first weeks in Vietnam coincided with this shift. He was twenty-two years old when he arrived, not much younger than I was when I made my trip.

The girl with the blond dreadlocks sat next to me on the bus. She told me that she worked for an environmental clean-up agency. She got college credit for participating in the program, she said, a whole semester's worth. She informed me that chemicals—white phosphorus and the rainbow of Agent poisons—still tainted drinking water and topsoil here, accounting for the abnormally high rate of birth defects among the village babies. She added that half a million people were still sick from chemicals sprayed during the war. The Red Cross reported over a million people disabled from Agent Orange and another half million dead. "That stuff was *way* nasty," she said.

71

I asked her what kind of work she did, imagining beakers and Bunsen burners, the elaborate equipment of a chemistry experiment.

"I go to the beaches," she said, in an offhand upsy-daisy tone, as if her job were the best all-expenses-paid vacation she'd ever had. "The South China Sea is the absolute best! You can scuba dive for next to nothing. It's a great gig—get college credit, see the world. Besides, the agency paid my ticket here."

She offered me half her sandwich. I took it. We exchanged autobiographies. We couldn't have been more different. She was the gold-card-carrying daughter of a man who did not fight in Vietnam, a man who had a student deferment. I was the daughter of a draftee, an ex-football star who had been kicked out of high school for punching a teacher. We sat side by side as the verdant landscape flashed by, two young Americans, filling up on cheese sandwiches.

"What did your dad do?" she asked, cracking open a can of Coke.

"In the war?"

"In the war."

I was unsure of what to tell her. My father was a grunt? A killer? "He was in the infantry," I said. "He was a tunnel rat."

"Wicked," she replied, offering me a sip of Coke. "That must have been some scary *Heart of Darkness* shit."

I agreed and asked about her father. "He's a professor," she said, rolling her eyes. "English literature. Berkeley."

"Wicked," I replied. "Mega-scary *Heart of Darkness* shit."

"Scary as hell," she said, and elbowed me in the ribs.

I pulled my backpack from under my bus seat and rummaged through it, looking for my camera. I'd been in Vietnam for days and had not put in the AA batteries or inserted a cartridge of film. Millions of images of Vietnam had already escaped me, recorded by nothing but the fragile medium of my memory.

I had a notebook I'd been keeping since college, a kind of scrapbook of the war. Pulling it from my backpack, I opened the cover to a photograph of a banyan tree I'd taped on the inside, its roots twisting like a hundred snakes. I had drawn a network of tunnels on the first page with a pencil, the levels folding and dissolving into one another, spiral after spiral of graphite. There were clippings from magazines, transcriptions of conversations I'd had with my father, and lines copied from a story by Tim O'Brien. The notebook recorded my Vietnam, the one that I had made distinct from my father's.

I'd bought the notebook in Madison on a cold evening, when I was a student at the University of Wisconsin. It was the night the Badgers won the Rose Bowl, and—despite the subzero temperatures—the streets were mobbed with half-naked football fans. To escape, I walked through the aisles of the university bookstore, past computer software and jars of pens, until I found a shelf full of notebooks. After sifting through a tangle of spiral-bound Meads, I discovered a heavy hardbound Clairfontaine. The cover was purple, the pages thick and honey-yellow. The price tag read $19.99, an amount that was, at a time when I was living off student loans, expensive. I paid the cashier with a credit card and walked outside, into the icy evening, happy. I didn't write in the notebook that night. Instead, I sat in a café on State Street, looking out a plate glass window, past a fist of icicles, at the state capital building. The umbrella of its dome rose into the black sky, moonlight rolling from it like luminescent rain.

The notebook also contained an article about Karl Armstrong, the man who—along with his brother and two other men—blew up Sterling Hall's Army Math Research Center in the summer of 1970. Seymour Hersh had exposed the My Lai massacre, four students were dead at Kent State, and Karl Armstrong was outraged. He trolleyed a van packed with fertilizer and explosives to Sterling Hall, parked it, and ran off. The explosion destroyed the building and killed Robert Fassnacht, a graduate student and father of three, who had been doing late-night research. Karl Armstrong went to jail, but later operated a juice cart in the University of Wisconsin pedestrian mall.

My notebook was full of what Vietnam begot—men like Karl Armstrong and Robert Fassnacht—killers and victims and protesters and fatherless children. It had timelines and statistics and photographs. But, turning the pages, I saw there was nothing at all about the families of the men who came home. What happened to them, after the war? When I told my mother I wanted to go to Vietnam, to understand what Dad had experienced there, she said the war was too horrible and I would be better off to forget it. And yet, I couldn't forget.

As I closed my notebook, I thought of the rickshaw driver's question: *What do you know about war?* Perhaps he was right. Maybe I didn't know the first thing about it.

My father certainly didn't understand my interest in history. When I told him, at eighteen, that I was going to college in Madison, he dismissed the plan as foolish. To him, education and books were a waste of money. He thought I would be much better off working in an office or waiting tables, making a real living. His father had worked construction; his father's father had worked construction. He promised I would receive no help from him. And although he eventually relented and paid half my in-state tuition, Dad always thought he was throwing money out the window.

Dad once told me he withheld his support so I would learn to fend for myself. He wanted me to make it on my own, to become strong. And I did. I learned to stretch five bucks into twenty, and more. I became, as my father hoped, strong. But I also became hard, never easy to befriend or to date; never able to accept anything from anyone—not dinner, not a movie, not a gift, not even a compliment. A college boy once told me I was beautiful, and my first reaction was anger. Pretty was too soft, too vulnerable. Warmth was a sign of weakness. My father had made it clear that only the weak needed other people. I learned to go it alone.

THE BUS PARKED BEFORE A CROWD OF PALM TREES. A tour guide announced the attractions: a water buffalo, a craft market full of woven baskets, a *pho* cart. We followed the guide to a sheet-metal shed, where a woman in a black *ao ba ba* ushered us to our seats. Rows of folding aluminum chairs had been stationed before a big-screen TV. As we sat, a video flicked on. It was a black-and-white film from the sixties featuring water buffaloes and armored personnel carriers, Kalashnikovs and M-16s, the Peace-loving Peasants and the American Devils. Women and children bathed in bomb craters. American GIs lit up with Zippos. The footage followed the movements of a girl guerrilla fighter, a beautiful child with a long glossy black braid who appeared to be as tough and sharp-shooting as her compatriots, all men. The screen darkened, and then the camera focused on the grainy, shadowy features of Vietnamese tunnel fighters, a group of ten sitting in an underground cavern. The camera panned over the room. I was fascinated: These were the first moving images of the tunnels I had ever seen, the first pictures I could compare to the ones I had imagined. A bullhorn-loud voice blared from the TV, announcing, *Patriots give their lives for freedom from the American Imperialist Devils!*

Although it was obvious that this was a propaganda film made during the war, an American woman behind me was shocked. She protested under her breath and shifted in her seat. Finally, after being called a devil one too many times, she stood and said, "Who do they think is spending money to visit these tunnels anyway?" and walked out. I watched the film for another minute, until the tunnel fighters were replaced by more footage of Peace-loving Peasants, and then I followed her.

The woman sat on a tree stump, a Louis Vuitton bag scrunched in her lap. She wore mini-shorts and, as I approached, she crossed her long tan wax-smooth legs. Her sandals were high-heeled, expensive, and impractical by any standard.

"Want a cigarette?" she asked, assuming I spoke English.

I took one and sat on a tree stump near her. The smoke rose into the rubber trees.

The woman told me her name, Patty, and where she was from, Mas-sachusetts, and said, "My husband was in Vietnam with the Special Forces. I wanted to go to Bali, but he needed to come back here."

My jeans were dirty, my hair cropped and messy, and there was not a bit of gloss or shadow or any other form of makeup on my face. I felt extremely young, all of a sudden, as if I were twelve and trying to impress a Roscoe's barfly. I told her my father had been in Vietnam as well.

"Is that why you came here," she asked, twisting a diamond ring on her finger, "because of your dad?"

"Because of him," I said, watching the thick green jungle, "and because of me."

"So," Patty said, as she picked a fleck of tobacco from her teeth, "you're one of those kind of people."

"One of who?"

"One of those people who think you can come to terms with it. It's so masochistic. I mean, Christ, it is time to *move on* already!"

I had never thought of it that way, but maybe she was right. Perhaps there was something masochistic about an American coming to Vietnam. I'd met a man earlier that day, in a café near my hotel, a heavyset guy in his fifties who told me he'd served in the Big Red One. It was his third trip back to Vietnam since he'd left in 1970. He had graying hair and owl-droopy eyes. A hive of beggar children descended upon him—as they do upon all foreigners—and he gave out dollars, perhaps fifty or so, before waving his hands over his head. "No more!" he said. "No more!" And still the children swarmed. The man must have had some terrible ghosts haunting him. He looked heartbroken. If he'd had a mint's worth of dollars, I'm sure he would have given them all away. Finally, he got up—his coffee unfinished—and walked down the street, a fat, limping man trailed by kids.

"Jim!" Patty waved over her slick manicured husband. He looked as young as his wife, but he must have been at least fifty, if he'd served in Vietnam. "This girl's dad was here," she said, proud of herself for finding me. "What year did he come, honey?"

"'Sixty-eight," I said.

"Her father was here in 1968. Maybe you knew him?"

"Not likely, sweetheart," Jim said, turning to me. "You're here with your dad?"

"No," I said. "I'm here alone."

The man looked me up and down, suspicion in his eyes. I knew that look. I encountered it many times in Vietnam, especially when I met veterans. The look was skeptical yet interested. The look said, *What is a nice girl like you doing in a joint like this?* It posited that he liked my style, that I was cute in a spunky way, but that I would be much more attractive if I stopped playing with boy toys and got back to girl stuff. Jim said, "Where'd your dad serve?"

"Here," I said, opening my arms. "Right here."

"Infantry Division?"

"Twenty-fifth."

"Tropic Lightning?"

"You got it."

The man nodded. He knew that division. I had passed his test.

The tour guide led the group into the forest. A tiny old man who had lived (our guide informed us) in the tunnels during the war accompanied us through a grove of rubber trees. We passed a sign that read: PLEASE TRY TO BE A GUERRILLA FIGHTER! Just beyond the sign, in a clearing, was a shooting range where we could, for a dollar a bullet, try our luck with any one of the Ms: -1, -3, -4, -14, -16, -30, -60. These were the guns of the American infantryman. I asked to handle the Russian AK-47 rifle, the most widely produced firearm in the world and favorite weapon of the NVA and VC. It was heavy and cool in my hands. I slid my fingers over the iron barrel and then gripped the selector lever. I tried to imagine the kick of the gun in automatic. I repositioned the lever; it made a thick *ka-chunk*. How many Americans, crouched down in the rubber trees, had heard this noise in the distance and feared for their lives?

The tour guide gave us a history of tunnel warfare, elaborating on the terrible pain the Western enemies suffered as they died in the depths of the earth. Patty, still feeling demonized, piped up from the back row. "There are some Americans in your audience, you know. Maybe you could tone it down a little?"

The tour guide told us that the tunnels began as small disconnected burrows under peasants' huts, places to hide weapons or extra food or even a person. When the war with the French began, the Vietnamese worked through the laterite clay at a pace of six feet a day, using hands, sticks, and small woven baskets. They scattered the dirt in the jungle under cover of night, to ward off suspicion. Over time, the tunnels connected through rooms—kitchens and sleeping chambers and hospitals—and plummeted sixty-five feet to the water table, forming wells. It was possible that the Vietnamese got the idea of building tunnels from the Chinese, who had made similar structures in the thirties, during the Sino-Japanese War. The Vietnamese complexes, however, surpassed the Chinese tunnels or any other tunnel system. They radiated from the Cambodian border to Saigon, allowing the Vietnamese resistance to plan battles, store weapons, and launch attacks. In fact, the tour guide claimed as he gave us this information, the Tet offensive was planned right there, in the Ben Duoc tunnels.

We stopped before a tunnel entrance. The tour guide rounded us up and said, a hint of challenge in his voice, "Please make two groups. Group one, those who would like to go into the tunnels. Group two, those who will stay aboveground." The girl with the dreadlocks flat out refused to go down. She stepped into the second group, as did Patty. But I, who until that moment did not know if I would have the courage do it, felt excitement growing in my stomach, a liquor-strong warmth that was part fear and part excitement. I stepped into the first group.

THE FIRST TIME A U.S. SOLDIER WENT INTO THE TUNNELS was in 1966, during Operation Crimp, when Platoon Sergeant Stewart Green accidentally sat on a nail protruding from a wooden entrance cover. Green thought he'd sat on a bee. In fact, he had uncovered the hiding place of thousands of Vietnamese guerrillas. As he was only 130 pounds and wiry, he took it upon himself to investigate the tunnel complex he had discovered and became the first American tunnel explorer. This discovery was the beginning of the U.S. military's understanding of how profoundly their enemy was entrenched. Once the underworld of the VC was exposed, the Americans—with their gas grenades and tracking devices and bombs and tunnel rats—began to shut it down.

In June 1967, the First Infantry Division—the Big Red One—created the only official tunnel rat squad, a brotherhood of thirteen men who were, like the Green Berets, highly disciplined, trained, and fully aware of what they were up against. According to *The Tunnels of Cu Chi*, the "dirty thirteen," as these rats came to be called, was composed of volunteers who "tended to reject most of the earthly pleasures available to men in war." These men didn't drink, gamble, or become involved sexually with the civilian population. They were soldiers with little patience for the usual rigmarole of search-and-destroy missions, who wanted to do more than Rome-plow the jungles or toss around cans of CS gas. These rats had their own swagger and a patch that read NOT WORTH A RAT'S ASS in Latin to match it. They also had "undergone considerable psychological and physical examination" before being allowed to join the squad.

My father and the other men who went into the tunnels for the Twenty-fifth Infantry Division had no such support. Although their base camp sat just south of the Fil Ho Plantation and slightly north of Cu Chi town—in the middle of one of the most densely tunneled areas in the war zone—tunnel exploration and destruction was not an official priority. The Twenty-fifth never got a squad together, and there was no standard operating procedure created for the tunnel rats, as there had been for soldiers in the Big Red One. The rats of the Twenty-fifth were all volunteers taken from the regular ranks of grunts. They tended to be go-it-aloners, guys with an extraordinary sense of self-reliance, maverick privates out to prove themselves. The Twenty-fifth was not picky—they took anyone who came. As a result, untrained, uninformed, unprepared privates died in the tunnels, clearing the way for other untrained, uninformed, unprepared privates to volunteer. One Sergeant Green could be replaced with another. There were always more: cowboys, rodeo stars, bone-dumb grunts who didn't understand the hell of the mission. Or men like my father, who wanted to do more than walk around in circles through the jungle, men who believed they could handle the worst the war had to offer and come out unscathed.

THE DAY DAD WENT DOWN HIS FIRST TUNNEL, HE WAS dehydrated and dizzy from the heat. His canteen was empty, and the Huey wasn't scheduled to drop more water until dinner. Humidity hung over the forest, a hallucinatory sway of green and beige.

The platoon hiked down a gulch with a thin stream trickling through it. Goodman spotted a tunnel entrance dug into the side of a hill and pointed it out to Pops. As Goodman ran his fingers over the entrance hole, he said, "You want VC communications, that's where you'll find them." He knew if there was one thing the brass always liked, it was recovered documents.

Pops limped to the hill and looked into the hole. "All right, Goodman. Smoke it."

Goodman pulled the pin and threw down a frag grenade, singing (with his thick southern accent), *Three blind mice, three blind mice. See how they run, see how they run.*

Fine dust rose from air holes in the ground ten, twenty, thirty feet away. Pops cleared Goodman to go, but he stayed, waiting for the dust to clear. Tommy was always joking around, and he cracked jokes while the rest of the guys dropped their rucks and ammunition belts to the ground. George walked off to piss. Rudy, a black guy who called himself the platoon's sharpshooting motherfucker, opened a can of C-rations as Pops pulled his socks off to give his infected feet some air. Pops had transferred up from the Mekong Delta, where he'd waded through the marshes, and a tropical fungus had embedded itself between his toes. At their worst, his feet were greenish blue with cracks of yellow pus running through them. The boys in the platoon were always surprised that Pops managed to keep up with them, but he did.

Weeds and brush grew around the edge of the tunnel entrance. "Don't worry, this ain't a live one," Goodman whispered, as my father squatted before the hole.

"How do you know that?" Dad asked, gazing into the darkness.

"With the entrance uncovered like this? It's definitely cold."

The earth was thick and hard around the opening, reddish

brown. "Just follow me," Goodman said. "Got your flashlight? I'll be checking out the nooks and crannies for booby traps." He pulled a rope from his rucksack and tied one end around my father's waist, the other to a tree just outside of the entrance. Goodman grinned as he knotted the rope. "Just in case someone needs to pull you out," he said. When he didn't tie a rope around himself, my father asked why. Goodman grinned, showing perfectly even teeth. "Don't worry about me, Trussoni. I'll pull myself out." He rigged a small flashlight to his bush hat with wire and duct tape. "Now, keep the big flashlight in your butt pack and be ready to backtrack if there's a problem. Got it?"

The tunnel opened around them in a whoosh of blackness. My father stumbled and fell into the darkness. His eyes died, became useless. He blinked, trying to adjust. His flashlight was weak, and his hearing began to subsume all his other senses. Sitting on his haunches in the entrance shaft, he felt too big for the space. The air was thick, without oxygen. For the first time, he felt utterly alone.

He crawled into a communication tunnel, a space even smaller than the entrance shaft, three feet high and two feet wide. Following Goodman's lead, he leveled out onto his forearms and knees. They moved ahead slowly, by inches. Roots brushed against his head. The flashlight beam played over the walls, and he felt the earth tilt away under him. He fell deeper and deeper, swallowed by the earth.

"No matter how cold a tunnel is," Goodman whispered, "never just go on through. That's when they get you, when you least expect it."

"But this one's cold, right?"

"There's no such thing as a hundred-percent-safe trip through the tunnels—there are only degrees of hot and cold." If a man respects the danger, Goodman continued, he's got a much better chance. Respect the tunnels and their rules. Rule number one: Always check for booby traps along the entrance tunnels. A guy never knows what's there. A VC might have rerigged a stretch just for the hell of it.

There was a rasp of metal on leather as Goodman sheathed his knife.

Goodman pulled himself up off his belly and onto his hands and knees. The tunnel seemed to widen, to open, but, when my father lifted his head, he hit the tunnel ceiling. His flashlight fell and rolled into the darkness.

They pushed forward, through the overwhelming heat. Goodman gathered speed. The flashlight beam diffused over the tunnel walls, revealing a bat sleeping in a crevice, a bump of black hair on the smooth brown wall. My father tried to keep up. The rope snaked behind him. It jerked, then cinched, becoming tighter and tighter around his waist.

"What about the rope?" my father asked.

"Untie it," Goodman replied. "Pick it up on the way out." Dad fumbled with the knot, loosened it, and left the rope behind.

Without it, he felt unprotected. Sweat fell into his eyes; his nose burned with dust; his uniform had shrunk to his skin. The darkness pressed upon him. He didn't feel scared, exactly, more like he was choking. He tried to breathe slowly, as if this might clear the dust or lighten the density of the air. His biceps burned; his wrists ached. There was nothing but dark as he moved forward.

"What do you smell?" Goodman whispered. When my father said that he smelled nothing, Goodman corrected him. "You smell dirt," he said. "You smell your own sweat. When you're down here, you always smell *something*."

My father went ahead. He put his flashlight in his mouth and dirt dissolved on his tongue, tasting mineral. Raising his .45 next to his ear, he pushed himself forward, into a room, hitting a mound of loose dirt. Goodman crawled in after, took the flashlight, and swung light over the floor, swift. "First, you check for movement," he said. "Then, for other tunnel entrances."

He moved the light across the walls.

"Take this," Goodman said, handing my father the flashlight.

Dad slid his gun under his belt and worked the light over Goodman's head.

Goodman pried at the clay with his knife. It fell in chips, creating dust clouds in the light. "This is damn solid," he said. "It probably takes forever to dig out one of these rooms." He pulled out his gun and hammered the knife handle, directing the blade like a chisel. Chunks of dirt flaked to the floor. "More light," he said, irritated, and my father leaned closer, so that a dull sphere of illumination fell across the wall. Goodman hacked at the dirt, sweat blooming over the back of his fatigues, turning the olive-drab black. My father wanted to know what in the hell he was doing, digging at the wall. All he wanted to do was get out of there, crawl back up to light and fresh air. How long would it take to get up to the surface?

It was always here in my father's story that he paused to take a drink of brandy and Coke, and I—who am an impatient listener, too susceptible to suspense—would beg him to go on. He'd swirl the ice in his glass and drag on his Pall Mall. "What do you think old Goodman found?" he'd ask, and although I had heard this story many times and knew exactly what he and Goodman found in the tunnel wall—a discarded NVA uniform—I wanted Dad to tell me that it was here, in his first tunnel, that he and Goodman dug out the skull. I wanted him to tell me how he carried the skull through the war, and why he brought it back home. Why had he been drawn to it? But when I'd say, "What else did you find? There must have been more down there," my father just shook his head. "I didn't want to stick around to find out. I told Goodman we needed to get the hell out of there, and quick."

Goodman climbed into the communication tunnel. My father followed, picking up the rope on the way back and tying it around his waist. He crawled through the dark until the entrance shaft gaped above him. The dull black of Goodman's boot swung through the weak sunlight, just missing his face. He reached up, grabbed the tunnel edge, and pulled. Light. Air. He wanted the surface like nothing he'd ever wanted before.

YET, HE NEVER LEFT THE TUNNELS FAR BEHIND. ONCE, AS a girl, I woke in the middle of the night to find my father bleary with booze, his war photos scattered across the kitchen table, a handgun (loaded, with the safety on) resting on a mess of spilled brandy and cigarette ash. As I stood behind him, so close I could see the fine hair at the back of his neck, I wondered what bad dream had scared him awake.

"I can't sleep," I said, yawning and brushing the hair out of my eyes. Dad jumped a little—I had scared him from his thoughts—and then pulled me to his lap. Chilled in my thin pajamas, I worked myself close to his chest, where I could smell the musty cigarette smoke, the tang of liquor on his breath. Resting my head against him, I drifted into sleep, half conscious in his arms. His words filled my mind, as if they were something I had dreamed.

"I'm sorry," he said, picking up a picture. "Forgive me."

As he spoke, confessing a crime I never understood, I did not know what he meant. He was apologizing (to Goodman? to God? to himself? I have never known to whom he was speaking), begging forgiveness.

"I didn't want to be there in the first place," he said, as he pushed a photo of his platoon (Goodman and Dad, their arms around each other's shoulders, front row center) across the table with his index finger. "I had to do what I had to do. I didn't have a choice. Nothing I could have done would have made a difference. Nothing at all."

SIX

The year I turned eleven, Mom started a new job as a clerk at the Onalaska Town Hall. She worked from seven-thirty until four during the day and then drove downtown, to her college classes, which sometimes lasted until eight. On weekends, she went shopping at department stores and brought home new clothes—gabardine slacks and silk blouses and three-inch pumps: work clothes, professional clothes. They suited her. From the way she held the pieces up, squinting as she examined herself in the mirror, I could see how happy they made her. She couldn't wait until Monday to wear them.

Mom had her hair styled into a pixie cut, giving her face a sharp angular beauty. I almost couldn't recognize her any longer. She had transformed, growing determined, more defiant. Despite Dad's grumbling about money, she had bought herself a pair of sparkly diamond earrings for her thirtieth birthday. And she kept her job, no matter what Dad thought. When he said, "You don't have any business working outside of this house," my mother looked him over, careful about which battles she would fight, and walked away.

It seemed to me she was leaving us an inch at a time. Mornings, she walked down the driveway with us to the bus stop, where she left us loaded with lunch boxes and book bags. *Kiss, hug, see you tonight!* We tucked our milk-money quarters in our pockets and waited for the school bus. Mom checked her watch, turned on her heel, and marched back up the driveway.

After school, when she was at work or her class, we let ourselves in the house through the garage door. The house was never locked. As we lived in the middle of nowhere, nobody would have thought of breaking in. If the door got latched by mistake, I would bust the door to the wood chute in the cellar and lower Matt down. At six, he was skinny enough to crawl through the narrow passageway. He would climb over the mossy logs, fearless, before running upstairs to the first floor, to let us inside.

One afternoon after school, when Mom and Dad were still at work and Kelly and Matt were toasting Pop-Tarts in the kitchen, I found Mom's green canvas backpack, filled with her schoolbooks. Spreading the contents across the floor, I found accounting and business textbooks, a pack of mustard-yellow Bic pens, and a spiral notebook. I opened the notebook and saw Mom's fat, loopy cursive writing. The top of each page had been marked with a date, and the middle of the page carried sentences peppered with the names Kelly, Matt, Danielle, and Dan. Reading it over, I realized I had found Mom's diary. I read her account of my sister's grades and my brother's daredevil injuries. Matt was a package of unstoppable speed, running as fast as he could, never looking where he was going, and slamming into walls, knocking himself down: a manic, bloody windup toy. But she also wrote of wanting more than life had brought her. More time, more money, more love, more freedom.

Flipping through, I came across a page in the center of the notebook filled with colored bars. Looking more closely, I saw that Mom had made a chart. Our names were written down the left margin of the page, vertically, and the numbers ONE to TEN were written above, horizontally. The names and lines were arranged in a fashion that quantified how much Mom believed we loved her. She had shaded the line next to Kelly's name all the way to the number NINE with blue pencil, signifying that she thought Kelly loved her 90 percent. Matt's line had been shaded to a little over NINE in green pencil, just inching past Kelly's line. My name, however, was colored only to FOUR, in red pencil, the same color as my father's line, which was also shaded to the number FOUR.

I stared at Mom's chart, feeling as if the wind had been punched out of me. I felt hurt by my mother's assessment and surprised that I didn't have a NINE like my sister and brother. But I also felt strangely proud to have been given equal footing with Dad. It was the first time I saw proof that I was like him. We were Dan and Danielle, two perfectly matched, inadequate red fours in Mom's life. I slapped the notebook shut, wishing I had not seen it. Mom had balanced the books, and two of us didn't measure up.

ONE WINTER EVENING, WE WENT SLEDDING ON THE HILL below the garden. Kelly and I pulled Matt up the slope, poised our red plastic sled at the edge of gravity, and—*one*, *two, three*—we hopped on and skidded down, all the way to the clothesline near the porch. Dad walked outside jacketless, a cigarette hanging from his lips, wearing nothing warmer than a Hanes T-shirt, arms exposed to the wind. Grabbing a shovel, he cleared the sidewalk. Although it was freezing, he didn't seem to notice. Our father had the constitution of a mule and never admitted to feeling pain. Despite his ulcer, and the steady stream of Tums he swallowed to soothe it, I rarely saw him sick. In the harsh beam of the floodlight, he shoveled a path through the snow, his breath freezing around him. When the sidewalk was cleared, he propped the shovel against the house. "Inside," he barked. Kelly and Matt rushed to the house.

I didn't follow them. My moon boots felt leaden, too heavy to lift over the snowdrifts, so I sat, letting snow fall upon my cheeks. Frozen air rose from my lips and disintegrated into the night. The sky was magnificent: black, threaded with stars. Spreading my arms and legs, I made an angel in the creaking snow. A fine-pared moon ascended from behind a hill, inching up. I didn't want to go back indoors. It was clear to me that nothing had been right in our house for months. Mom was out again and Dad was grumpy, yet no one talked about it. It was as if a sheet of glass had fallen between my parents and us. We saw them and they saw us, but we could only watch as they drifted apart.

When I went inside, Kelly and Matt were thawing on the living room floor. Dad sat in a recliner, a drink in one hand, the remote control in the other. Dad didn't know how to cook, so when we got hungry, he cracked walnuts, picking the meat with a steak knife and scattering the puckered nuts across the coffee table for us. We thought the walnuts looked like little brains, so we snatched them up and screamed, *I'm eating your brain! Now you don't have one! I'm eating Matt's brain! Now he don't have one!* We chewed overdramatically, with mannered self-satisfied chomps. Kelly cracked a can of Dr Pepper and gave me a swig. This was our dinner. When Mom got busy and didn't have time to go shopping, the fridge would be empty and we would munch on whatever was left in the pantry from Mom's last shopping trip. Peanut butter and apples. Rice Krispies soaked in Kool-Aid. Matt curled up with Tootsie, our fat calico cat, to share a pint of ice cream. Tootsie licked the spoon clean.

It was long past dark. At the window, Dad lifted the lace-trimmed curtains and peered out, looking for Mom's car. Knocking the lip of his beer bottle against the glass, *tap, tap, tap, tap,* he looked like a deserted little boy. No matter how much he drank, Mom's nights away from home didn't sit easy. He would only go so far as to admit she was changing, now that she'd gotten a different set of friends and a paycheck she spent as she liked. "I'm not the kind of man who lets his wife run around," he said, as he gazed through the window at the dark night. When I leaned against his arm, our pale reflections stood side by side. We were insubstantial, ghost people, waiting and waiting.

"Fuck a duck, I'm hungry!" Kelly said, bounding into the kitchen.

"Watch your language, young lady."

"Where the heck is Mom, anyhow?" she asked, her finger shoved up her nose, but she already knew the answer: Mom was out with her friends. Or she was at her university lecture. Or she was at her aerobics class. Or she was at the mall. She was always somewhere else. We didn't understand why she was never home or why we had been left to Dad, who couldn't do anything as well as Mom did. We watched, waiting for him to figure out what to do, but he just sat—wounded and pissed off—as the ship sank. Dishes piled up, and Mom grew more daring in her escapes. Dirty laundry spilled from our bedrooms. The prow tipped and the cabin filled. The water rose higher and higher. Mom had jumped ship. Nothing we could do. *Gurgle, gurgle*.

At eleven years old, I did not see my mother's nights out the way Dad must have seen them. It took me years to recognize what was happening in the months before she filed for divorce. Yes, I missed her. Yes, I felt let down that she wasn't home to tuck me into bed. But I expected us all to be together forever. My father, however, knew he was losing her. All the signs were there, bright and flashy: new high-heeled shoes; fresh manicure; evasive, sullen, annoyed manner with us. And, of course, there was her growing absence. It was as if she had kept track of all the hours my father had left her at home alone over the years—his hours at the bar, his hours on the job, his hours dillydallying with whatever woman caught his attention—and was taking them back, minute by minute, her due.

Maybe during the months my mother was building herself a new life, Dad could have changed things. Perhaps if he had talked to her, she would have stayed. But it was probably too late for talking. At that point, little could have been done. And besides, my father didn't believe in negotiation. *Jabbering doesn't solve anything*, he would say. He would never, for any reason, have admitted that he had driven her away.

BY NINE O'CLOCK, KELLY HAD FALLEN ASLEEP ON THE couch and matt had curled up on the recliner, tucked under an afghan. The house was quiet, Mom-less. "Half brandy, half Coke," Dad said, instructing me on how to make his drink. "And use the crushed ice, not the cubes." He was particular about the strangest things—the brand of soda, the kind of ice in his glass—and I tried to be careful to get it right. I filled a tumbler with crushed ice, measured the brandy, and then the Coke. I carried his drink to the table, careful as I balanced the tumbler in the palm of my hand, feeling as though the fate of the world depended on getting it to him without spilling one drop.

"It's like you don't have a mother anymore," Dad said, taking the drink from me.

"Maybe Mom just needs a vacation from us," I said, sitting down next to him. Although I was trying to be reassuring, Dad got so angry I thought he'd knock me off my chair. He gritted his teeth. "Nobody takes a vacation from marriage."

After a few more drinks, Dad picked up the phone, punched in some numbers, and handed the receiver to me. "Ask to speak to your mother," he said, gruff.

I put the phone to my ear, confused. "But Mom's at the mall."

Dad stubbed out his cigarette and lit another. "She's not at the mall. The mall closed at nine. Do as I say."

Before I had time to argue, a female voice answered. "Hello?"

"Hi," I said, unsure of whom I was talking to or what I should say. "Is my mom there?"

The voice was as confused as I. "Well, I don't know. Who is this?"

"Danielle," I said, swallowing hard.

The voice repeated my name, and I recognized it. It was Sherry, my mom's best friend. Sherry, who had a daughter my age, and invited me over to swim in her pool and drink bottles of Mountain Dew and watch *Dance Party* on cable. "Danielle?" Sherry said. "What's the matter?"

"Nothing," I said. "It's just that Mom's late getting back from the mall. Is she over there? Can I talk to her?"

Sherry paused, and I heard (in the background) Mahogany, the golden retriever, clipping across the tiles of their kitchen. Sherry said, "She's not here. I haven't seen her all night. I hope everything's OK."

"Everything's great," I said, hoping my voice didn't quiver. "Everything is just perfect."

I hung up the phone, turned to Dad, and shrugged my shoulders, a *what-can-we-do-she's-not-there-who-knows-maybe-she's-still-at-the-mall* shrug. Dad's face darkened, but he was not surprised. He put out his cigarette and chewed a Tums, then pulled a red address book from a drawer. Flipping through the pages, he began to dial numbers, an unlit cigarette dangling from his lips. We called Mom's sisters, her friends, her parents. Dad dialed and I did the talking, feeling him behind me, listening: *Is my mom with you? Have you seen her tonight? Do you know where she might be?* I asked questions until I was on the verge of tears. When I was so worried I could not call another person, I looked at Dad and said, "What if Mom was in a car wreck? Should we call the hospital?"

Dad smirked, suppressing his anger as best he could. "She hasn't been in any car wreck," he said. "Don't worry about your mom. I'll track her down."

Dad left Trussoni Court in his truck. I sat at the kitchen window, drawing spirals in the frosted-over glass. The tail-lights of the truck burned sharp and hot as Dad drove into the snowy night, hunting Mom.

WHEN MOM CAME HOME, TWO HOURS LATER, I KNEW SHE had not been at the mall. As she unwound a chenille scarf from her neck, the car keys jingling in her hand, I saw that she was too made up (with her lips and her fingernails painted sports-car red) to have been shopping, too beautiful for Sherry.

As Mom walked through the kitchen, Dad (who had passed out in his recliner with the walnut bowl in one hand and the steak knife in the other) woke suddenly, as if he'd been caught sleeping on guard. "Where've you been?" he demanded, brushing his fingers over his shirt, to smooth it.

"Out," she said, evasive.

"Out?" Dad repeated, as if he had never heard this word before, as if he had not used this same explanation for all his own late nights and lost weekends over the years. "I drove all over hell, looking for you."

"I went ... "—Mom paused, examining her drunk, disheveled, knife-holding husband—"shopping. With Sherry. You know that."

It was obvious, by the way Mom carried herself and the fact that she had no packages to show for her trip, that she had not been shopping. She set her purse on the table and unbuttoned her long wool coat. "What, Dan?" she asked. "What do you want me to tell you?"

As my father stood before her, helpless, I remembered a trip Dad and I took the year I started kindergarten. We drove fast on two-lane country highways, as Dad chain-smoked and chewed Certs mints, the radio cranked. After ten minutes of driving, Dad parked in front of a house. It looked like nobody was home—the lights were off, and no car sat in the driveway—but a woman with red hair stepped from the door, as if she'd been waiting. She led me into her living room, set a bowl of pretzels before me, and turned the TV to *Sesame Street*. Then I was alone.

I wandered through the house, looking at crystal knick-knacks (mice and kittens and clowns) and Hummel figurines displayed in a cabinet. Along one wall, a series of photographs had been hung; kids with the same auburn hair as the woman smiled from wooden frames. Where were these children? I wondered. Why weren't they at home?

Letting myself out a sliding-glass door, I walked onto a deck. A bright blue inflatable kiddie pool sat at one end. Although it was October, the pool was full of water. Red and orange maple leaves floated upon its surface. I took off my shoes and stomped in the water, kicking the leaves. When Dad came downstairs, full of piss and vinegar, tucking in his shirt and checking his watch, he saw me and stopped in his tracks.

"What in the hell are you doing?"

I hopped out of the pool and stood, soaked, on the deck.

"What's your mother going to say?"

"Better towel her off," the woman said.

Upstairs, in the bathroom, the woman took a blow-dryer to me. She wrapped me in a towel and wrung out my clothes. I was too young to fully understand what was happening, and I probably would not have remembered the incident at all—not the house or the kiddie pool—if it weren't for the odd way the woman looked at me as she combed my hair. Something was wrong about her. She was too attentive, studying me as if looking for flaws. I was not used to such scrutiny. She squatted down, staring at me full in the face, and said, "She looks like her mother, doesn't she."

My father wasn't paying any attention to the woman or to me; he was anxious to leave the scene of the crime. "Spitting image of her mother," he mumbled. "Spitting image."

I STOOD IN THE HALLWAY, WATCHING, AS MOM FOLDED her chenille scarf and laid it on the kitchen table.

"Danielle called Sherry," Dad said, his face growing red. "You sure as hell weren't with *her* tonight."

Mom paused, taken off guard. She set the car keys next to her scarf, too careful, too deliberate. "And just why was Danielle calling Sherry?"

Dad ignored her question. "First, you're gone all day at

that job of yours, and now you're traipsing around all night. Look at this house. Do I work all day to come home to this? What's next? You're gone weekends, too?"

It was then that Mom noticed me, watching from the sidelines. She didn't speak to me, and for a moment I thought she was angry that I had called Sherry. She pointed her long red fingernail in the direction of my bedroom and mouthed one word: *Bed*.

IT WAS SNOWING AGAIN. DRIFTS PILED UP INTO FROZEN waves of white, two feet high. When the snowplows didn't come, we were all stuck inside, for a snow day. Dad didn't work much from November to March, anyway—it was too cold for masonry—but Mom, who had grown to love her routine (up and out of the house by seven-thirty, work until four, off to the university, home by ten) didn't know what to do with a snow day. She walked through the house, her lips pursed, forced to face our messy rooms, the mountains of unsorted socks, the catastrophe of unpaid bills and unmade beds. She stood at the window, watching the snow barricade the road. Everything she wanted was on the other side of that glass. Finally, she changed out of her work clothes, tied a bandanna over her hair, and made us breakfast.

We were thrilled to have our mother all to ourselves, so we followed her around the house, bugging her. Oatmeal, pancakes, cookies—we wanted whatever she could give us. After breakfast, she set up our coloring books and paints on the living room floor and fell into a plush recliner near the window, a stack of *Better Homes and Gardens* magazines at her side, watching the snow fall. By lunchtime, she'd had enough. She sent us outside with pails and shovels to make a snow fort.

Winter was our native season. I was a winter baby, my first months of life filled with ice. Dad was born in a snowstorm. As my grandmother told it, she went into labor with my father three weeks early. No doctor would drive to Genoa on ice-covered roads, so they found a neighbor (a DeFlorian cousin) to assist with the birth. My father was born quickly, without complications, and although he had come ahead of schedule, he weighed over ten pounds. Grandma once said that his premature birth was an example of my father's personality, his *let's get on with it* approach to life.

My grandmother said that in his first moments of life, he was silent, as if getting used to the idea of the world. He opened his large curious eyes and lifted his arm, experiencing gravity's resistance. A rime of ice on the window comprised the lacy-white landscape of his first minute of sight. He was blood-coated and still warm from the womb. A cold draft reacted with his heat, and the tiniest bit of steam rose from him. He shivered, had his first notion of nostalgia, and screeched. The DeFlorian neighbor wiped the blood film from his bullfrog belly with a hot cloth, squeezed (dispersing pink into a porcelain basin), and gave him back to his mother, ready for the world.

When we came inside, Mom was cleaning our rooms. She picked the toys up from the floor, dusted and boxed them before brushing the vacuum over the rug.

It had only been half a year earlier, the previous spring,

when Mom had been laid up in bed, stricken by a mysterious illness. Every day, when we got off the bus from school, we would walk through the unclean house, past Tootsie, to my parents' bedroom. "Bring me a glass of tomato juice, would you?" Mom would say, and we'd sit at the foot of the bed, watching the tail end of *The Bold and the Beautiful*. My parents' bedroom smelled warm and musty, as if something were decomposing under the bed. Matt would snuggle at Mom's side, working his head under her armpit, his shoes crumbling mud on the sheets. Mom was pale; her eyes had dark rings under them.

"What's wrong? What's wrong?" we asked.

"Nothing's wrong. I'm just resting, that's all."

As I eased myself next to her, I felt safe and secure, as if nothing bad could happen. I ignored the fear I felt, seeing her sick. Mom wouldn't lie to us. If she said nothing was wrong, nothing was wrong.

One day we came home from school to find her bedroom empty. Maureen O'Brian, our regular babysitter, sat in the kitchen, talking on the phone to her boyfriend. Maureen had had an accident the year before; she had fallen asleep driving and flipped her Pinto into a ditch. The window had been open, her arm resting on the ledge, and her left hand had been mangled in the crash; she always tucked this scarred fingerless hand under her armpit, so it looked like she was hugging herself.

Maureen finished her call and said, "Your mom is in the hospital. Your dad will be home in an hour or so. He'll explain everything."

When Dad came home, we ran down the driveway,

meeting his truck. He climbed out, grabbed his toolbox, and walked inside to the kitchen, where he took a can of beer from the fridge, popped the top, and flicked it into the trash. Kelly and Matt and I gathered around him, barraging him with questions. *Where is Mom? Why is she at the hospital? Is she sick?*

Dad said, "I have some good news and some bad news."

Good news first! Good news first!

"Good news: Your mom had a baby."

Dad paused while Kelly, Matt, and I whooped and screamed. *A baby? A boy or a girl? What's its name? A baby!*

Dad took a sip of his beer, waiting for us to quiet down.

"Bad news: It was born too soon and died."

The three of us looked at our father, too stunned to speak. Dad leaned against the countertop and tapped a Pall Mall filterless from the maroon-and-white pack. He lit the cigarette and looked out the window. A slow, sickening sensation of loss grew in my body. A new baby had been given to us and taken away, all in five seconds. I hadn't even known that Mom was pregnant—she had hidden herself in her bedroom and wasn't far enough along to show, anyway. But now, knowing that a baby had been on the way, I thought of it as stolen. It would have come home, wrapped in a white blanket, and I would've helped change and bathe it. I would've picked out a name and taken the stroller down Trussoni Court. Although I had never imagined another one of us before, now I felt robbed. An extra place setting formed at our table, another set of shoes appeared at our doorstep, one more giggly-voiced kid rode in the backseat of Mom's car. A new face appeared in every family picture and then disappeared, leaving a blurry, indistinct hole. Maureen looked away, her hand tucked behind her, embarrassed and uncomfortable. Kelly's eyes filled with tears. Matt said, "We can fix the baby, right? The doctor will make it better, right?"

Dad did not respond. Annoyed by our whining, he dug in his pocket for cash, which he gave to Maureen, her pay. Ignoring Kelly's tears and Matt's questions, he took one last swig of beer and walked to the front door. "I'm going to the hospital," he said. "To bring your mom home."

When Dad left, I took Kelly and Matt to the living room, where we sat cross-legged on the shag carpet.

"Where did the baby go?" Kelly asked.

"Don't worry," I said. "The baby is in heaven. It's OK. Don't cry."

Although I was as confused as they were, I felt it my duty to supply the words and the expressions and the gestures that Dad had withheld. I tried to explain. Lying to my sister and brother and to myself, I created a Dad code. I told them Dad's annoyance meant he loved us more than words could express; his drinking meant he suffered more acutely than other people; his coldness was a cover for intense feeling. I apologized for Dad and forgave him in advance. I interpreted Dad and spoke for Dad. I convinced myself that I was capable of this. And sometimes I was.

AFTER THE MISCARRIAGE, WE ACTED AS IF IT HAD NOT happened. Nobody spoke of the baby. Nobody mentioned that Mom had stopped doing all the things that made her Mom. This was when she started going out more than ever, and Dad turned mean. One evening, on her way out the door, Mom turned to me and said, "You're in charge of cleaning your bedroom. It better be spotless when I get home."

I looked out the window as Mom backed down the driveway, did a Y turn, and drove away.

Dad was sitting in the recliner, his feet up, the phone cord wrapped around his tube socks, on the phone with one of my uncles. I stood in the doorway, listening. *I found her the other night at some bar with friends I didn't know she had. This place is a goddamned pigsty. She's got no time for us anymore. I told her she doesn't need to work. She should be home, raising these kids. They run around like a pack of goddamned ragamuffins. There's no discipline around here. Danielle and Kelly are the mouthiest little shits I've ever seen.*

When Dad saw me in the doorway, he covered the phone with his hand and said, "Your mom told you to clean your room. Is it clean?"

I kicked the carpet with my sock. "Not yet."

"Then get your ass in gear and clean it."

I did not get my ass in gear. I squatted in the doorway, pulling strands of the shag carpet, eavesdropping. Dad smoked and looked into the distance, his eyes dark and intense. Dad's eyes were the same color as mine, only a slight blue circle had developed around his brown iris, forming an off-colored ring. The ring was congenital, a genetic gift from my grandfather. Dad didn't always have it. The ring came slowly, developing like a photograph under the spell of a chemical solution: The black edge of the eye dissolved into points of light, becoming the loveliest hazel (almost butterscotch), and then gunmetal gray, until the eye congealed into its final concentric composition. Dad's doctor said the ring signified cholesterol, the accumulation of lipids under the slight membranes of the eye, but I always thought of it as a family mark. The day before Grandpa Trussoni died from cancer, when I went to his room to say goodbye and his oxygen tubes were at the side of his pillow and his skin had gone yellow, he looked at me and said, *I'm always going to be watching over you, wherever I am*, and I did not wonder where he was going or how he would get there. All I saw was the pretty blue ring around his black eyes.

Dad covered the phone with his hand and said, "What are you looking at?"

"Nothing much," I said.

"I don't need your lip. I told you to clean your room. Now go. "

But I did not go to my room. I tried on Mom's shoes and kicked around in the hallway and was in the process of tap dancing in the kitchen (Mom's Dr. Scholl's *clip-clopping* on the yellow linoleum), when I felt Dad's hand grab the back of my neck. It was so sudden, so jarring, that I did not have time to scream or kick or protest as he dragged me to the hall toward my room.

"What did I tell you?" he said, as he lifted me above the carpeting with a firm grip. He held me by the neck with one hand and swiped with the other. Cold-hot slaps stung my legs, my thighs, my back, my face. I wiggled in his grip, unable to breathe. "Nobody gives a shit about this house," he said. "It's a goddamned pigsty. I work all day to come home to this. Go. Clean. Your. Room."

For a moment, I was lost in the momentum of Dad's anger. I was backpedaling, sinking. The hallway reeled from under me; it flashed black and brown and red. I tried to breathe but choked on the air. It was not until I stopped struggling that Dad dropped me to the floor. I looked up at my father, astonished. His body was taut, constricted, ready to come at me again. And then, when I began to cry, he transformed. It was as if he had surfaced from the depths of a dark dream. His body softened, and a look of recognition crossed his face: *Don't I know you? Haven't I seen you somewhere before?*

He turned on his heel and walked away, mumbling, "I don't have time for your bullshit," which meant (in Dad code) *I love you.*

seven

In the months before the divorce, Dad drove us to school in the morning. Kelly, Matt, and I crunched into the cab of his white Ford pickup, trying to fit. Dad had moved "the books"—thick binders filled with records of his company's transactions—into his truck, where they sat, stacked on the seats and under the glove compartment. He had begun to carry his home around with him in the past months, as if afraid that my mother would burn the place down while he was gone, incinerating everything precious—marriage, kids, business. Kelly, Matt, and I packed ourselves inside the truck, ready for school.

Dad used the truck as his main office, conducting his business in transit. At red lights, he answered his phone, a handbag-sized mobile phone—the kind that required a huge antenna attached to the roof—bolted to the truck's floor. A notepad had been Super-Glued to the glove compartment door; pens sprouted from the built-in ashtrays. Invoices and bills and paycheck stubs were strewn over the floor. The only thing the truck lacked was a filing cabinet and, perhaps, a secretary. With the phone wedged to his ear, a cigarette in one hand, coffee in the other, he would turn to me—*Quick, write this down*—and I took dictation. Dad sipped his coffee, careful not to spill, and worked the mug into its dash-top holder.

Dad dropped us at church to attend mass with the other students. Saint Patrick's Christian Grade School was small, private, and run by Franciscan nuns. Children ages five to fourteen spent their days moving between a church, a school, and a caged-in blacktop playground. Despite the fact that it was below zero, we stood outside, glaring at the building. We hated going to church in the morning and would have rather frozen to death than walk up the sidewalk and go inside. I buttoned my coat, wrapped my scarf over my chapped lips, and stared at the stained-glass windows. They were so luminous, so perfectly lit, that the whole church seemed fashioned from sparkling glass, as if someone had thrown a bucket of water to the sky, and by some miracle of winter it froze in midair, becoming a light-filled ice sculpture.

My fifth-grade class sat at the center of the nave. Although we were all eleven years old and should have been alive with energy, my classmates were prematurely aged, soporific, ready to die of boredom. We attended church service every morning before class, mass on Sunday with our families, religion classes all afternoon. When we weren't in school or in church, we were out fund-raising. The nuns sent us door-to-door with catalogs featuring scented liquid hand soaps, cubic zirconia earrings, and potpourri jars. We carried a little card that read: *I am a student at Saint Patrick's Grade School. Please buy this scented hand soap to support the teachings of our Lord.*

Every spring, I rode my bicycle to all the houses near Trussoni Court. There were not many, and I had to ride for miles to reach them. I pushed my bike up steep hills, my eyes and throat swollen from pollen. When I reached the top of a driveway (my white cotton blouse mud-spattered) I pulled out my sweat-soaked catalog and my crumpled card and said, *I am a student at Saint Patrick's Grade School. Can you help me out and buy something?*

My best friend, Serenity, saved me a seat in her pew. She said, "Hey, what's up, Doc?" her voice Bugs Bunny wry, her eyebrows two thin wings. Serenity, who had a strawberry-blond pageboy haircut, the ends blunt as if they'd been hacked by gardening shears, was smart and worldly and new at Saint Pat's. When she introduced herself, she said, "I know, I know, Serenity is a strange name. My parents were a pair of hippies. Too much macramé or something."

As I sat next to her, Serenity smiled, wickedness in her eyes, and flashed a *Playboy* magazine hidden in her hymnal.

She said, "How much do you want to bet Father Rossitor gets it on with Sister Mary Jane?"

I laughed, drawing evil looks from the nuns.

Serenity continued. "Of course, he's probably not in big demand—most of the nuns don't want him." She raised a pale eyebrow. "If you know what I mean."

I had no idea what she meant. I listened to Father Rossitor's sermon, trying to figure it out.

I shifted my gaze to Father Rossitor, our priest. Father Rossitor had spent a year in Vietnam as a chaplain, where he damaged his feet following soldiers through the swamps. He wore black plastic orthopedic shoes and walked with a limp. Dad always liked Father Rossitor and considered him a family friend. As far as I knew, Father Rossitor was the only outside person my father spoke to about Vietnam. Sometimes they talked after church, and Dad would say, "Father Rossitor is just a regular guy, like the rest of us. He isn't like those other priests, always trying to make you something you're not. He knows where I'm coming from."

Father Rossitor finished his sermon, the words *sin* and *payment* and *forgiveness* floating through the church. My mind drifted through standing and kneeling and praying until it was time for Communion.

"Before we leave this morning," Father Rossitor said, at the end of the service, "I would like to ask each of you to direct your thoughts to a terrible problem in our congregation. It has come to my attention that some families are having difficulties, and so I would like to have a moment of silent prayer for the members of our community who are going through a divorce."

Silent prayer filled the church like a clear, dizzying gas. I looked around, horrified. Did everybody know about my parents' problems?

After mass, our class was herded to the confessional. I'd been confessing my sins since after my first communion, in the second grade. At seven, I had had little of interest to say; by eleven, I considered myself a fountain of sin, a veritable juvenile delinquent. I slid the confessional door shut, bent into the thick cushions of the kneeler, and told a shadowy figure the inner secrets of my soul. *Forgive me, Father, for I have sinned. Since my last confession, I copied Jenny's math homework. I talked during church. And, worst of all, I think my family is getting a divorce. I know I should pray, but I always forget. Don't tell anyone. Except God. But he probably already knows. Anyway, forgive me, Father, for I have sinned.*

I didn't confess that I'd lost faith in my family. If I said a hundred Hail Marys and Our Fathers, pushing the plastic beads of my rosary through my fingers all day, would it make a difference? Mom had been sleeping on the couch and Dad didn't come home until late at night. I didn't tell Father Rossitor that, when I felt the ceiling and the walls would collapse in on me and my stomach twisted so I was on the verge of throwing up, I would bite the skin on my arms until great kidney-shaped welts appeared. When bruises blotched my skin, I wore long-sleeved shirts to cover them. I colored the bruises with a red marker, drawing hearts and curlicues and song lyrics. I didn't tell Father Rossitor this. What would he have said if I did?

My time at Saint Patrick's ended abruptly that spring when a disgruntled member of the congregation named Brian Stanley entered the nave of the church (just minutes after mass had ended) with a hunting rifle. He descended to the church basement and shot the janitor, Mr. Hammas, whose wife (a crossing guard) was standing just outside, policing a sidewalk; he shot a lay minister, Ferdinand Roth, whose grandson was in my class; and he shot, execution style, Father Rossitor, who was kneeling in prayer before the cross. When the man had finished his gruesome business, he left the church, his hunting rifle in his hand, his mission accomplished, and sauntered down Main Street, where he was apprehended fifteen minutes later. He did not fight when he was arrested. He surrendered his weapon and told the police he was performing God's will. He was self-righteous, full of conviction. The newspapers called Brian Stanley a fanatic.

On the day of the killings, Kelly and I left the school grounds. The church was roped off with yellow tape, and there were TV people doing live reports. Police cars had blocked the road; blue-and-red lights spun across the church entrance. Parents were buckling their crying children into station wagons. Kelly, who had the baffled expression of a doll, stood by my side, biting her fingernails. She looked up and down the road, waiting for a white Ford truck to appear and carry us away.

MEANWHILE, MOM HAD BECOME THOUGHTFUL. SHE WAS calm, distant, all-her anxiety gone. She had made her decision, and now it was just a matter of time. She ironed our clothes too perfectly, stacking our jeans in neat crisp piles in our dresser drawers. The pantry was always stocked. Our socks always matched. I would catch her watching, waiting for the right time to tell us.

One afternoon after she got home from work, Mom called Kelly, Matt, and me together in the kitchen. Leaning against the wall, her hands in the pockets of her gabardine trousers, she said, "Danielle, why don't you go to the fridge and get everyone a Coke."

"But we're not supposed to have Coke," I said. "Only on special occasions."

"It's a special occasion," Mom said, keeping her voice low, as if not to wake a baby.

I poured out glasses of Coke for Kelly and Matt, and I knew (as I sat in a chair, facing Mom) what was coming.

"I have something to tell you," she said, although she was looking not at us but out the window, into the yard, at the three trees in the lawn. Dad had planted those trees after we were born, christening each one with our name. Danielle was a thick-branched oak tree whose bark swirled with knots and fissures, Kelly was an ash whose lithe branches lifted toward the opaque sky, and Matt was a sapling apple tree, still too young to produce more than knobby green fruit. The trees sat all winter, blanketed in snow. Now it was April, and they were just beginning to bud.

"I know! I know!" Matt said. "We're going to Wisconsin Dells this summer!"

"Of course we'll go somewhere this summer," Mom said, turning from the window and looking at us. "But what I have to tell you is a little more *serious*."

"Let me guess," I said, deadpan. "You're getting a divorce."

When Mom looked at me, surprised, I smiled at her, sarcastic. *No fooling me.*

"Not exactly," Mom said, a little too quickly. Adjusting her tone, she continued. "We're not getting a divorce. Not right away. We're going to try a separation. Just to see how things work out."

"What's a divorce?" Matt asked.

"We're *not* getting a divorce," Mom repeated. "Nothing is certain yet."

"A divorce," Kelly announced, as if reading from a dictionary, "means you have go to court."

"Kelly," Mom said, her eyes filling with tears, "nobody is going to court."

"So, are you leaving?" I asked, my voice steely, angry.

Mom took a deep breath and said, "Your dad is moving to a house on the North Side for a few months. He's already rented it. He's moving his things out this weekend."

Crossing my arms across my chest, I stared at my mother. All these arrangements had been made over the past few weeks without us knowing.

"Don't look at me like that, Danielle. We're just trying this out."

"So you're getting back together then," I asked, "after Dad moves out?"

"Maybe," she said. Although her tone implied optimism, tears ran down her cheeks. She wiped them with the back of her hand. "Anything is possible."

Ten minutes later, I found her sitting on the edge of her bed, her head cradled in her hands. Her back was slouched and her neck soft, as if someone had taken her by the shoulders and shaken the strength out of her. When I sat by her side, she brushed her hand across my leg. There were no rings on her fingers. "Why don't you and Kelly and Matt go for a walk," she said. "The fresh air will make you feel better."

WE MET ANDY FOR THE FIRST TIME AT THE WARD AVENUE movie theater two months later. When Mom spoke of him she told us that the man in the yellow sweater was a Very Important Person. She said that we should be on our Very Best Behavior. We must try Very Hard to be nice. Even before we left home I knew, by the way Mom had dressed and the way she had dressed us—all in clean pressed clothes—that we would be meeting her boyfriend.

When we got to the theater, however, it was as if we'd run into Mom's lover by accident, a bit of happenstance at the multiplex. "Oh, hi there," she sang to a heavyset guy with a black mustache, as if to say, *Fancy meeting you here.* But as Andy walked across the lobby it was clear that this meeting wasn't a coincidence. He made a quick businesslike half wave, leaned across the red velvet rope to kiss Mom on the cheek, and shoved a twenty in her hand to pay for our tickets.

In the weeks after my father moved out, Mom filed for divorce, killing all hope that the trial separation would lead to reconciliation. Dad, who packed his truck and left Trussoni Court, angry and sullen, fell into a pit of drinking. Now Andy, the man Mom had been seeing on the sly, was meeting us at the movies.

I looked Andy up and down. He was a big guy, not much different from the lumberjack Dad beat at Roscoe's except, perhaps, that he was better dressed. He wore polished leather shoes with a fringe on the vamp. His skin was tanned dark brown, his black hair neat-trimmed, his yellow cable-knit fisherman's sweater the kind I'd seen only in the JC Penney catalog. Kelly stood at my side, looking at Andy, honestly confused. She wrinkled her nose and said, "And who the heck are you now?"

"I'm Andy," he said, a big smile on his face, trying his best to be friendly. "Which one are you?"

After Kelly had introduced herself, I said, "I'm Danielle.

Named after my dad. His name's Dan. You know my dad, right?"

I hadn't seen much of Dad lately. The day Mom announced the separation, he came home from work, riled on booze and indignation. He stomped through the kitchen (not bothering to remove his work boots), pausing at the counter, where Mom stood, washing dishes. "They know yet?" he asked, anger making his voice crack. Mom scrubbed the dishes, looking willfully into the sink, as the three of us kids ran to our father, hugging his legs. Dad looked straight ahead, as if we weren't there at all. With all of us clinging to him, he couldn't move an inch. That was how we wanted it. If Dad left, our world would topple.

Andy held his smile, but he was unsure of how to respond to me. He said, "Well, it sure is nice to meet you girls."

I folded my arms across my chest. Kelly wove an arm through mine, so that we were connected side to side, Siamese twins interrogating a prisoner. "So," I said. "How long have you known my mom?"

"*Our* mom," Kelly said, correcting me.

"Our mom," I said, corrected.

Andy took a deep breath, as if he'd been rehearsing the exchange for a month, and said, "We work together at the Town Hall. I've known her quite a while."

"You've *known* her a while? Or you've been her *boyfriend* awhile?"

Andy bit his lip, sending his mustache into a kink.

Kelly was with me one hundred percent. She nodded. *Go get him, sis.*

"Because if you've been her boyfriend for a while, why are we only meeting you now?"

Mom, who had been struggling with the zipper of Matt's spring jacket, appeared at Andy's side. She cleared her throat, embarrassed. "Girls," she said, narrowing her eyes. "*Shhh.*"

We took seats deep in the center of the theater. Red velvet drapes hung over the walls. Andy, Mom, Matt, Kelly, me—all of us sat in a row, almost like a family.

"What are we seeing here, anyway?" Andy asked, squinting to see his ticket in the dark.

"This should be a good show," Mom said, overcheerful.

"Who's in it?"

"John Travolta, I think."

"Oh, this will be great then," Andy said. "You kids like movies?"

We stared at him, silent, scrutinizing. After enduring us for a minute, Andy wiped his sweaty hands on his pants and announced he was off to buy popcorn. When he was gone, we turned upon our mother, who sat ill at ease, as if she didn't know how this whole movie situation came about in the first place, as if *oops* we'd all just ended up here together. It was a Tuesday afternoon in May, after all, and we were the only ones in the theater. Other kids our age were in school until June. Our summer vacation had begun early. Saint Patrick's Christian Grade School was dealing with a personnel problem.

"Here we go, kids," Andy said, when he returned. He was really trying to impress us; he had two large popcorns, a jumbo-sized Dr Pepper, a box of Dots, a box of Starbursts, a bag of Twizzlers, three Snickers, a Mars Bar, and a king-size Kit Kat. His arms were so full I could not see his face. He sat, flustered, and passed out this treasury of junk food.

Kelly took a tub of popcorn and a couple of candy bars. As the lights dimmed and the curtains retracted, she elbowed me and said, "Hey, maybe this guy isn't so bad."

I took the wet, waxy cup of Dr Pepper from her hands. I scooped a handful of popcorn, shoved it in my mouth, and filled the remaining space with sugary Dr Pepper. "Who?" I asked, my mouth full of sludge.

"You are so gross!" Kelly said, trying not to laugh. "This Andy guy. Maybe he's not so bad after all."

I swallowed the mucky mixture down, almost choking myself, and looked down the row, past Mom, at Andy. I might be eating his popcorn, but I was not easily bought. "Yes," I said, my heart full of Dad loyalty. "Yes, he is."

WHEN ANDY MOVED TO TRUSSONI COURT, I BEGAN TO sleep in the basement, in protest. I moved my things into an empty room near the wood chute, where Dad used to keep his business papers. A dull, earthy smell met me as I lugged boxes down the stairs. I carried them past the furnace, past Dad's workbench (which was now filled with Andy's drills and hammers and power saws), and deposited them on the moss-green carpeting. I filled a twin-size waterbed with water from a garden hose; I hung a poster of The Cure on the door. Mom had promised me I could do whatever I wanted to do in my new room, so I pierced my ears five times with a hatpin. I painted the concrete-block walls black and played depressing music at all hours of the day and night. I'd decided to never come out.

It was around that time that my uncle Dick, the three-tour marine, started calling our house in the middle of the night. When Andy picked up the phone, Uncle Dick would say, *Who do you think you are, sleeping in my brother's bed?* Andy walked through the house, dark circles under his eyes, his bathrobe tied slack over his stomach. There was the sense that we were all in danger, that the sharp-edged Trussoni wrath would soon fall upon us. We knew that with one wrong move our precarious family would collapse.

It was only a matter of months after Andy moved in that I decided to live with Dad. My father had told me upon leaving that I was free to come to his house any time I wanted. When I told Mom I was going, she had the same look of fear I saw once, when she caught me taking her best china into the woods for a picnic. It was clear that my decision hurt her, but I was angry. Since Andy, she had had no time for us at all. She and Andy would go away for the weekend, leaving us with Maureen, and they were planning a trip to California. Where was my place, I wanted to know, in Mom's new life? The last weekend in June, Dad loaded the back of his truck with my things. Mom drove me to the North Side, to drop me off.

THE EL CAMINO WAS SHINY PEA GREEN, AND MOM A reckless ready-for-anything driver. She turned up the radio and pushed her pink-painted toenails to the gas pedal. She drove sixty-five over mud bumps, rode the railing around long curves. The dirt roads near Trussoni Court—open and clear as we approached—changed as we drove over them, became closed and cloudy. The barbed-wire fences unwound alongside us, droopy as telephone lines. Speed whipped the heaviness of the world light, and I almost believed, for a moment, what my mother believed—that a quick engine and a jolt of speed could wipe the past clean.

Mom was a mess—no shoes, no lipstick, scraggly-fringed jean shorts—but happy. Her black hair blew over her face and snarled, but she didn't care. She smiled as I had never seen her smile before, the promise of freedom giving her a new kind of beauty, a crystalline other-timely beauty that I studied from the passenger seat, a bottle of Mountain Dew between my knees.

For the first time in years, Mom was happy. Even I, who never paid attention, could see the flush that love put in her cheeks. Other people saw it too. They stared when we stopped at the bank to cash her paycheck. They moved aside as she sauntered to the teller. I doubted that all the money in that bank could buy even a little of the *I'm starting over* joy my mother felt.

Outside the bank, Mom wove her long fingers between my short skinny ones, and we skipped across the smoldering parking lot. I steered her clear of the tar veins on the blacktop's surface. At the El Camino, Mom lifted her still-bare feet (vanilla-milkshake-white on top and blacktop-tar-black on the bottom) up and down, up and down, as if skipping rope. "Ouch! Ouch! Hot! Hot!" she said, as I tried not to cry. I blinked my eyes and blinked my eyes again. The crisp world of the parking lot and the El Camino blurred watercolor fuzzy. Would she miss me at all when I was gone?

"I want to stay with you," I said, but I realized, even as I said it, that this was not true. The Trussoni Court I used to know had changed. Although I loved that house, I did not want to live there anymore.

"You can come back anytime you want to," Mom said. "After the summer, things will settle down." Mom had hired Maureen O'Brian to stay with Kelly and Matt for the summer, while she and Andy went to Vegas and then California, to a wedding and then a honeymoon. Everything had been planned. The tickets had been bought. "Give me that," she said, nodding at my untied tennis shoe.

I lifted my foot to her, as if forking over something stolen. As if I were still a baby and not an almost-grown girl of twelve. Mom tightened the laces and rebowed the bow.

"This is your decision, you know," she said. "I know you're upset with me. But try to understand."

I eased off the hood of the El Camino, straightened my sundress, and slid into the car. Although I was doubtful that I would ever understand anything—not my mother's remarriage, not my new home on the North Side—nevertheless, I kept the promise before me like a door that would open (and open again and again) and lead me far away.

Gravel skidded under the tires as we parked next to Dad's house. The El Camino's hood captured my mother's reflection: the obsidian hair, the white skin. Mom walked through patches of afternoon sunlight and banks of shade to me. As I hugged her goodbye, I felt her soften and then become resolved. She would leave the past behind her. She would leave the world she had made with my father. And no matter how difficult it was for her to turn and walk back to her car, she would leave me.

She waved as she drove away. I waved back, halfheartedly. Caledonia Street, lined with maple trees, canopied the receding car. Patterns of bark pulled my eyes up, by way of branches, to open-fingered leaves that shifted and dipped in the wind. When she was gone, I flopped down on the curb, my yellow sundress spreading from my legs like a daffodil. The afternoon light distilled itself over my skinny arms and legs, dappling them pink and silver and cream. For a moment, I was an illuminated, fire-speckled girl. My arms would not move. My legs would not move. My body was still and broken, as if the El Camino had backed over me. I knew, for the first time, what it meant to be alone. I made a promise to myself, one that I would keep. I said, "Someday I'm going to leave this stupid place."

SIX MONTHS LATER, I WAS STILL WORKING OUT THE details of my escape. The curb before Dad's house was my favorite place for scheming. It was also where I would wait for him to come home from work. If his truck appeared at the stoplights down the street, I would jump up and wave my hands, signaling. When the truck rolled to a halt before me, I would wrestle the door open and climb into the cab and we would be off, two outlaws heading for Roscoe's. But my father didn't always come for me. Sometimes he went to Roscoe's alone. When he did, I was left on the curb, waiting.

Dad's house was on Caledonia Street, one block from

the Mississippi River and three lots down from a pawnshop called DEAL WITH THE DEVIL. His house was squat, gray, and cheaply made. The siding was plastic; the windows were covered with plastic; the mailbox was plastic. The lawn, the only nonplastic thing in sight, was mottled with muddy snow. I sat on the curb before the house, waiting for my father to come home.

North Side bars buttressed each end of our block. The corner bar to the right of our house was called Track II, the one to the left, Fishes. I looked from one neon sign to the other. I wrote the bars' names with a stick in the snow: *Track II, Fishes*. In the months since I'd left Trussoni Court, I'd spent too much time thinking about the meaning of these names. Did Track II refer to railroad tracks? To the owner's favorite songs? Where was Track I? I rearranged the words' letters, thinking that perhaps they were anagrams of a secret message. I believed, even at twelve, that there was meaning in the world, that there were patterns to it, no matter how hidden. As I studied the letters scratched into the snow at my feet, I wanted to capture the melancholy, the sense of hopelessness I felt on the North Side. *Track II. Fishes*. I looked into the empty street before my new home and wondered, *How in the hell did I end up here?*

When Dad didn't come for me, I stayed on the curb, angry and stubborn, until it was after dark and I could no longer see my breath freezing into arabesques around me. The chill crept up my legs, settling in my knees. I twirled my key chain (a loop of telephone cord) around my wrist. On these evenings, when I had been forgotten, I felt waves of desperate isolation wash over me, a sensation I would one day call *depression* but which, at the time, I designated as pure, pervasive cold. There was no remedy for it, no prescription, nothing I could do to nurse myself to warmth. I was utterly, hopelessly bone-chilled on a blasted-out moonscape sidewalk. It made no difference that I had a room packed with books and clothes and CDs in the house behind me. I would not go inside. I would sit and wait. I would absorb the ice and the snow and the wind until I was frostbitten blue. I would hold out until the end, continuing the game of chicken I played with my father, wanting (for once) to win.

OFFICIALLY, MOM AND DAD SETTLED UPON JOINT CUStody. In reality, Kelly and Matt stayed with Mom and Andy, and I with Dad. On weekends, however, all three of us would go to one house or the other, to visit. Mom took us one weekend, Dad the next. My sister and brother and I lived out an existence that was divided and scheduled. In my mind, there was something physical about joint custody. I always associated the idea with the body, as if time had been made skeletal. Our family was not held together by love or loyalty but by cartilage and ligaments. Time with my mother was one bone (perhaps the femur), time with my father was the other (perhaps the tibia), and we, the kids, the knee, the movable part that brought things together that would otherwise be separate.

One Friday night of Mom's weekend, Dad picked us up from school. Mom had to work late, so Kelly, Matt, and I sat in the living room, watching TV and waiting for her to come and get us. Dad had plans for the evening; he wore his best cowboy boots, and Old Spice filled the air. "Where the hell is that mother of yours?" he shouted from the kitchen.

When Mom arrived at eight o'clock, we had been waiting for hours.

Dad didn't hear the bell. I ran to the door and flung it open. Mom stood in the doorway, dressed for the weather. Her ski jacket was a mélange of blues: baby blue sleeves, navy collar, periwinkle trim. A bright red hat was pulled to her eyebrows. Mom was always a little afraid of my father during the divorce. Never certain of what he might do, she was careful not to confront him, especially when he was mad. I gestured for her to come in and, when she hesitated, I realized that (for the first time in my life) I was giving my mother access to a room. It was up to me to say, *Come in, can I take your coat?* It was me, her daughter, who had the power to bring her deeper into the house or—with a flip of the wrist—slam the door in her face.

She did not accept these terms. She stood at the doorway, peering in. Dad's house was small and exposed, and Mom saw everything: the kitchenette/dining area, the living room barely big enough for the (secondhand) love seat and TV, the exposed Sheetrock and woodlike plastic paneling. Dishes were piled in the sink, the floor was stained with mud. Ashtrays formed little volcanoes on every surface. She saw the wet T-shirted Bud Light girl poster/calendar tacked near the phone and the sack of Wonder bread on the counter. The whole thing, from the front door to my shoebox bedroom, was the size of the Trussoni Court house's garage. There was nothing to signal that my father was once a landowner, an inhabitant of a house with many rooms. The only things Dad had from his former home were the gun case and his box of war mementos. And me.

Dad hadn't registered Mom's presence and so, when he turned and saw her in the doorway, he was startled. He touched the kitchen table, to restore his balance, and smiled at her, a forgetful *where have you been my darling* smile, a grateful *you've finally come to save me* smile. In that topsy-turvy moment, my father forgot that he was living without her. There was no divorce, no other man, no battle over kids and property and pride: There was just him, in love with her.

Dad's smile filled the kitchen with radiance. I wanted to capture it (and all of its joy and all of its hope) in a glass jar and keep it in my room at night, so that it would blink in the dark like a firefly. Although I knew it was a mistake, I didn't want him to give the smile up; it was the only glimmer of happiness I had seen for weeks and weeks.

When Dad realized his mistake, the smile wobbled and tipped on its axis, shattering on the linoleum floor, a million shards of happiness.

"Come on, kids," Mom said. "Let's go."

"They're not going anywhere," Dad informed her. "You're late. I'm keeping them this weekend."

Mom did not leave the doorway. She said, "This is my weekend. I've made plans."

"Your weekend or not your weekend, these kids are mine. They're staying with me."

Kelly and Matt, who were putting on their hats and winter coats, stopped and looked from our mother to our father, miserable. Dad walked to the door, brushed past

Mom, and headed out to the street, where he opened the hood of her El Camino. We stood in the doorway, watching as he rummaged around the engine. Mom folded her arms across her chest and sighed. Her sigh held in its skin the remnants of every battle she had fought with my father. Her sigh said, No amount of talk, no bit of logic, will change this man.

Dad returned to the kitchen a few minutes later and threw the El Camino's spark plugs on the table. "I paid for that car," he said, hooking his fingers through the belt loops of his jeans. "It's staying here too."

Kelly began to cry. Matt, who was made of stronger stuff, stood next to me, wary. All three of us watched our parents, wondering what they would do. We knew that they were both miserable.

"Fine," Mom said, offering a hand to my sister and brother. "We'll walk."

Kelly and Matt zipped their jackets, took Mom's hands, and walked out into the snow. When my mother realized I was not following her, she turned. She said nothing, but I knew, by the emphasis in her pause, exactly what she was asking of me: *Will you brave the wind and snow and winter bitterness and come with me?* She was asking, *Who's it going to be, him or me?*

The choice was mine. I felt my loyalties collect into opposing sides of myself, a maternal side and a paternal side, a separation I had felt growing since before the divorce. Half of me wanted to walk with my sister and brother into the snow and follow my mother wherever she would go, to walk any road, no matter how cold, with her. The other half wanted to stick it out, there with Dad. These two new parts of me—one in white tights, the other in red—drew swords, hopped back, cantered forward, and parried. There was the thrust, the riposte. The fencer in white may have had my love, but the fencer in red had my loyalty and, in the end, won the match. My mother raised an eyebrow. Our eyes remained locked for a second of perfect understanding. And I knew, by the way she turned away—pain giving her an elegance she did not have five minutes before—that she accepted my choice and that my first step away from her would remain forever between us.

AFTER MOM LEFT, DAD FOUND HIS COWBOY HAT AND pocketed his keys. He didn't say where he was going, although I knew he would be at Roscoe's. He slammed the door when he left.

I tore the lid off a box of macaroni and cheese, poured the noodles into a pot of boiling water, and waited for them to soften. When they had expanded into overblown crescents, I drained the water through a colander and then—in an orchestration of perfect timing—cut butter into the pot, added a splash of milk, and returned the noodles, while (with the other hand) I shook a packet's worth of electric-orange processed-cheese powder over the mixture. With the right amount of stirring, I whipped the chunks of powder to a watery, iodine-colored sauce. I sat at the window, eating my dinner with a wooden spoon directly from the pot.

I set the pot of macaroni on the windowsill just as a rusted-out orange truck stopped before the house. Andy got out of the driver's-side door. He fumbled for something in his pocket, and I imagined a sleek black pistol emerging from his jacket. I imagined him polishing it with oilcloth, preparing for a duel on the front lawn. A neighbor would pull aside her lace curtains, light a cigarette, and watch as Dad and Andy paced off and turned, backs straight. They would shoot to kill and kill for love. The bullet would spin through the air, revolution after revolution of hot metal. Mom, the contested creature, the center of gravity of all of this passion, would lean against the truck, yawning as they carried the bodies away.

But there was no pistol and there would be no duel. Andy pulled a set of spark plugs from his pocket, lifted the hood of the El Camino, fumbled with his gloves, and went to work. Mom climbed out of the passenger-side door and stood next to him. I moved closer to the window and, as I did, some shadow of me must have caught my mother's attention; she studied the house and then me, sitting behind the dirty windowpane. She smiled slightly, raised her mittened hand, and waved. I waved back. The plate of glass between us was smeared with grime, and for this I was thankful. She could not see how much I missed her.

eight

Grasping the edge of the tunnel entrance, I pulled myself into the darkness. The guide was ahead, somewhere, and so I worked myself inside, past the entrance, where I sat on my haunches, feeling the cool crumbling walls, looking forward and then behind, sizing up the dimensions of the hole.

If the tunnels began as a haphazard network of underground hideouts, they were transformed by the Vietcong between 1954 and 1968 into a regulated, standardized city under the ground. A captured Vietcong tunnel manual (translated and held by the American Defense and Intelligence Agency until 1968) gave the official instructions for tunnel construction. In it, every dimension was prescribed. Communication passages between chambers were required to "zigzag at angles between 60 and 120 degrees," in order to divert chemicals, explosives, and bullets. The passages were to be "no wider than 1.2 meters, no narrower than 0.8 meters, no higher than 1.8 meters, no lower than 0.8 meters." Each tunnel was expected to conform to exact measurements, all of them smaller than the tourist tunnel.

Other mandates of tunnel construction were similarly

precise. A-shaped shelters—small conical grooves in a tunnel wall—were designed to withstand bomb and artillery fire. A snake-shaped curve, or U-bend, was molded into the passages to cleanse the air. Each room was supposed to contain two or more entrances, to ensure a quick escape. Even the layer of earth that separated aboveground from below had specific requirements: Each tunnel ceiling had to be 1.5 meters thick (about five feet), which according to the manual was the appropriate thickness to absorb the aftershocks of bombs. As the tunnel manual made clear, a tunnel system should be used not as a bomb shelter but for the transport of food, munitions, and guerrilla fighters. Each entrance, passage, and chamber must contribute to the larger purpose. Every tunnel was a small part of a large weapon.

When Dad was in Vietnam, locating an entrance was the most difficult part of tunnel destruction. Soldiers would Rome-plow the jungle or singe the foliage with flame-throwers and still miss them. When they did find an entrance, they used a commercial air blower called the Mighty Mite to pump down smoke, which rose through other entrances and into the air, creating a misty aboveground map of the network. Smoke spiraled in ringlets every ten, fifteen, or twenty feet. To clear the tunnels, men flooded the entrances with river water and acetylene gas. They threw down grenades and crystallized CS-1, to contaminate the air. With every technology available, they smoked the guerrillas out.

But today the tunnels were nothing like they had been during the war. They had been filled in, neglected, ignored. Most had filled with monsoon rains and collapsed. Jungle claimed the rest, piece by piece. Only the Ben Duoc tunnels had been preserved, and although I knew they were just a memorial, a tourist trap, a Disneyland kind of history, I could hear something ahead, breathing. It crouched in the dark beyond, waiting.

Perhaps my guide was closer than I thought. Lowering myself onto my palms, I crawled forward to find him. Rats knew that entering a tunnel was the most dangerous part of exploration. Sometimes they sent German shepherds in first—trained to sniff out the enemy—to clear the way. The dogs would go blind with dust and excitement and set off booby traps: boxes of bees, trip-wired grenades, red ants, punji sticks dipped in poison or urine, each one sharp enough to slip through the body, impaling soft unprotected organs. The dogs fell prey to scorpions and boa constrictors and vipers. Injured dogs whimpered in the darkness, helpless and forlorn as sick babies.

Not three paces in, I bumped into a wall, brushing my cheek against the rough clay. During the war, micro-organisms lived on the damp earth near the entrance. They would fall upon the exposed skin of tunnel fighters as they passed, dig through layers of skin tissue, and lay eggs. In the moist wet underground, the skin would erupt with stinging, crawling, biting chiggers. The only way to remove these parasites was to burn the skin with a sterilized knife. Chiggers, the Vietcong said, were their worst enemies. They feared them as much as they feared the Americans.

The tunnel was quiet. Although my guide must have been nearby, I could not hear him. Well trained, he had melted into the network. I rested my head against the wall, unable to go forward. Perhaps I had come too close to my father's past. I could almost see him—white T-shirt soaked with sweat, .45 cocked at his ear. He was just ahead, and I was a girl again, running to keep up. He paused to light a cigarette outside of Roscoe's, his face tinted blue from the neon light. The door swung open, my father's fingerprints smearing the glass. *After you, Danielle-my-belle.*

MANY YEARS BEFORE, I HAD TAKEN A GREYHOUND BUS home and walked through the wintry streets to Roscoe's. I was in college at the time and had become obsessed with the tunnels. I wanted to write about them for a history class I was taking, and I was sure I would find my father on his usual bar stool, smoking and rolling for a drink during happy hour. Sure enough, his cowboy hat stood out at the far end of the bar. After pushing through the crowd, I pulled up a stool next to his. My father's third wife, Debbie, a tall pretty Roscoe's regular with perpetually shocked blue eyes, put a Virginia Slim between her lips, grabbed her lighter, and sauntered to the jukebox to play Kenny Rogers songs.

"Well, my dear," Dad said, as he made room for me at the bar, "how's college been treating you?"

I'd been having a rough time, working to pay for rent and books and tuition while maintaining an A average, and my father knew it. "Great," I said, nonetheless. "School is great."

Dad ordered me a beer. A bartender I did not recognize (Jan had long since quit) placed a bottle of Old Milwaukee before me. I told Dad about my classes (I was double majoring in history and English) and about an award I'd received from the English department. After we had a few drinks, I told him I wanted to write a paper about the tunnels for a history class. Would you mind doing an interview with me? I asked him, placing my notebook on the bar. "I want to know," I said, "what it *really* felt like in those tunnels."

My father gazed at the television, unsure of what to say. He didn't know why I was so interested. He sighed and said, "The truth is, I'm sick of thinking about that place. The day I left Vietnam was the best day of my life. I didn't think I would ever get out of there. I got in the plane and pinched my arm, like this—"

"Ouch!" I said, pulling my arm out of Dad's reach.

"I told myself, *You are a lucky man, Trussoni.* I decided then and there I was going to forget Vietnam. Some guys couldn't make it after they came back. I know those guys. They don't work. Can't have a family. Don't do anything but think about where they were. But I'm not like that. I never used the war, or my disability, as an excuse for anything. I let it go. I don't keep none of that war with me."

"Where is it then, Dad?" I asked. It was painful for me to see that my father did not realize how much the war had damaged him. He seemed to really believe that all his experiences had been shelved away and forgotten. But I knew my father better than that. I had seen how hard it was for him to forget. "Where is it?" I asked again. "Where has it gone?"

My father cleared his throat. He was quiet for a moment, and I suspected that he might be gearing himself up for some confession, a bit of self-reflection about how the war had changed his life. But he gave me a devious look—half love, half malice— and flicked my notebook with his finger. He said, "I gave that war to you."

DAD WAS SITTING ON THAT SAME BAR STOOL A NUMBER of years later when he told me he had throat cancer. The first symptoms had surfaced a month before, when he lost his voice. The harsh buoyancy of his speech calloused over and became husky, muted, whispery. He went to a hospital in La Crosse, where he was told he was experiencing a reaction to his stomach acid. A few months later, when his symptoms had not abated, he went again, requesting a more thorough examination. Although his doctor performed a biopsy, Dad was told he was fine and was sent home. This continued for a year, until my father could not swallow or eat food properly. He could speak in only a hoarse croak and was in so much pain that he took off time from work. When he went to the VA hospital for another opinion, the doctors asked him questions about his tour in Vietnam. They asked him when and where he had served. They asked him if he had had contact with defoliants, especially Agent Orange. They questioned him about his level of stress, the health of his children, his premature balding, the ulcer he developed before he was thirty. Had he, they wanted to know, ever had a psychiatric evaluation? When they finished asking questions, the VA doctors told my father that he would need to go into surgery at the Mayo Clinic in Rochester, as soon as possible. They had located a tumor the size of a bird's egg tucked behind his larynx.

Over the next few years, my father's cancer disappeared

and returned. He would go into chemotherapy and into remission and back into chemotherapy. Just when he believed he'd beat it, his doctor at the Mayo Clinic would call to inform him that they'd found something unusual in his scan, and another round of exams would begin. When it was time to go, Debbie backed their pristine white Cadillac from the two-car garage, careful not to nick the paint. Dad's Caddy had a vanity plate that read CIB68, which stood for Combat Infantry Badge 1968, the year he was awarded it. Debbie drove my father over the skeletal ironwork bridge that traversed the Mississippi River. They drove through Minnesota with the radio on a country music station. My father had a jade-green scarf—a python of a scarf that I knitted for him one Christmas—around his neck and a cowboy hat tipped over his eyes. After chemotherapy, a net of fine red veins had opened over his cheeks, as if his skin were experiencing a second youth.

His life changed after his diagnosis. He closed his construction company and retired early. Although his work truck (the tank filled with gas) was left unused in the garage, Dad still woke at five in the morning and looked out the window at the cold snow-covered streets, ready to go. He was a creature of habit. He hated to change his routine.

At night, Debbie cooked, setting her cigarette at the edge of the sink as she opened a can of Campbell's string beans. Debbie had a weekly menu, one she never varied: Monday hamburgers, Tuesday spaghetti and meatballs, Wednesday casserole, Thursday frozen pizza, Friday steak, Saturday wild card—either leftovers or delivered pizza or a restaurant dinner. Dad and Debbie no longer went to

Roscoe's. They mixed drinks at the kitchen counter. If I was there, Dad would pour me two fingers of brandy. He'd say, *Shit, I should've made my own drinks years ago. Bars make three hundred percent profit on liquor. Think how much money I'm saving!*

One evening, over drinks, my father showed me his post-traumatic stress disorder diagnostic report. In order to receive medical benefits from the government, he was required to undergo a mental health evaluation. He had gone to see a psychiatrist the previous month and had just received the results. As he had recently finished another round of chemotherapy, his voice was barely audible when he said, "Bet you never knew your old man was nuts."

He gave me the report. I looked over the list of symptoms, written out point by point. The report listed my father as suffering from the following:

Being overly alert

Feeling emotionally numb

Experiencing feelings of paranoia, excessive sensitivity, or that life has "backed you up against a wall"

Experiencing physical reactions when you are reminded of the traumatic event

Reliving the traumatic event, acting or feeling as if it is happening again

Trying not to think about, talk about, or have feelings about the traumatic event

Having bad dreams or nightmares about the traumatic event

Not being able to remember an important part of the event.

The bottom of the report read: *Mr. Trussoni's Symptom Severity Score is 41 with a Symptom Severity Rating of* SEVERE. *His level of impairment in functioning is recorded as* SEVERE *as well. His GAF score is 43.*

As I read the report, I felt a wave of recognition wash over me. Problems I had been grappling to understand for years seemed, suddenly, clear. I'd never had a language for Dad's illness, and simply seeing his diagnosis written on a piece of paper made his pain somehow manageable. I believed, as I studied the report, that Dad would finally accept that he was sick and get help.

The psychiatrist who performed these tests recommended extensive individual and group therapy. Dad, of course, had no intention of going. He had agreed to do the diagnostic test only to get medical benefits. After he'd qualified for the benefits (which included a monthly stipend of over two thousand dollars and full medical coverage for the duration of his illness), he did not plan to go back for counseling. Despite the report, he believed he didn't have a problem. In his mind, he had survived the war intact.

My father's PTSD diagnosis was made thirty-five years after he served in Vietnam. I wondered, as I looked over the report, what his Symptom Severity Score would have been in the early years, when he was fresh from the jungle, in the years of my childhood, when he drank to keep his depression away. In those years, we watched our mother struggle to understand a man who had built a wall so solid, so protective, that she could not break through it. We watched her turn around and go back to him, again and again. We struggled to be close to him and were shoved away. All of us absorbed the radiation of our father's memories, all the sad things he said late at night, after the bars had closed and he sat at the kitchen table having a nightcap. We absorbed all the things he didn't say too. We knew, when he shook his head and mumbled *Things were fucking crazy over there*, that some of the things he experienced in Vietnam were too terrible to talk about.

When I asked my father why he would not go back for counseling, he smoothed the edges of his PTSD report, clearly embarrassed that he had gone to see a psychiatrist in the first place. "I don't feel comfortable," he said, "telling a stranger about what happened." He didn't think he had a right to complain. "What do I have to bitch about," he said, "when I lived?" He did not consider that his problems had affected all of us, and this made me angry. I wanted him to get help. I believed that, if he did, my relationship with him would improve. I took the report and read it again. "Why didn't you get therapy when you came home? You could have been happier. Things could have been different."

Dad sipped his drink, set down the glass, and gave me a cocky half-smile. He had always been contemptuous of pain, especially when it was our own. "I didn't want their help," he said. "After I left Vietnam, I wasn't going to be a part of that again. Ever. Besides, I was too busy raising you kids for all that emotional hogwash."

THE TUNNELS STRETCHED AHEAD, ENDLESS. MY FATHER'S voice—the voice of my childhood resounded through the darkness. I crawled forward to meet it. The air was sticky-wet, without oxygen. I touched my arms and face, as if trying to brush away a cobweb, but the air clung to me as I moved. Why hadn't the guide returned? Please, I said to the tunnel, to my father, to no one in particular. Please, get me out of here.

The tunnel floor was rock-hard clay. I pressed my hands flat on its surface. I had nothing to dig with, so I pushed my fingernails into the earth—pointer, middle, ring—and pried. Small chunks gave way. I clawed deeper, scratching out a tiny hole. Drops of sweat rode my forehead and fell across my nose. I dug until, after a too-vigorous scoop, part of my fingernail ripped. Out of instinct, I put the wounded finger in my mouth. The sweet-salty taste of blood suffused my tongue.

Then, as if smelling blood, the guide was upon me, tugging at my arm to hurry, hurry, follow him. I placed my hands over the tunnel floor, feeling the contours of the small hole I'd made. Fumbling through my pockets, I found a few wads of paper, some *dong*, and a AA battery. I put these things in the hole, an offering, and covered them with the loose dirt. I had nothing else to give.

The guide turned a small flashlight upon me, shocking my eyes. When he moved the flashlight to the wall, I saw nothing but blobs of orange. Blinded, I reached for him. He took me by the arm and led me through the tunnel, to the exit.

MY FATHER USED TO SAY THAT TIME MOVED DIFFERENTLY in the jungle. Nobody could keep the days straight. You'd think it was Tuesday, he would say, and it would be Sunday.

You'd think it was July; it was March. A week would pass, then two, but it always felt like the same damn week.

George, the platoon's machine gunner, marked his days in-country on his helmet with a black marker. When it rained and the lines washed off, he would begin again. He said, "It feels like I start my tour over every time I get wet."

"But it's the monsoon," my father said. "It rains every day."

At night they camped in the jungle, digging foxholes or sleeping under ponchos. During the day, they patrolled, humping over hills, through jungle so thick the rain didn't make it down to them. Droplets spattered above their heads, pounding like a machine gun that never jammed.

Scotty, a grunt halfway through his second tour, said the VC were slippery little fuckers, invisible yet ever-present, and my father believed him; he'd been in-country two weeks and hadn't seen the enemy. Their platoon was instructed to find them and destroy their operational bases. They never stopped moving, sleeping half awake under canopies of palm leaves and spiderwebs. In the thick of the jungle, among snakes and swamp and indistinguishable peasants, they searched for an invisible enemy who, they believed, saw everything.

On the Fourth of July, they sat on listening patrol, dug into the side of a hill overlooking the jungle about a hundred yards outside camp, as their platoon shot off rockets and tossed grenades into rice paddies. Someone hiked a boom-boom girl up from the nearest village, and she stationed herself against a tree about fifty feet from camp. A platoon a couple of klicks west sent up flares and sang the national anthem. Red streaks reflected in black pools of water. It rained, on and off, and wasn't much different from any other night out in the boonies, except for the fireworks and all the singing.

It was late before the grenades and rockets faded into the nervous stillness they faced every night. My father had set up a couple of claymore mines fifty feet away, just in case. Claymores, my father liked to say, had two advantages: They were mobile and small. He held the detonator in his hand, running his thumb over its surface. Goodman was restless, pacing and chain-smoking, slapping mosquitoes and looking into the night, as if he could see past the monsoon clouds blocking out the moon and stars.

Rudy and George hiked the hill and sat down. Goodman examined the jungle, as if the VC were right there, camouflaged, hanging from the trees. "Look at this," he said to my father, bending down. "There's an entrance back here."

Goodman turned on his flashlight, pushed away a bank of leaves, and found a tunnel entrance, camouflaged with weeds and sticks. Bamboo was embedded in the clay around the entrance hole, strengthening it. Rudy and George joined them, Scotty sauntered over, and soon all five soldiers stood over the hole. "See how the bamboo is all straight here?" Goodman said, as he shook one tree and three others moved. "They've been tied together to look natural."

Suddenly a shot went off, the distinctive pop of an AK-47. A Vietnamese soldier ran to a tunnel entrance about thirty feet away. Making a quick vertical descent, he dropped fast and graceful into a space that couldn't have been more than two inches wider than his body. Watching him was like watching a pole, greased with oil, slide into the earth and vanish.

Goodman threw down his bush hat. He was decisive, gung ho.

"You don't need to go down, man. You're relieved," Scotty said, but Goodman stuck his flashlight in his belt and shrugged off his rucksack. "Take this back to camp for me," he said.

Watching Goodman, my father felt excitement growing in his chest. Although he didn't understand why he wanted to go down—he knew it would be better to leave this one to Tommy—he felt that this tunnel was his. He tucked his pants into his boots and loaded his pistol.

"This one isn't cold," Goodman said, as he crouched near the entrance, touching the edges gently, feeling for wires or bamboo triggers. He pushed himself in headfirst. His boots rested at the entrance for a moment, and then he was gone.

Scotty and my father walked up the hill, toward camp. George and Rudy stayed near the claymores, on watch. It was near sunrise, and the darkness had changed from black to light gray. Scotty said, "You have no idea what you're dipping your ass into, Trussoni. Your buddy, he knows what he's in for. Shit, he's praying for it. But you're just following after him like a stupid country boy."

"I don't follow anyone," Dad said, and left it at that.

As they hiked the hilltop, the sun rose in the distance. Dad always said he'd seen more sunrises in Vietnam that he had seen on the farm in Wisconsin. He watched the sky, when, all at once, he knew that he was alone. Scotty was a hundred yards back, crouched, watching. Branches broke at the base of the hill. A group of NVA soldiers—between ten and twenty of them—crept below them.

Scotty was on his belly, his M-16 before him. "Stay the fuck away from me, asshole," he whispered, so my father crouched down where he was, above the NVA soldiers. He couldn't distinguish much more than their strangely shaped hats and the shape of their AK-47s, but he knew he was in trouble.

Scotty let go of his weapon and slowly, quietly, tied his hair back with a bandanna. The NVA moved around the base of the hill, toward George and Rudy. My father stayed flat against the ground, hoping they wouldn't see him. He knew his odds—he was alone, in the open, an easy target. He held his weapon close, too terrified to move. He hoped Goodman wouldn't come up anytime soon.

At the top of the hill, Rudy and George smoked and talked, unaware of what was happening below them. Scotty began to crawl around the base of the hill. Near the bottom, he jumped up and ran, closing on the NVA soldiers from behind. Before my father had a chance to follow, Scotty opened up on full automatic. One, two, three, four NVA fell instantly, the entire back of the group. Rudy and George heard the gunfire and started shooting, taking out another two or three.

My father opened up from his position. Bullets sputtered rhythmically. George scaled the side of the hill, fast and steady. Scotty had once said it was better to be high than drunk during a firefight, that pot doesn't immobilize you like beer. George, who was so stoned he never came down, was living proof of this; his movements were fast and precise. He hit the ground not twenty feet away and started picking off the right flank.

Rudy, alone on the hill, threw down his gun and went for the claymore detonator.

Suddenly, Scotty backed off. Perhaps he'd gone through his ammo—two magazines wasn't much in a firefight—or maybe he simply wanted to see how many NVA were left. George, as if taking telepathic orders, stopped firing as well, and in the brief silence that followed, Rudy set off the claymores. A terrible scream rang through the jungle. Somehow, although nobody knew how they had pulled it off, the VC had turned the claymores around. The mines fired backward and Rudy got it all, ball bearings and C-4 plastic explosive. George ran back, over the hill, to Rudy. Rudy's fatigues were all but gone from shoulders to waist, and his back was a shredded, bloody mess.

The remaining NVA ran off into the bush, leaving their dead and wounded. Scotty walked slowly, almost languidly, to the bodies, stopping to kick a dead NVA and rummage in his pockets. One of the wounded groaned, and Scotty finished him off. The shot seemed somehow more terrible than the barrage of shots before. It echoed through the trees.

"Fuck, man," George said, as he cradled Rudy's head in his palms. "Go back and radio a dust-off."

Half an hour later, Pops walked through the jungle, a clipboard in hand, taking the all-important body count. My father always said that the war fed itself on the body count. *Stars and Stripes* published the numbers; the papers stateside published the numbers. Before my father had come to Vietnam, he thought our side was surely winning the war.

How could we be losing, with a kill ratio like that? He found out soon enough that the numbers were inflated. His platoon could get little extras—beer or better food or time in the rear—and Pops could get promoted if the numbers were high.

Pops said, "OK, boys, how many dead? How many wounded?"

"Got twelve dead NVA, Pops," Scotty said.

"Any wounded?"

Scotty smiled. "Not anymore."

"How many you see?" Pops asked George.

"I saw twelve dead." George was shaking and looked sick.

"How about you Trussoni? Twelve?"

"There were twelve dead," my father replied.

Pops said, "Nice work, boys. Four times twelve. Forty-eight confirmed dead. Eat. Rest. We're heading out in an hour."

THE BUS DROPPED US ON DONG KHOI STREET BEFORE THE tour office, among swarms of rickshaw drivers. Jim bent to tie the shoestring of his Nike trainer. As he did, a black nylon money belt (tucked in the back of his khaki shorts) rose above the waistband. Patty tucked the belt back into her husband's shorts and pinched his bottom. Her mood had improved since we'd left the tunnels. She ran her fingers through her curly auburn hair and checked her pink Swatch. "Cocktail time!" she said. "What do you say? Our hotel has the best view in Ho Chi Minh City."

We crawled into a dilapidated Lada taxi. Masses of people—kids in school uniforms, tourists with tie-dyed

T-shirts, vendors carrying baskets of mangoes—blocked the road. As the driver eased into first gear and the taxi inched through the street, the crowd displaced itself onto sidewalks and alleyways. Jim and Patty paged through their guidebook, looking for the address of an ex-pat nightclub called the Apocalypse Now Bar. They wanted to see if it lived up to the movie.

Rickshaws and bicycles moved by my window. I focused on the slow revolutions of a bicycle tire; it moved round and round and round. It would have been easy to fall asleep like that, warm, hypnotized, especially with jet lag setting in. But then, from behind a group of backpackers, I saw the man with the aviator sunglasses. He leaned against a telephone pole and crossed his arms, staring at me. I sat up straight and pressed my hand against the window, as if to block him from view. When he saw that he had my attention, he eased his baseball cap off, so that his long black hair fell over his shoulders. He nodded at me, letting me know that he had been waiting.

Abandoning the telephone pole, he began to walk at our pace, on the sidewalk, just in line with the taxi's window. With each step closer, I felt a tightening in my chest. I almost believed that if I looked straight ahead and pretended he was not there, he would disappear. I told myself it was a simple coincidence. If not, how could he know to find me at that particular place at that particular time? Had he been waiting at the tour office all afternoon? Did he know where I was staying? What did he want from me?

"Here, give me that," Jim said, taking the book from his

wife and turning to the index. "You can't read a map to save your life."

"That's true," Patty said, winking at me. "I can't."

I pushed the lock on the door and rolled up the window. The air in the cab became hot and stagnant. The taxi driver looked over his shoulder and said, "This car has no air conditioner, mademoiselle."

The man with the aviator sunglasses moved closer to the taxi. Agile, he slithered through the crowd toward me. Fear, pure and simple, took over inside of me, but all I could think to do was to sink into my seat. Suddenly, I felt something that I had never expected to feel—that Vietnam might not let me off easily. However illogical, I was sure, suddenly, that I had inherited a debt and this man had come to extract it. As he walked closer, I believed in fate, retribution. That nothing of the past was forgiven. Or forgotten.

Jim held the guidebook toward his wife. "Maybe you'll like this restaurant, Sweetie. It's called Bibi's. It's French."

"Pass," Patty said. "I'm in the mood for Vietnamese."

The taxi paused as a rickshaw driver filled his buggy with clients. Our driver pounded the horn, and it sounded to me, with my heart beating and the blood quick in my ears, like the low, suffering *baa* of a sheep. *Baa, baa, baa. Baa, baa, baa.* I sank farther into the metal-sprung cushion of the backseat as the taxi driver unrolled his window to dispel the unctuous heat. When the man with the aviator sunglasses appeared at my window, leaning close, as if he would press his thin lips to the glass, I turned toward Jim and Patty, panicked. I said, "Why is the taxi moving so slow?"

"Hey," Jim said, studying me. "Everything OK?"

"Did those tunnels give you have a headache?" Patty asked. "I've got about a gallon of Advil in my purse."

The man was so close to the window I could have unrolled it and run my fingernails across his pockmarked skin. Then, he raised his hand and—opening his pointer and middle fingers in a V—he pressed them on the glass and walked back into the crowd.

Jim said, "Do you know that guy with the Yankees cap?"

"Who?" Patty asked, angling her head toward the window, to get a better look.

"Some native," Jim said. "He waved at us."

Patty found the man in the crowd, looked him over, and said, "Now there is a guy in need of a new T-shirt." Turning her attention to her handbag, she pulled out a hairbrush, a tube of lipstick, and a hand-tooled leather wallet and came up with a bottle of Advil. "I hope he's not a friend of yours," she said, as she tapped the bottle in her palm and gave me two pink pills. "They wouldn't allow that guy within a mile of our hotel."

THE TAXI PICKED UP SPEED AT THE END OF DONG KHOI and turned onto Nguyen Du Street. Shifting through a number of small unmarked roads, we exited upon Dai Lo Le Duan, a capacious boulevard spiked with palm trees. Across the way, there was a huge park that housed the Workers' Club and Reunification Palace. I remembered reading that the North Vietnamese Army came here on the morning of April 30, 1975, to claim the South. An NVA soldier climbed the palace stairs and hung a red flag with a yellow star at its center from a fourth-floor balcony.

Wind whistled through the cab as we drove past lush hotels with topiary-sharp lawns, many of which had been built during the mid-nineties. For a few years, after the United States lifted sanctions in 1994 and the Communist government eased strictures on trade, Vietnam was a place for optimism, joint ventures, and cases of champagne. Luxury hotels and ayurvedic spas opened in Da Lat and Nha Trang. For a little while, Vietnam was a paradise of opportunity. When the bubble popped in the late nineties, many investors were left to fall without a parachute.

I waited in the hotel lobby as Jim collected the room key from the reception desk. A red-uniformed doorman opened the door for a group of businessmen. They walked past, sending a ripple of Japanese through the lobby. Patty browsed the gift shop, examining a display case filled with Vietnamese antiques. There was a water puppet and a wooden Buddha. She asked to see a carved jade bracelet and bought it.

A vase of pink and yellow orchids, hundreds of them tangled around one another, bloomed from a marble pedestal. There was a full-length mirror beyond, and, when I looked into it, the explosion of color doubled. I saw myself (behind the orchids), a woman with short messy hair and a smudge of tunnel mud on her cheek. My tennis shoes were dull against the glossy marble floor, my jeans scuffed and dirty. When my hair was long, and there was a little more roundness in my cheeks, I looked like my mother. Family friends would always compare us, saying how lucky I was to look like her. But now, with my hair sheared and my face gaunt, I saw what I had inherited from my father: the high cheekbones and an overwrought expression around the mouth. The pale skin and dark circles under my eyes. I looked closer, examining my black eyes, checking for a slight blue penumbra. I hardly recognized myself, but I was not surprised. I always expected to see someone else when I looked into a mirror. I always expected to find a girl of twelve, tanned and crooked smiled, staring back.

nine

It was four o'clock in the afternoon, and already it was dark. Fat wet snowflakes fell through the cavernous sky, collecting upon mailboxes and fence posts. Wrapped in a huge wool coat, more Eskimo than schoolgirl, I stomped down Caledonia Street, cracking the frozen puddles with my boots as I went. Looking down, I saw the sheer glassy panes explode into shatter-line fissures. I couldn't explain why this simple act of destruction was so thrilling, so satisfying, but it was. I cracked the crisp top layers of ice, step after step, accepting cold water in the boots as my due.

After the divorce, I often felt like an only child. Sometimes I saw Kelly in the hallway at school. As we passed, she would smile and I would smile, both of us still uncertain of how to view our separation. The way it was, she could have been any other fifth-grader, coming from any other family. And although I didn't see Mom or Andy or Matt often either, my circle of acquaintances was growing. Every weekend, Dad brought home women to our house after bar time: married women, divorced women, women with kids, women with tattoos, women with twin sisters: more and more women. They kept me awake at night, screeching and moaning from his bedroom.

Dad's truck was parked outside of Roscoe's. I walked past it, dragging a finger through the salt that had condensed on the steel, and pushed open the door to the bar.

"Jan," I said, "where's your best customer?" Although I was not the only kid who came to Roscoe's around dinnertime, I was the only one on a first-name basis with the bartender.

"He's got a game of darts going," Jan said, as she wiped her hands on her jeans and nodded toward the back room. "He's been here all afternoon."

The back room of Roscoe's was nearly empty. A pool table and a low-hanging plastic lamp filled the center of the room; pinball machines lined the walls. Dad stood near an electronic dartboard with Slash Monti and Frankie Lefebvre (pronounced, by his friends at Roscoe's, La Fever). Slash was an old friend of my father's, a Genoa boy who had known Dad since before the war. About ten years before, Slash had run his snowmobile into a barbed-wire fence, nearly decapitating himself. As a result, a ten-inch scar ran across his face and neck. When fresh, it had been a bright and startling zag across his features, but eventually the deep red faded to pink. A ghostly ridge marred his cheek, giving him an aura of ruthlessness, not that he needed it. Slash Monti was the toughest guy in the bar. This was exactly why Dad liked to drink with him. It was an asset to have such a man at your table, but (of course) only if he was on your side. Slash Monti had never found out about Dad and his wife, Mary (my godmother), and all the problems she had caused Dad the year I was six. I wasn't about to tell him.

Dad pulled up a stool, and I sat next to Frankie La Fever, a tall wiry guy with fuzzy blond hair that curled over his ears. Frankie was in Vietnam in '67 and came home to work at the La Crosse Rubber Mill on the North Side, making rain boots. Frankie was single and had never been married, a rare thing among the regulars, whose weddings and divorces made up the major dates of the North Side social calendar. He lived in a small apartment above the bar and paid his tab each month along with his rent.

Frankie, Dad always said, was a loose cannon. Sometimes he would deal a game of blackjack, putting a stack of cash on the rim of the pool table and calling for players: *Come on, you pussies, put your money where your mouth is!* He would deal the cards, calm, collected. Players would gather; money would exchange hands. It would appear that Frankie was having a great time, until he began to lose money. Then it was as if a daisycutter had gone off in his mind. He would scream and swear and kick over the bar stools. He would smear the cards on the table, throw his money on the floor, storm out of Roscoe's, and sit in his truck in the parking lot. When that happened, Dad laughed and said, "That La Fever's got a screw loose." The regulars tried to ignore Frankie's mood swings. They stepped aside when he off-loaded. But none of them really knew Frankie. They were all in the dark about who he was, underneath the mop of frizzy blond hair and the mood swings.

Frankie shocked the entire Roscoe's community one drunken evening when he confessed that he was gay, outing himself before a room of people who had no idea of what, exactly, he meant. His revelation shocked them, not so much because of what he revealed as because he had been able to keep his secret so well for so long. In Roscoe's, there was a ratio between drinking and talking: The more one drank, the more talking he did. And Frankie La Fever always drank more than most.

Dad stood and threw his darts, one after the other.

"Hey, La Fever," Slash Monti said. "Show us your toes."

Frankie stepped to the white tape, next to my father, aimed his dart toward the bull's eye, and threw it left of the mark. "Shit, Monti," he said. "Go look at your own toes."

Slash turned to me and said, "Frankie lost his toes in the war."

Frankie rolled his eyes. "I've got most of them."

"Take off your boot," Slash ordered. "Come on. Show the kid your toes."

"Aw, shit," Frankie said. "You know I don't like to talk about that stuff."

"No one's asking you to talk," Slash said.

Frankie leaned against a stool and unlaced his boot. He eased off his sock and wiggled the two remaining toes, the big and the pinkie, for me.

"Those little piggies got lost in 'Nam," Slash said, his voice full of wonder.

As Frankie slid his foot into his sock, Dad slapped him on the back and said, "Lucky that's all you lost, La Fever."

"Shoot," Slash said. "A couple of toes ain't much. Now a scar like mine is what you should bring back from a war. A scar like mine says, *I met the devil and he don't like a soldier.*"

"You're as sharp as a rubber hammer," Dad said, eyeing Slash up. There had always been an element of competition between the two of them, and Dad didn't like to be out-done, especially when it came to his military service. "You've never left the goddamned Coulee Region, let alone gone to war."

Slash picked up his darts and walked to the white line. He said, "Well, I could've gone."

Frankie said, "Sure, and you could've been the King of France, too."

"Maybe that's so," Slash Monti said, throwing his darts, one after the other. "Maybe that's so." He collected his darts and slammed the rest of his drink. Then he dug in his wallet for a five-dollar bill, which he gave to me. "Make yourself useful, sweetheart, and get a couple of thirsty soldiers another round."

It was happy hour, and the front room was packed. Regulars, poised on their stools like gargoyles, met my eye as I walked past. The neon lights were yellow and dim. The dark wood paneling was cluttered with the remains of birthday party decorations. Red streamers curlicued from the ceiling. A water-stained banner read OVER THE HILL AND UNDER SEXED! Even Jan had overdone it; her makeup was garish, as if she'd been cut loose from the circus.

"Is that eye shadow?" I asked her. "Or did you run into a door again?"

"Better watch it," she told me. "I eat kids like you for breakfast."

"You wouldn't like me," I said. "Too sour."

I placed the five-dollar bill on the bar and told Jan I

157

wanted to roll for a round of drinks, a double-or-nothing wager that only the brave and foolhardy attempted. She pushed the dice box my way and crossed her arms. It was obvious that she wasn't impressed with me at all—not my scam confidence or my over-the-head shaking technique. Yet, despite all logic, she liked me. She scooped a bowl of popcorn and set it on the bar; she made a cherry Coke and slid it my way. When I shook three dud rolls in a row (paid for with Slash Monti's five-dollar bill) and I was heartbroken from misfortune, she refunded the money. She said, "Come on, now! It ain't like a stray shit on your sidewalk!" She mixed the round of drinks. "You're too young to be rolling for drinks. This round's on the house."

As Jan surely knew, I'd been rolling for drinks since the third grade. It was thus a small act of charity that she let me off easy. Sure, I was young, but it was too late—Roscoe's had already got me. It churned in my bloodstream, sliding over platelets, infiltrating organs and bone marrow. Roscoe's was so much a part of me that, years later, a certain smell (sawdust and whiskey), a certain sound (the side-winding groan of a Gretch guitar), would bring tears to my eyes and I'd be there again, sitting on a vinyl stool, heir apparent of a barroom. Once Roscoe's got its fingernails in, it burrowed deep. Nobody's skin was clean of bruises. Jan knew this as well as anyone.

I set the drinks before Dad. He took one, finished half of it in one gulp, and lit a cigarette. Slash Monti racked the balls for a game of pool. "Hey, Trussoni, break this mother-fucker, will you?"

When Dad did not respond, Slash Monti chalked his cue

and bent over the table, leaving my father to his thoughts, leaving my father in a place where the air was hot and wet and thick.

"You couldn't see anything," he said, "the air was so damned thick. We crouched in the elephant grass all day long, but no matter—we couldn't breathe there, either."

"George sat in the grass ahead, with the pig propped on its legs next to him, the barrel tipped slightly up. The man had timing. He always knew when to sit it out and when to go. The rest of the platoon was God-knows-where, maybe ahead, maybe behind. We'd tracked a group of NVA to Trung Lap village, supposedly a strategic hamlet, but you know those fuckers weren't anymore on our side than the others. We were ordered to wait, and we did what we were told. We sat there all afternoon. The sun rose high and then fell. Didn't mean nothing, though—we were hot as ever. When the sun had nearly set, I inched my way to my buddy, Goodman. *You see the signal yet?* I ask him, and he says, *When Pops goes, I'm going.*

"We split a can of C-rations and the last of the water and tossed the cans into a paddy. Pretty soon, Goodman sees Pop's steel pot lift from the grass, and we move out, quick and low to the ground, following Pops toward the village. *Here we go, Trussoni,* Goodman said, and, before tossing his cigarette to the ground, he looked at me real slow. He liked me, for some reason, and was always watching out. *Be careful in there,* he said. *This is the real show.* I gave him some distance and then followed.

"The silence broke all at once. Pops rounded up a group of village boys and ordered the platoon to search the hootches. I followed George past a series of small fires—each one illuminating hands and eyes and pots of rice—and into a hut.

"*The fuckers are in here*, George said. *I can feel them*.

"A woman with a baby in a sling across her chest backed away from George, into a corner, as a little girl ran out the door. I didn't know what to do, except search the place, so I pulled up a wattled hatch in the floor and found bags of rice and packets of army-issue malaria pills. George tried to clear the woman out of there, but she started shouting. *Get the fuck out of here, lady!* he said, moving his M-16 from the woman's chest to the door. Maybe the woman didn't understand English, but she sure as hell should've understood the M-16. Anyway, she wouldn't budge. She stood against that wall for what seemed like forever, one hand on the baby, the other behind her back, until George moved toward her, ready to take her out physically. Then, she sidestepped, leaving, in her place, a grenade the size of an apple, and scurried out of the hootch seconds before the explosion. I was far enough away to get out with some shrapnel in my back. George wasn't so lucky."

Slash Monti pulled the pool cue back, as if drawing an arrow in a bow, and released. The triangle of balls sprang out, solids and stripes bursting to the edges of the table.

I hit my father's arm. "Hey, Dad? Maybe we should go, huh?"

"Go where?" he said, his voice gruff.

"Maybe we should go home," I said, trying to sound grown up but coming off, in the end, sarcastic. "You know—

home? That place where families go to eat and sleep and watch TV?"

"I don't have a home," Dad said. "Your mom took that."

We watched Slash Monti sidestep around the pool table, angling for a shot.

Dad pushed a pretzel across the table, picked it up, and examined the Möbius strip curves. "I don't have a home and I don't have a family either. It was your mother who wanted you kids in the first place. I told her, *No more damn kids!* And what does she do? Gets pregnant whenever she wants to. Pretty soon, we've got three kids. And she planned it! How do I know? Because once she said she hated to be pregnant in the summer, and you know what? She was never pregnant in the summer again. Your sister and brother were winter pregnancies! I'll tell you something else. That baby she miscarried last year? That wasn't mine. I got a vasectomy years ago, right after Matt. Your mom got that one on her own. I didn't have anything to do with that baby."

I picked up a pretzel, brushed it free of salt, and put it in my mouth, whole. This was the first time since the miscarriage that anyone had mentioned the baby.

"You kids belong to her," Dad said. "Your mother got the house and the land and the family and I"—he opened his hands to the pool table, the TV set, the dreary, smoke-filled backroom of Roscoe's—"I got this. Go call your mom. She'll take you home."

I slid off my bar stool and walked into the main barroom, where I fell into the dark corner of a booth. There were voices—boisterous, happy—but I was tired, exhausted, so without energy I felt as if I had been submerged in a deep pool. How, I wondered, as I looked through the smoke of Roscoe's, would I ever make it to the surface?

I pulled myself out of the booth and walked to the bar. As I pushed past the regulars—past Wrangler labels on corduroy pockets, stitched arabesques on denim pockets, wide-handled combs peeping like paddles from pockets—I heard Jan say, "This is Dan Trussoni's daughter." A man turned to look at me. The intensity of his stare, and the assumption of what my name made me, filled me with rage.

"For your information," I said, with a pugnacity that gave me away, "I am *not* his daughter."

I walked to the door, where I placed my hands to the glass, feeling the pressure of my fingertips on its cool surface. I did not know if it was the distortion of the door's thickness, or my sleepiness, but the outside world was disintegrating. The North Side was a blur before me. My father's image appeared in the glass, a clouded hallucination. I rapped at the reflection, hoping for the smallest sign of reconciliation, a smile, an apology, anything that might give him back to me. What could I do but watch as he turned away? What could I do but accept his absence?

I pushed the door open and walked into the cold night.

MONDAY MORNING, I WOKE TO THE SOUND OF WATER running in the kitchen. Dad washed the coffeepot and filled the automatic coffeemaker for twelve cups, enough to fill a thermos. The heat had been turned low overnight, and the air was chilly. My bed, heavy with blankets, retained the warmth and moisture of my body. When I looked at the wall, I saw a fine network of lines where termites had eaten through. The house, we had recently discovered, was infested. I burrowed down deep, wanting nothing but to be back in the oblivion of sleep, if only to keep the comfort of darkness, if only to dream.

When I walked into the kitchen, Dad was packing his HungryMan cooler. He took the same lunch every day: a stack of white-bread sandwiches made with Miracle Whip and Oscar Mayer lunch meat, a bag of potato chips, and a can of Mountain Dew. He would change this set menu only slightly over the years, replacing the Mountain Dew with Gatorade, or the potato chips with Twinkies or Ho Hos or Ding Dongs. Dad didn't like to change his routine.

Although it was a school morning, my uniform was crumpled in a corner of my room, wrinkled, unwashed, unwearable. I'd spent the weekend devising a method to stay home from school. I had stayed home sick at least one day every week since moving to the North Side, sometimes even two days. I'd discovered that, if strategically placed on a Thursday, my sickness would buy me a long weekend. The secretary at my school had recently pointed out this pattern to my father, and he prom-ised to get me to class. I knew that if I wanted to stay home, I had to come up with some-thing good.

I sat at the kitchen table. Dad sat next to me, reading the morning edition of the *Tribune*, a thin daily paper with articles about property taxes and the local wrestling rivalries. Winters were slow going for us. Dad got most of his contracts in the summer, and from May to September he worked ten hours a day. By November, the work dried up. Occasionally, however, he took a winter job. He wrapped the space in plastic, heated the air under the tarp with an electric heater, and then poured concrete into the small warm space. If he was able to keep the temperature even, he would sculpt a set of steps or refashion a chunk of broken sidewalk. If he could pull it off, he was able to earn a living through the cold season. This wasn't always possible. Cement was unstable and easily manipulated. It froze and thawed and contracted and expanded, absorbing temperature like a piece of aluminum. If he was not careful, the cement cracked. Even in the artificial biosphere of an enclosed site, the wind and ice had their effects.

I stared at the front page of the newspaper. There was a report of an epidemic of lice in the local public school. The headline read: LOCAL KIDS CARRIERS OF PESTS.

I tapped the newspaper. Dad lowered it below his nose. I said, "I hate to tell you this, but I think I have lice."

My father's first reaction to everything was skepticism. He said, "Don't talk nonsense."

I scratched my head, to prove that I was, indeed, infested. "It's going around school. It's everywhere."

He looked wary and then angry, a sign that he was considering the veracity of my story. Mom would never have bought this. She knew I was very particular about my hair and washed it nearly every day, lathering it with shampoo and detangling it with conditioner. According to my mother, I spent too much time in the bathroom doing something she called *primping*. But Dad didn't know this. He went to the counter and finished packing his lunch, stacking his sandwiches (each encased in a Ziplock bag) in his cooler. He said, "How in the hell do you get rid of lice?"

"Poison," I said confidently.

"Poison? What kind of poison?"

"Lice killer."

He was almost impressed. "You know where to find that?"

"No problem," I said. "You go to work. I'll handle it."

Dad shook his head, dismayed. He wasn't used to dealing with sick kids. Leukemia? Lice? It was all the same to him. But then, my father wasn't used to making dinner or helping with homework or buying groceries or washing clothes or anything else that touched upon raising children. He was a busy man and expected someone to take care of him. He sifted some money from his wallet and gave it to me, for the lice poison. "You need me to call your school?"

I handed him the phone. "Tell them I'll be out all week."

"You've got two days. Tops."

THERE WAS A STRIP MALL ABUTTING CALEDONIA STREET, a single-story brick building with a movie theater on one end and a Shop-Ko at the other. The parking lot was shot through with cracks; in the summer, dandelions grew through the kilned blacktop. The bright yellow weeds burst toward the sun, disavowing their bleak garden, which always made me wonder how something of such a transcendent color could make it through the thick, mucky sediment of tar and oil.

There were no dandelions on that windy January morning. Streetlights rose from the parking lot, their lanky metallic bulbs stretched like grasshopper antennae. I walked past iced-over American-made pickup trucks and Japanese compacts. I didn't know much about cars—there was no particular make or model that I liked—but I knew I needed one. I'd be happy with a junker, so long as it started in below-zero temperatures. In the Midwest, a car was freedom. I looked forward to turning sixteen, when I would be old enough to take driver's education and test for my license. I wanted to drive up the ramp overlooking the North Side onto I-90 and speed out, out, out into the world beyond. I was thirteen and three months old: 993 days shy of my sixteenth birthday. I scratched numbers into the snow: 993 days until freedom. Give or take a day.

I'd spent a lot of time at the strip mall since moving in with my father. On weekends, when Dad wanted me out of the house, he peeled a five-dollar bill from his wallet and sent me to the theater at the far end of the mall. On long calm days of Dad-lessness, I stood before the movie posters, beautiful airbrushed faces of actors staring down at me. I pulled back the sleeve of my coat and examined the imperfect skin of my arm, with its dappling of freckles and chevrons of fine hair. If my reflection superimposed itself upon the poster—my pale face and stocking cap layering over the starlet's radiant features—the combination was comic. Was it possible, I wondered, that such flawless people existed?

Sometimes I bought a movie ticket and sank into the dark unmoored space of the theater, giving my imagination up to the play of shadows across the screen. But most of the time I didn't go inside. I snubbed the hope and heartbreak of the movies for a bag of hard candies. I hung out on a bench, or I walked through the warm hallway, sloshing through puddles past a pharmacy and a Coney Island hotdog stand. I spent my time alone, feeding quarters into the bottomless stomach of a MS. PACMAN machine.

When Serenity was with me, we played a game. I dared her to steal something worth twenty dollars. She bit her lip, thinking over the risk; then, accepting the challenge, she walked though Shop-Ko's electric doors as I waited outside.

Serenity strolled through the store, making her way to the underwear department, where she sifted through a bin of satiny bras. When nobody was looking, she hid a bra in her pocket and walked out to me.

It was my turn. Serenity dared me to lift a lipstick, so I drifted through the aisles of the toy department, packed with shelf after shelf of bright plastic objects, to the cosmetic department, careful and unhurried. The sales assistants, each in an orange lab-coat uniform, watched me, suspicious. Every minute a new employee approached me: *Can I help you find something? Just let me know if you need some help. Is there something special you're looking for today?*

I passed under the neon lights, fending off sales assistants. *No, thank you, just looking. No, thanks. Just looking. No, thanks!*

As I caught my reflection in the mirror—the black trench coat (picked up at the North Side Salvation Army), the beat-up Doc Martens, the silver shoulder-length duster earrings brushing my collarbone—I worried that I looked like a shoplifter, but that was precisely what I was, so I decided to act brash and confident. Impervious to danger, I chose a

Maybelline lipstick and stuffed it in the inside pocket of my trench coat.

A respectable-looking woman breezed past me. She was old enough to be my mother, so I followed in her wake, hoping to look like I belonged to someone. My boots squelched on the shiny floor. The electric doors were just beyond a rack of cassette tapes. As the woman walked toward the exit, I stayed close behind. A man in a gray suit standing near the music department counter watched me as I approached. This man (I was certain) was an undercover cop, ready to tackle me and take me to the Shop-Ko back room. He stepped into the aisle, directly in front of me, and reached in his pocket for a walkie-talkie. He checked his watch, waiting for backup. It is only a matter of time, he was thinking, before I take this punk into custody.

I took a deep breath, bracing myself for whatever might happen, and left the store. The buzzing, dizzying thrill of sure ruin blurred my eyesight. My knees were weak; my hands shook. I ran all the way down the mall to Serenity, who was waiting near the gumball machines.

But today Serenity was in school. I walked to the medicine aisle, found the RID lice ointment, shoved the box into the inner pocket of my trench coat—no dare needed—and walked out, unhurried.

DAD WAS DRINKING COFFEE FROM A WISCONSIN DELLS mug when I returned. He took the brown glass bottle of RID from my hands and placed it on the counter. He was brusque, businesslike. I stood before him, dumbfounded. He was supposed to be at work. I had depended on his absence so I could dump the lice poison down the drain and spend the day watching MTV. Instead Dad directed me, with a fine-toothed comb in his hand, to a chair. He had ruined my grand plans for a day off.

The kitchen was warm and smelled of coffee. A small portable TV on the counter was tuned to Channel 8, and the low hum of the local weather report stapled itself around us. Dad lit a cigarette, placed it in an ashtray next to the RID, and began working through my hair with the black plastic comb.

The weather report woman turned to her electronic map, tapping it with a metal rod: *Temperatures will hold steady at ten degrees Fahrenheit throughout the Coulee Region, dropping to below zero over the next week.*

I fell into a fit of scratching my scalp. If Dad realized I had no lice to kill, there would be hell to pay.

"Quit wiggling," Dad said. "These suckers are hard to see." He stabbed my scalp with the comb.

"They're *impossible* to see. They're microscopic. Why look for them at all? Just pour the RID on!"

"Sit still, I said!"

Dad didn't have patience for squirming or complaining or any of my childish behavior. I sat straight and stiff and perfectly still, watching our reflection in the glass door of the gun cabinet. Dad, in dirty jeans and a quilted flannel jacket, stood over me, tweezing through my hair with his big fingers. There was something of the primate in the scene; I felt, for a moment, as if I were viewing a clip from a National Geographic film: Dad, the big gorilla, picking tiny creatures from his baby gorilla's fur. I almost expected him to put the lice in his mouth and chew them. Maybe he would have, if there had been any lice to be found.

"I can't see a damn thing," Dad concluded. He set the comb on the table, next to the ashtray, and rummaged in his desk for a flashlight. He put a small Black and Decker in my hand, lifted my arm up, angling it like a lamp, and dove back in. He pulled strands of my hair, pushing my head this way and that. The phone rang, but he left it to the answering machine. My father would not be distracted. He was going the distance. He would hunt down the lice and destroy them, ridding my head of all licelike creatures. He was going to exterminate the race of infectious pests that had infiltrated his home. If these lice could infest his daughter's hair, why, they would soon infect the beds and the rugs and the furniture until his house—no, *all of the North Side*—would be infested. This was Dad's Domino Theory of pest control. This was my father's War on Pests.

My father pressed his finger into my scalp. "There, I found one!"

"You did?" I asked, trying not to sound too surprised.

"Sneaky little shits," he said. "They've dug way in there."

"Really?" I asked. "You saw one?"

"Of course I did," he said. "You think I don't know lice when I see it?"

He shoved the box of RID into my hands and told me to read him the treatment instructions, printed on the back.

The weather woman finished her forecast: *There will be scattered snowstorms tonight, piling up a good five inches by morning. You can sure bet those snowplows will be out and about by breakfast time tomorrow!*

Dad poured the ointment on my scalp, rubbing it behind my ears and above my neck. He finished and rinsed his hands under the tap. My head began to tingle; after a few minutes, the tingle grew to a steady burn. I chewed on a fingernail, trying to ignore the pain. I must have looked uncomfortable, because Dad slapped me on the back and said, "No pain no gain, sweetheart. Those sons-of-bitches don't stand a chance."

Dad smoked his cigarette and watched TV.

I asked, "How long do I need to sit here?"

"What does it say on the box?"

"Ten minutes."

"You sit here ten minutes, then." My father checked his black plastic Casio wristwatch, his work watch that had concrete solidified in the tractor-tread grooves of the band. "You know, Danielle, I don't have time for this shit. I've got to check out a job up in Sparta."

I looked up at my father, humbled. But as the lice poison dripped down my forehead and ran into my eyes, I had one more request. "Could you get me a towel before you go?"

Dad opened a closet next to the gun cabinet. He pulled out a Mickey Mouse towel and, in the process, knocked over a cardboard box. The contents spilled over the blue shag carpet. He lifted a chain with dog tags, an olive-drab canteen, a small photo album. A tin box spilled a confetti of multicolored bars and insignias, his red-and-yellow Twenty-fifth Infantry Tropic Lightning patch, and his medals.

He tossed me the towel, picked up the photo album, and leaned against the counter. As he turned the pages, the album's plastic binding creaked like the hinge of an old car

171

door. He leaned toward me, showing me photographs of tanks and soldiers in fatigues, strange huts with thatched roofs, pigs and chickens surrounded by red mud. Dad pointed to an aerial shot and said, his breath all coffee and cigarette smoke, "That's the base at Cu Chi from a Huey."

I shifted in my chair. The heat spread through my scalp and expanded. My father touched a picture, another aerial shot, this one of a river. "That's the horseshoe," he said. "Men would get trapped in there all the time. I saw sappers mow down a whole platoon once. I was right overhead, in the chopper, and couldn't do nothing but watch those poor bastards fall."

Dad pointed to a group picture.

"That was Rudy; he got hit just after this picture. And this guy was our medic. He was an Italian kid from New York. Went loony. Talked day and night about the devil and the black angels. That kid right here, George, smoked dope all the time. He was injured too. And that good-looking guy in front is me."

I took the album from my father. It was true—Dad was handsome in the picture. There was something vibrant in his smile, something bright in his eyes. At first I thought this magic was simply youth, the result of smooth skin and a full head of hair. But after closer examination I saw that what was different about my father had nothing to do with time. There was an innocence in his face I had never seen before, something hopeful, trusting.

Dad sipped his coffee and turned the pages. I saw a picture of a Vietnamese woman with heavily painted eyes.

She wore a blond wig and a blue babydoll dress that billowed and ruffled like layers of Kleenex. There were three, four, five pictures of the same woman. In one, Dad had his arms around her. In another, she kissed his neck. In another she sat on his lap, leaning her cheek to his cheek. He took the photo album from me. He said, "You don't need to know anything about her."

Dad turned another page. A photograph showed Vietnamese soldiers on their backs in the dirt, each one laid out like a crosstie on a railroad track. The bodies wore army-drab cargo pants and no shirt. They were bloody and mutilated. Every eye was closed, as if the boys had been given a moment to prepare themselves for death, to shut their eyes and wait to be relieved of the world. All except for one. His eyes were open. He stared blankly up from a bed of red mud. A shadow—the grainy outline of the photographer—covered half the boy's torso. I had seen the picture, many years before, but—as Dad poured himself another cup of coffee and lit yet another Pall Mall—it was not the bodies in the photo that I saw. This time, it was the outline of my father's shadow that burned itself into my imagination. It was my father's shadow, wavering liquidly over the bodies of the men he had killed, that I could not stop looking at.

Dad pulled a stick of beef jerky from his back pocket. He peeled the plastic casing and took a bite. "That was a firefight," he said. "We didn't have backup. First thing Charlie took out was the machine gun and radio. That's what they liked to do—kill our firepower and stop us from radioing for help. Usually we didn't let them do that, but the little fuckers snuck up on us. I got recommended for a Purple Heart in that one. We weren't expecting them at all. But we got them in the end."

The atmosphere of the room had changed, and although my scalp was burning I did not notice. I pointed to the photo of the dead boy. "Did you ever shoot anybody?"

"Damn right I did," Dad said. "If we didn't shoot them, they'd sure as shit shoot us."

It was 11 A.M. *The Young and the Restless* theme song played from the TV. Dad checked his watch and grabbed his cooler. "I've got to go," he said. "Better rinse that shit off your head." He shoved the album into the cardboard box and grabbed his cooler. "I'll be home by four. Clean up this mess before then, will you?"

He slammed the front door on his way out. I was left to put the house in order. After I washed the RID out of my hair, I cleaned the kitchen. I emptied the ashtray of cigarette butts and washed the coffee cups. I picked up the dog tags from the floor. And I returned the album of war photos to the closet, determined to forget my father's shadow.

ten

Through the years that we lived together, the women in my father's life came and went. They arrived, all heat and smoke, and they left, snuffed. There were the women who stayed only one night, whose shoes I discovered on the couch or under the bathroom sink, whose cigarettes (snapped snug in faux-leather cases) lay on the coffee table when I got up to watch cartoons on Saturday morning. When they woke, these women sauntered across our tiny kitchen, barefoot, snarly-haired, and went directly to the fridge to scrounge their Diet Cokes. Sometimes they even hung around to smoke, but most often they took off early, just as the sun was rising, hoping to sneak home into their beds without waking their (a) husbands, (b) kids, (c) dogs, or (d) all of the above. I never remembered the names of these women. I never remembered their faces after they had gone. What I remembered was the streaks of sadness they trailed behind them, smears of purple-gray hopelessness that spoke of middle age, indigence, and exhaustion. These sensations colored our house for days after they had left.

And then there were the women who stayed in our lives

for more than a night. These were a special breed, the kind with fire in their eyes and silver caps on their teeth. None were beautiful or solvent. They lived hard and loved hard, saving nothing for morning. If my father told one to get lost, she would show up at our house at bar time and alley-cat at the window until my father unbolted the door. When Dad showed her in, he informed her (as he took her coat and made her a drink) that he was done with women. He announced (as he escorted her to the bedroom) that he had undergone a vasectomy, and if she hoped to rope him into marriage by getting knocked up she was shit out of luck. My father gave the women in his life all he could give, and that (he made clear as he locked the bedroom door) was nothing. He said, I'm a worthless son-of-a-bitch, but I'm all yours. Take it or leave it.

The year I was thirteen, the women in Dad's life had been taking more than he could handle. With the answering machine jammed full of messages, we would sneak out the back door, to the alley, and climb into Dad's truck. Every weekend, we hit the highway, leaving the North Side behind.

Dad cracked the windows and punched the built-in cigarette lighter. It popped; he brought its hot coils to the end of his cigarette. "Put on some music," he said, and I snatched an eight-track (Willie Nelson's greatest hits) and shoved it into the rectangular mouth of the player. Country music drifted through the cab, a concoction of guitar and desire that made me feel free, as if the whole world were wide open before us.

Although there was a crisp sheet of ice on the road, my

father drove sixty. We barreled full speed ahead into sunshine, the highway switchbacking with the quick sidewinding turns of memory. Faster and faster we went. We were free. Nobody would catch us.

The truck fell over the snow-dusted hills. We turned onto Highway 35, a north-south two-lane road that ran along the Mississippi. Locals called the highway the River Road, but I always thought of it as the glacier road. It was there, hundreds of thousands of years before, that the swollen ice sheets that leveled most of the Midwest had halted. Across the river, in Iowa, the land was flat. On our side of the river, the sandstone bluffs lifted into sheer snakeskin escarpments. As we drove by, the rock face leaned to the road and retreated. Maple trees grew through the ledges of porous rock, their roots descending like veins of mineral. When it was high summer and the leaves were heavy, the branches brushed the tops of passing cars. As it was winter, the branches were as bare as broom handles. We passed unimpeded.

We drove past fishing shacks, a full-service gas station, and barn after barn capped with snow until we saw a placard: ROMANCE, UNINCORPORATED. Romance, Unincorporated was one of many tiny towns scattered up and down the Mississippi that grew around stagecoach stops. Romance, Unincorporated (just down the road from Victory, Unincorporated) was little more than a pocket of land with a tavern and a baseball diamond, but during the winter, every ice fisher from Stoddard to Prairie Du Chien lugged tackle and bait to the ice. During the winter months, Romance, Unincorporated was the only place to be.

Romance was not unique. There were similar hot spots every weekend. There was the Coon Valley Canoe Races, La Crosse Riverfest, Holmen Cornfest, La Crescent Applefest. My first real taste of these festivals occurred at eleven, when I won the Annual Onalaska Sunfish Days Button Design Contest (1985). My winning drawing (a smiling sunfish standing before a rainbow) was transposed onto shiny laminated pins; my picture appeared in the local newspaper and I became (overnight) the most celebrated preteen girl in all of Onalaska, Wisconsin. I was given a cash award and a place on the official Sunfish Days Parade Float, where I sat high above the street, waving to the crowd, a white-gloved plastic girl on a white-tiered plastic wedding-cake float. A high school band marched before us; the fire department engines rolled behind. The parade bottomed out at the VFW hall, where I jumped from my throne, shucked the tiara, and tromped through the beer-guzzling crowd to Dad.

Today, the river's surface was swarming with ice fishers. Their bright-colored snowsuits sprinkled the ice like candies on whipped cream. Sleds packed with ice augers and propane heaters, with spud bars and bait buckets and freeze-free tip-ups, were parked next to half-ton Chevys. The ice must have been thick, because trucks had been driven out mid-channel and left waiting, as their owners drilled holes and set up portable shanties.

Although there were at least ten trucks mid-river, and the ice appeared sturdy, everyone knew that the Mississippi should not be trusted. When it was liquid, in the long stretch of thaw from March to November, the sough and shake of the current, the pressure of its swell, the glitches and gushes and the go of it, sucked deer and escaped cattle and the occasional drunk teenager into its undertow. In winter, if the sheets of ice weakened and floes spun like tops over its surface, the river claimed snowmobiles and foolhardy cross-country skiers. Yet everyone (more out of resignation than benevolence) overlooked the river's murderous nature. In summer, they motorboated on its surface and camped on its banks. In winter, they drove clear to the river's center, risking their lives on the timorous ice sheet. Many trucks had cracked the ice and, tire by tire, sunk into the water, yet nobody held a grudge. They drove onto the ice every winter.

Dad steered the truck onto a bank of snow and cut the engine. We walked over the highway and through a patch of birch trees, to the bar. Although there were some die-hard ice fishers in Romance, the main attraction was always the tavern. Fishermen, fisherwomen, fisherkids, and random drivers-by ended up Bermuda-triangled at the bar, where they warmed themselves with whiskey and plates of fried smelt. All the local beers (Pabst Blue Ribbon, Schlitz, Old Milwaukee) were on tap. Dad and I went inside, where we were greeted by a room of familiar faces. Everyone was there: the Roscoe's crowd, my uncles, and (to my father's dismay) the very women he was trying to escape.

Maria Vargas waved at us, trying to get my father's attention. Dad tipped his cowboy hat to her, but I could tell, as she pushed her way through the crowd, that he wanted to turn and run.

"Hi there, stranger!" Maria said, wrapping her arm around Dad's waist and rubbing against him. "Where y'all been? No hanging around the neighborhood these days?"

Maria Vargas was our neighbor. She was a hard-drinking welfare mother and the proud owner of a husband in a Houston correctional facility. Maria banged on the front door of our house one cold December morning the year I was twelve. *Anybody home in there?* she said, her voice deep and hoarse, as if she were recovering from laryngitis. She rattled the door. *Come on, now, your lights are on. I know somebody's home!*

Dad had good instincts; he was wary of Maria Vargas from the beginning. Working his cowboy hat over his head, he opened the door just a crack. "You looking for somebody?"

Maria scratched her scalp and tucked a strand of black hair behind her ear. "You got any jumper cables?" she asked, pushing the door open.

"Your car's dead?"

Her eyes drifted to Dad's Stetson. "Sure is, cowboy. Deader than a frigging doornail."

"Where're you at? I'll pull my truck around and give you a jump."

Maria pointed out a monstrous seventies Buick with expired Texas plates marooned next door, in front of her apartment complex. The Buick was covered with ice and snow and looked as if it hadn't been driven in a month. "You mind if my kids wait inside? They're freezing their butts off out here. This isn't Corpus, know what I mean?" She ushered Juan (a tubby boy my age), Amy (a girl of six with black hair that curled to her waist), and Jose (the baby, who was so fat that Amy could hardly hold him) into our living room and then led my father into the snowy afternoon.

Over the winter, we got to know Maria Vargas. She came over daily, asking me to babysit her kids while she and Dad drank tequila. They would do shots until the early hours of the morning and then stumble to the bedroom, leaving me and the Vargas kids camped out in the living room in front of the TV. We would all wake the next day, groggy and hungry. Maria would give me food stamps and send me out for groceries with Amy and Jose. If Dad discovered the food stamps he would snatch them from me and throw them in the trash, mumbling, "My taxes pay for these goddamned things. No daughter of mine is showing up at Kwik Trip with food stamps."

Dad's status as a taxpayer gave him the right to complain about almost everything. The percent of his wages taken by the state and federal government, his property taxes, the tax he paid on cigarettes—he complained about them all. If his mail was late or a check got lost in transit, he called the post office and asked to speak to the manager. He was a Taxpayer Goddammit and Everyone should Snap to It when he needed something done.

Maria Vargas was not in our tax bracket. She was, Dad said, the kind of person who lived off of decent hardworking folk like us. Although Dad had known her over a year, and she still slept at our place from time to time, he never took her to Roscoe's. If asked, he would say that Maria Vargas was a married woman, he didn't believe in infidelity, and there was nothing between them but a certain friendly understanding. "My daughter babysits her kids," he would say. "It's good for Danielle to learn the value of hard work and earn a little pocket money to boot." In the end, Dad never acknowledged his relationship with Maria Vargas. She was his secret, married, welfare-mother girlfriend.

"I got some free drink chips," Maria said now, showing us three small plastic coins. "What you drinking, Danny? It's on me. Don't you move a muscle. I'll be right back."

While Maria was at the bar, Dad sneaked into the back room. I followed close behind, hoping Maria hadn't seen us flee. Suddenly, a hand grabbed my wrist and yanked. I found myself face-to-face with Suzie, Dad's official Roscoe's girlfriend. "Hey there, squirt!" she said. "Who lit a fire under your dad's ass?"

Suzie was part of the North Side scene. She played softball for Sloopy's, drank twenty-five-cent taps at Fishes, and had a way with words that only a resident of Loomis Street could have. Suzie was pale and freckly with strawberry-blond hair and an all-American smile that implied a Kewpie Doll childhood and a hula-hoop adolescence. And, to Dad's great approval, Suzie had regular employment. She worked at a North Side construction company as a nine-to-five secretary, answering phones and filling work orders. She wore poly-blend power suits and large plastic earrings. Suzie was organized and able to pay her bills, and she was always up for a drink. As she lived just three blocks from Roscoe's, she was also convenient. Dad never worried about a DUI when he spent the night with Suzie.

Suzie and Dad would go to Roscoe's after work and

drink a dozen brandy and Cokes between them. She could keep up with him, drink by drink. She was a happy drunk, so good-natured that, when he was with her, Dad's bad temper dissolved. This made me love Suzie. As she was much younger than Dad, I saw her as a perpetually drunk school friend. She gave me the inside information on boys and tampons and sex and the benefits of Diet Coke in mixed drinks. She was the older sister I didn't have.

I kept this image of her until Kelly showed me (one night after she'd been snooping in Dad's filing cabinets) a sheaf of Polaroids of Suzie naked. Although my father's photography was amateurish and unfocused, it appeared to me that Suzie was out-of-her-mind drunk. The pictures were variously hilarious and disgusting. Kelly and I covered our eyes in revulsion, giggling, but our father's homemade porn stayed with us. Kelly mentioned the pictures from time to time, saying things like, "Suzie sure looked funny naked!" After that, we could not stand to see Suzie. At Roscoe's, we avoided looking her in the eye. She was demoted to Dad's centerfold girlfriend.

Suzie dragged on her cigarette and blew the smoke slowly out her nose. "Your uncles are playing cards in the back room," she said. "I'll give you five bucks if you take me back there with you."

I pocketed the money, and Suzie and I joined my uncles, who played euchre at a card table.

"Well, well, if it isn't Suzie-Q!" Dad said, pretending to be pleased to see her. Dad had been dealt into the game. I leaned over his shoulder; he held a king of diamonds, a queen of clubs, and three low spades, a bum hand.

Uncle Dick led with an ace. John trumped it with the right bower. Gene and Dad threw down their cards, and John, the winner, swept the trick. Gene said, "My deal," pushed the cards into two neat piles, and shuffled them, card-shark deft. He flipped the cards to his brothers and turned up the king of hearts, a wishy-washy card and (therefore) an inprovidential beginning lay. John, victor of the last trick, lifted two quarters from a silo-shaped stack of coins at the corner of the table and gave them to me. *Get yourself a soda, a bag of popcorn, a bus ticket, a new life.*

"What in the hell are you dealing, Geno?" Dick said, folding his cards before him. "Bullshit is all I got."

"Sometimes you got to win with bullshit," Gene said.

"A bullshitter like you should know," Dick countered.

"I know one thing," Gene announced. "I'm going it alone."

Going it alone was a risky venture, one that excluded all help from a partner. My uncles loved going it alone. All of them played euchre with the secret hope that they would either get the magical cards that allowed them to win the hand alone, shaming their opponents and cleaning up the pot, or foil somebody else's attempt to go it alone.

"You aren't going to win this one," Dick said, placing a dollar on the table, upping the ante. "You've been bluffing all afternoon. Once a bullshitter, always a bullshitter."

"That might be true," Gene said, laying out a perfect hand of red cards: left and right bowers, ace, king, and queen of hearts. "But a bullshitter don't need to bullshit when he's got a spread like this."

There was a communal groan as Gene brushed the stack of quarters to his corner of the picnic table. He snatched Dick's ill-staked dollar and tucked it in his baseball hat. "Sorry about that, Richard."

Uncle Dick scowled. He was not generally good-natured when he was drunk, and (like all of us) a terrible loser. Once, when Dick lost at cards, Dad got a phone call from a bartender in Coon Valley, requesting that he come and collect his brother. Dick was drunk and belligerent, the bartender said, and in the mood to fight. When we got to the bar, Dad walked behind Uncle Dick, slow and tentative. "Hey, buddy," Dad said. "What you doing here, all by yourself?" Uncle Dick blinked, trying to place us. There was a strain of madness in his eyes that scared me to the bone. He raised his drink and gestured toward the television, which played a rerun of *The Jeffersons*. "I'm just sitting here, Danny," he said, his voice calm and woozy, "watching some niggers on TV."

Gene shuffled and dealt. John played a queen; Dick an ace. Dad placed a left bower on the card table. "That's my trick," he said, and swept the hand. He was gloating over his win when Lolly Parsons, the wildest, craziest, and most wicked of Dad's girlfriends, walked in.

Lolly Parsons was pure evil, and we all knew it. She was the kind of woman who flirted with married men in front of their pregnant wives, the kind of woman who spent a man's entire paycheck on a pair of shoes, the kind of woman who would do anything to get her way. Lolly had dated most of the available men in Dad's crowd and had broken up more

185

than one marriage. Her reputation fanned from her like plumage. Any man in his right mind would have stayed away from her. Dad did not.

He stuck his nose in his cards, hiding, but Lolly didn't buy it. She strutted to the Trussoni table. Lolly looked the same as always. Her hair was a mess of curls that sank over her cheeks in frizzy blond layers. Her face was plastered with makeup. Her jeans were tight and faded and ripped in all the right places. In fact, Lolly looked exactly the same as she did two months before, sitting in a squad car in front of our North Side house after she (and her sixteen-year-old son) had been arrested for breaking and entering.

Lolly edged close to Dad. She lit a cigarette and blew the smoke in his ear. "What's your problem, Dan? You don't return my calls, my letters, my telegrams, my ads in the singles column, my telepathic messages, nothing. What am I, last week's fireworks?"

Dad arranged his cards carefully, meticulously. He said, "Hello, Lolly. How was jail?"

"I was out the next day," Lolly said. "As you would know. If you returned my calls."

"Actually," Dad said, his voice playful. "I've been meaning to call you. You owe me forty-nine fifty for a new door."

Lolly had jimmied the lock on our front door with a screwdriver, scratching the paint and denting the jamb in the process. The implication that she should pay for damages sent her into hysterics. "New door? I'll give you a new door, asshole!"

Dad tried to ignore Lolly and Suzie and play cards, but when he spotted Maria Vargas walking our way with her hands full of beer cans he knew he was outnumbered. He did what any hunted creature would do: He wiggled into his jacket and snuck out the back door.

Dad's girlfriends sat at the card table, next to me.

Lolly cracked open a can of beer. "Your dad can't ignore me forever. You tell him I said that."

Suzie, who had heard every angle of the Lolly Parsons breaking-and-entering gossip, said, "You broke into his house. What do you expect him to do, buy you a drink?"

Lolly said, "He didn't even call to see if I got out of jail OK. No bail. No call. Nothing. Then he slaps a restraining order on me!"

Suzie said, "Guess that means he doesn't want to see you again, Lolly."

"You think so?" Lolly asked, sarcastically.

Maria Vargas said, "Where I come from, that's exactly what a restraining order means."

"And just where are you from?" Lolly asked. "Iowa?"

Maria was offended. "Texas," she said. "Houston."

Lolly flicked her cigarette ash on the floor. "Well, isn't that a million miles from nowhere!"

Suzie laughed, almost choking. Maria handed her a can of Pabst Blue Ribbon, to help clear her throat.

Lolly said, "A restraining order was unnecessary. It isn't like I'm a *criminal* or something. Like I'm some kind of *psycho* or something. All I wanted was to have a drink at his place, and next thing I know the cops are there and I'm spending the night in jail. My son gets hauled off. As if *my son* should be taken away by police!"

"*Your son* broke into Dan's house," Maria said. "Jesus,

that kid is lucky to be living up here in the Midwest. You break into someone's house in Texas, you get the electric chair."

"Darn tootin'!" Suzie said.

Lolly lit another cigarette, thinking over her son's luck.

Maria fumbled with her vinyl cigarette case. It was empty. She turned to Lolly. "Hey, girl. Mind if I bum a smoke?"

Lolly narrowed her eyes. "Do I look like a vending machine?"

Suzie shrugged. "Sorry. I'm all out."

Maria nudged my arm. She said, "Juan is out on the ice. Why don't you be a sweetie and tell him to bring his mother a smoke?"

JUAN WAS WITH A GROUP OF BOYS AT THE RIVER'S EDGE. They were taking turns riding an old Schwinn bicycle down a precipitous twisting path and out onto the river. The bike was heavy, and when the tire's rubber met the iced-over trail the boys picked up so much speed that, by halfway down the hill, the bike was careening and unmanageable, an out-of-control toboggan whooshing past tree limbs. The path was long and dangerous, but the boys had been practicing all afternoon. The chrome rims scattered light over the snow as Juan pushed the bike up the hill and gave it to Tony Dimantilo.

Tony had black hair, with a sweep of bangs that angled over his chin. He was two years older than I. He wore Vans and baggy Vision Street-wear T-shirts and smoked Marlboro Reds. I first met him one Sunday afternoon at Roscoe's, when he beat Frankie La Fever at pool, a feat that had given him a certain status in Roscoe's back room. I'd had a crush on Tony for months.

Tony took the Schwinn by the handlebars. He looked me over and said, "Come on. I'll give you a ride."

I scooped a fistful of snow, squeezed it into a ball, and threw it at a tree. It exploded in a burst of powder.

"Come on," Tony said. "What are you afraid of?"

We were at the top of a steep, icy, winding hill. From that height, I could see clear across the river. In the distance, the hills looked pasted onto the sky, one row of peaks superimposed upon the next. Tony steadied the bike as I edged my feet onto the rims. I had no choice but to lock my arms around his waist, a closeness that produced a deflation in my body and a sudden sharpness through my stomach. He wrapped his hands around the plastic handle grips, stood on the pedals, and muscled the bike to the root of an old oak tree. It seemed to me, as I sat back on the seat, that the balance of the world was suddenly perfect; the downswing of the hill and the backswing of myself created a nice equilibrium, with Tony as its center, a balanced scale of hill and girl and boy. I pressed my chin in the squish of his neck, my lips resting on the scruff of his hairline. He edged the tire over the root, and—*whoosh*—off we went. He pedaled for a few seconds, until speed overtook the iron frame of the bicycle. We plummeted down the hill, faster and faster.

The bike tire skimmed the trail's edge, occasionally slipping into the packed snow. Tony wrestled with the handlebars. He pumped the brakes when we slipped off the path, and thrust his weight forward when we were on. I

189

didn't know if it was the danger of falling or the way Tony eased himself back next to me, but I could not breathe, not at all, until we had flown down the entire hill. When we cleared the trees, riding out the thrill of the decline to the last dizzying revolution of the tires, and slammed out onto the ice, I was left with the tingling frost-bitten sensation of a crash landing. I was left with my first inkling of love.

As I dismounted, Tony winked at me. He pushed the Schwinn up the hill, to Juan.

The sun was going down. The snow was dappled dark gray, as if a rain of ash had descended on us. I sat before an abandoned fishing hole, pulled the sleeve of my coat to my elbow, and thrust my hand past the rim of ice, into freezing water. My hand burned for a moment and then, finger by finger, slipped into dead numb sleep. In the distance, I heard Juan laugh as he rode the Schwinn through the trees.

Suddenly, Dad was standing at the back door of the bar, his hands shoved in the pockets of his jacket. His beard was unclipped and his jeans were speckled with concrete. He was not wearing his cowboy hat, and his face looked thin and battered. He stared out at the frozen gray river.

I pulled my numb hand from the river, shook it free of water, and started toward him. "Dad!" I yelled.

He didn't hear me. He stepped over the rusted iron beam of the railroad tracks and walked alongside the highway. From behind, he looked like a hitchhiker, tough-skinned and dangerously hungry. When an old red Mustang drove past him, shivering his clothes in its wake, he did not flag it. Instead, he crossed the highway and walked toward the lot where he had parked the truck. Panicky, I followed after him, afraid that he was leaving me in Romance.

The air was cold in my throat. "Hey, Pop!" I said, out-of-breath quiet. "Wait up!"

Dad walked on, slow and steady. The sky (ashen, immense) didn't seem to be itself at all but implied a dream sky, too dim for the waking world, too endless. I steadied myself and scrambled up a bank toward the parking lot, but Dad was walking too fast. My lungs (too full, too empty, too full) filled with heat. He walked past his truck to the forest edge, snow and branches crunching under his feet. He flicked a burned-down cigarette into the snow and searched his pockets for a fresh pack. Cupping his hand over the lighter, sheltering it from wind, he lit the cigarette. The orange-yellow flame flared and reacted with his breath; smoke dispersed, twisting in the frozen air. The cigarette dangled in Dad's lips as he unzipped his jeans, adjusted himself, and took a piss, staining the phosphorescent snow deep yellow.

I walked back to the river's edge, past black walnut trees, past birch trees, past ash. My jacket snagged on the hooks of a blackberry bush, so that a tiny poof of stuffing hung from the sleeve. I sat on a felled log near the ice. I asked Tony Dimantilo to teach me to smoke and we shared a Marlboro Red, watching as the frozen sun fell behind the Mississippi. Beside him, the bleakest evening would have been beautiful. Tony passed me the cigarette. He laughed when I coughed and punched me in the arm when I didn't.

*

DAD WAS AT A BEER TENT IN BANGOR WITH MARIA VARGAS on the day of the accident. Mom was not in town either; she had gone with Andy to New Holstein, a town four hours east of us, to spend the weekend with his parents. Dad hired my cousin Laura (who, at fifteen, was two years older than I) to babysit. There were six of us kids and one of her, and by these odds we ran the show. We were Dad-less and Mom-less ragamuffins, free to do as we pleased. We spent the day watching movies and emptying the fridge of Dad's lunch staples—Mountain Dew and Ho Hos and Oscar Mayer lunch meat. By late afternoon, we were restless and ready for an adventure.

The older kids—Juan Vargas, Laura, and I—walked ahead, while the younger ones—Kelly, Amy, Matt, and Jose—trailed behind, trusting as a line of ducklings. Juan Vargas wore cowboy boots and a T-shirt that read DON'T MESS WITH TEXAS. Amy lugged Jose around on her hip. On Dad weekends, we were usually a mess. Kelly was snarly-haired and chubby. She had recently started biting her nails again, something she'd given up the year she turned six. Matt had mismatched socks and a dirty face. His uncut hair hung in his eyes.

We walked to Kwik Trip, a gas station and convenience store a block from Dad's house with tinted windows that wrapped around it like a high-security prison. The exterior was plated with space-age white plastic paneling; a concave metal canopy hung above the gas pumps. In the parking lot we gathered around Juan, who had a fistful of Vegas Boards, card-stock lottery tickets shaped like a slot machines. Maria Vargas hadn't had any cash, so she gave Juan the Vegas

Boards before she left. If he won, he'd have enough money to buy something to eat.

Juan pulled back the little doors of the Vegas Boards as we waited, full of anticipation. Three cherries could be traded for $1, three lemons for $2, and the $10 oranges would buy us all a feast. There were larger sums to be won with the bananas ($50) and the once-in-a-lifetime Vegas Board, the $100 pineapple. But nobody we knew had ever got a banana or a pineapple. They were exotic and coveted. We could not even hope to find one.

"My dad got a pineapple once," Juan said.

"Oh, yeah?" I said, impressed. "What'd your dad do with all that cash?"

"Don't know," Juan said, kicking a rock across the sidewalk. "Probably bought a car or something."

I never asked Juan why his father was in prison. Although he talked about his dad all the time, he never ratted on his dad's crimes, a quality I admired in him. Juan told us that his father was a huge man, with muscles like a World Wrestling Federation star. In fact (Juan said), his dad was the Tex-Mex Hulk Hogan. Juan and I had spent many afternoons eating Captain Crunch in front of the TV, discussing the superhuman qualities of Mr. Vargas. He was always changing occupations. One afternoon, Mr. Vargas was a trucker. Another day, he was a rodeo star. Over time, Mr. Vargas inflated before me, transforming from a flimsy unanimated presence into a blown-up figure hovering above, as big and unmanageable as a hot-air balloon. I knew that Mr. Vargas was a nobody, like all of us. More than likely, he was just an average man, living an average life, not unique

193

to anyone but Juan. And yet his absence made him special. Juan could make him into anything he liked. Loving a ghost, he lent it flesh and bones. He invented muscles and crimes. The only way for him to love his absent father was to create a new one.

Inside Kwik Trip, the walls were lined with glass-doored refrigerators. Juan went to the counter to exchange his Vegas Board cherries for cash. The rest of us went for the food. In the elongated reflections of the overhead mirror, I saw Kelly (snarly-haired) and Matt (dirty-faced) and a gang of hungry Vargas kids. Behind the glass, there was a stunning array of food: sandwiches, cartons of pudding, a hundred varieties of soda: 7-Up, Pepsi, Fanta, and the local favorite, Jolly Good Soda, which had flavors like grape, pink lemonade, and lemon-lime. There were wands of beef jerky, cheese sticks, bottled water from La Crescent, bottled water from Madison. The selection was endless, and we were in love with the options.

Earlier in the year, when Dad didn't know how to feed us, he set up an account at Kwik Trip and told us to charge our dinner. Kelly and I would walk to the gas station after school and stack Twinkies and chocolate milk on the counter. Sue, the clerk, would tally the total, bag it, and send us on our way.

In the beginning, we were moderate in our purchases. We would buy a bag of potato chips, a two-liter bottle of Cherry 7-Up, and a frozen Tombstone pizza. But soon we began to branch out to the candy aisle, filling our arms with taffy and bubble gum and pop rocks. We would buy everything we wanted, everything that had been banned by Mom:

tabloid magazines, lipstick, Cheetos. We even bought tampons, although we had no use for them. I was such a skinny adolescent I didn't get my period until I was sixteen, and even then it came only once or twice a year until I became "regular," in college. Kelly, Matt, and I would sit up at night, while Dad was out at the bars. We would eat bags of junk food and smack one another with pillows, too slap-happy to do anything but jump on the couch and wave our hands around, our eyes rolling back into our heads. Kelly and I stayed up until the early hours of the morning, watching R-rated movies on cable, while Matt, who normally went to bed at eight, would yawn and rub his eyes, trying to keep up with us.

Our Kwik Trip sprees ended abruptly one afternoon when my father stomped into the house, the bill in his hands. He said, "What do you kids think—I'm made of money?" Later that day, he canceled our account.

Once we were no longer Preferred Customers at Kwik Trip, we scrounged change to buy candy. When there were no coins hidden in the dust-bunnied carpet near Dad's waterbed, Kelly took a butter knife from the silverware drawer, sat cross-legged in front of Dad's gun cabinet, and cracked the lock. She dug through papers and packages of bullet cartridges in the base of the cabinet and pulled out a stack of cash, bundled and rubberbanded. We'd had a safe at the Trussoni Court house, and we knew how to work it open, but there had never been as much cash as this.

"Holy cow," I said, impressed, but Kelly (who had been taking five dollars here and five dollars there, small amounts that would never be noticed, for many months) informed me that this was not just Dad's money. Debbie, his most recent and serious girlfriend, who was a manager at the South Side Shop-Ko and had a huge salary of forty thousand dollars a year, kept her money there too. Dad's cash was stacked on the right; Debbie's was stacked on the left.

Kelly took a five-dollar bill and shoved it in her pocket. "Don't ever take any of Debbie's money," she said, making a face of repulsion. "She counts it all the time. She knows what she's got, down to the last cent."

But we didn't need gun-cabinet money that day. We had pocketfuls of change that we found in Dad's bedroom. We paid for our candy with 216 pennies. Sue stood behind the cash register, framed by cigarettes, newspapers, and a rack of country music cassettes, glaring at us as she counted the copper pieces and stacked them in towers of ten. Sue worked double shifts on weekends and holidays and had been the Kwik Trip Employee of the Month two months standing. An Employee of the Month photo of her (smiling) hung behind her real self (frowning). Sue gave us a receipt and slammed the register drawer shut. She said, "Have. A. Nice. Day."

There was a busy road next to Kwik Trip, the only one we had to cross before Dad's street. Our pockets were full of junk food as we ran down the sidewalk on our way home. Kelly skipped ahead, a bag of Fritos swaying in her hand. My cousin Laura had a huge domed lollipop in her mouth, the kind that had a wad of gum at its center. At a crosswalk, she pushed the lollipop to the side of her mouth, so that it jutted her jaw out like a tumor, and tried to get our attention, yelling for us to follow her: *This way! Come on! In the crosswalk!*

Juan Vargas had never been one to follow orders. He ignored the crosswalk and ran full speed into the street. Matt, who imitated Juan in everything that he did, from games of Nerf football to Frogger, darted after him. Juan made it to the center of the road, skipped over the centerline (two solid yellow stripes, a no-passing zone), and landed at the other sidewalk. Matt, however, was slow. He was seven years old and had the skinny, wobbly, uncoordinated jaunt of a baby giraffe. He was just off the curb when a brown Mercury (going, the police report would later confirm, too fast for a twenty-five-mile-an-hour street; going, the police report suggested, at least thirty-five) clipped him with its bumper. My brother popped into the air, just high enough for the grill to get him full on. I saw a sparkle of sunlight on chrome. I saw a blur of Matt movement as my brother was thrust backward. He hit the pavement headfirst and rolled, stopping at the curb, a few feet from where he started.

In the moment of silence that followed the accident, the texture of the air—which had become thick and luminous—bent around me. I saw Kelly screaming, but I did not hear her voice. I felt Amy Vargas's hand, pulling my arm toward the curb, but I couldn't move. I saw Laura drop her lollipop and sink to the sidewalk. She covered her eyes with her hands, as if to block what had just happened from her vision. And I saw the driver of the Mercury, horrified, run to the front of the car, look at the bumper and then at my brother—*What has happened? What has happened?*

When the moment snapped, and time moved again, it was crisp and new-paced. My lazy-eyed vision of things had been shattered. I saw and felt everything with a sharp overbearing clarity I did not have before.

I ran to the edge of the curb, next to Kelly, and squatted at Matt's side. His body was twisted and contorted. One leg bent under him at a funny angle, the knee jutting the wrong way, skin and muscle stretching where the thighbone had fractured. His arms were splayed over his chest, and his neck was twisted back, so that his head of bloody hair looked like a red flower, broken at the stem. My brother's eyes were closed, but his finger twitched out a Morse-code reflex: *Tap, tap tap. Tap, tap, tap. Tap, tap, tap. Tap, tap, tap.*

Blood pooled under Matt's body. It collected in the groove below the curb, a black-red pond, almost the color of the pavement. Laura's saliva-slicked lollipop (an elbow of gum poking from the side) had fallen nearby, a spattering of sand clinging to it. Kelly screamed, and the high-pitched desperation of her scream spoke its own language. Her scream said, *We cannot save you from this. No matter how much we want to snap the bones back and wipe the blood from your lips, we cannot. We are helpless. You are on your own, little brother. To your fate we give you.*

eleven

Jim ordered another round of huge tropical drinks. The waiter walked swiftly around the curves of the rooftop swimming pool, past a table of German tourists, to the bar. Five minutes later, Patty and I had flamingo-pink frozen daiquiris with chunks of strawberries dangling from the rim. Jim's drink was swimming-pool blue, dressed with mangoes.

Patty slid a cigarette from a new package. "Isn't this great?" she asked, as she lit up. "I can smoke wherever I want here!"

Jim fished a mango from his drink, lifted it over his lips, and bit.

From a five-star rooftop, Ho Chi Minh City could be any city in the world. Clusters of streetlights flecked the darkness; buses and cars distributed horn noise and pollution. On the streets below, I had been overwhelmed by the mopeds, the heat, the unending stream of people. But up here, Vietnam was serene. Lights cracked on the surface of the swimming pool and refracted, broken. My daiquiri was sweet and strong. Alcohol seeped through my throat. I felt drunk and jet-lagged and wanted, suddenly, to fall asleep on the rooftop, to curl into my cushioned chair and surrender to the tropical night.

Patty took off her high-heeled sandals and propped her feet on a chair. "You know what?" she said. "A pedicure in the hotel salon costs fifty bucks. If I go around the corner to a Vietnamese place, it will be five. And you know what? Tomorrow, I'm going to march down to the lobby and get a fifty-dollar pedicure. That's the kind of mood I'm in."

"A dangerous mood," Jim said, clearly in love with his wife.

"Better believe it," she said, as she flicked the ash of her cigarette onto the tiled floor. "I live for danger."

"What did you think of those tunnels?" Jim asked. "They were something else, weren't they?"

"They were a little less . . . dramatic than I imagined them to be," I said.

"Well, it wasn't like you had someone waiting down there with an AK-47," Jim said, smiling.

I remembered a day I had sat with my father at the kitchen table. It was mid-afternoon, the glare of winter sunlight sending waves of brightness over the grain of the table's surface. I pushed a small red button on the tape recorder and set it between us. "Tell me about the tunnels," I said. Dad lit a cigarette and shifted in his seat, clearly uncomfortable. He took a breath and began talking, his voice slow and hesitant.

"The way my father described them," I said, returning Jim's gaze, trying to find the right words, "was so perfect. When he talked about the tunnels, I was scared to death."

"See, that's the difference between my generation and

my father's," Patty said. "My dad was in World War Two but he never talked about it. Never. He just acted like it had never happened."

"You can't compare World War Two veterans and Vietnam veterans," Jim said. "Your dad's generation came home winners. We did not. I got back in 'sixty-nine after two tours, and let me tell you—I felt like a loser. The world had changed. I enrolled in college, but I was so out of touch. You wouldn't believe it."

"That's not true," Patty said, ruffling Jim's hair. "Not true at all."

"So tell me," Jim said, finishing off his drink, "what did your dad have to say about the war? Was he okay when he got back?" Jim's voice was tender, as if asking after the welfare of a brother. I would have liked to tell him that my father was fine, that the war didn't really affect him, and that Dad had left combat in the jungles and moved on.

"The reason I'm asking," Jim said, "is because coming back here can really help. This is my second trip, and I find it very . . . relieving."

I had asked my father to come to Vietnam. Thinking that such a trip would help him, I called and offered to book the tickets. We could walk through the village of Tay Ninh, I told him, and go to the grounds of the old Twenty-fifth base camp, near the Cu Chi tunnels. As I talked to Dad about the trip, excited about the possibility of seeing the scenes of my father's war stories up close, he was silent. "No," he said, finally. "No, I'm not going there. I can't. Not again."

"That's just what I used to say," Jim said. He took Patty's

cigarette, dragged deeply, and returned it. "But I'm glad I came. It put a lot of old demons to rest."

I stretched in my chair, only half listening to Jim narrate his previous trip to Vietnam, taken with a group of veterans. I knew he was right. My father should have come with me, but he did not want to visit his past. He wanted to forget it.

Jim and Patty listened as I told them about my father's life after Vietnam, even about the skull my father brought back from the war.

"Wow," Patty said. "How did he get it into the States? Wouldn't a customs official take it away from him?"

"I've heard of guys doing shit like that," Jim said. "But I can't imagine where he would've gotten a skull. You sure that thing was real?"

As an adult, I sometimes thought I'd made the skull up. I could not believe that my father (no matter how disturbed by the war) would bring human remains into our house. But the memory had left an impression upon my mind, one that returned every now and then as a dream, so I called one of my uncles, to ask him about it. Yes, he said, he remembered the skull. My father had brought it back from the war and had been strangely attached to it. "Your dad was a different man when he came back from Vietnam," my uncle said. "He beat the shit out of me one night because he thought I was coming on to his girlfriend. He didn't know then that I was gay and wasn't interested in his girl in the least. He just snapped. All of a sudden, he's got me on the floor, beating the hell out of me. Your dad would never have done that before Vietnam. Sure, he'd been in his share of fistfights, but never with one of us. Us younger kids used to see Danny as our protector. He was right in the middle, the sixth kid. He'd always stick up for us when the older ones tried to pull something. When your dad came home, he wasn't the brother I knew. He was a different man."

I had heard stories of my father's transformation from many of my relatives. They all said the same thing: *War was the first thing to change your dad; the divorce was the second.* The first scarred his soul; the second broke his heart.

"Your dad was living with Albert on the South Side, before their big blow-out. He put that skull on top of his TV set and kept it there," my uncle continued. "I couldn't even watch a football game at his place, with that thing staring down at me." When I asked my uncle if he thought a skull was a strange thing to keep on a TV set, he said, "I sure as hell thought that your dad should get rid of it. That skull was damned weird."

I was glad I had called my uncle. He helped me to see that my father had been unwell for a long time, and that the discomfort I felt in his presence—the sense that he was always just off-center from the rest of us—had been felt by other people. The skull disappeared when I was very young, I never knew exactly when. My uncle guessed that my mother had thrown it away.

For Mom, the past was something to be tossed out and forgotten. If I tried to talk about the past with Mom, she stopped me cold. She spoke about the Trussoni Court years as if they were a story she once heard. If I asked her about my childhood, she paused, her face perturbed, and confessed that she didn't remember. If I told her something I remembered—like about the nine stitches I got in my thigh in first grade—she would look vaguely interested, as if I were speaking about another girl from another family, and say, "Is that so?" If I asked her about the divorce, she looked dismayed. She did not want to think about that part of our life. "Why talk about this?" she would say. "It was such a long time ago."

"Because it is important to me," I would reply, irritated.

Mom fought to remain on the safe, solid pathway of the present. "It's better," she said, "to go forward and never look back."

After the divorce, I fought my mother with a fury that only a teenage girl could fuel and maintain. I was angry that she had left my father, but I was equally angry that she had remarried only a few months after the divorce went through. Andy was not perfect; he had a Dr. Jekyll and Mr. Hyde quality to him and was often moody. He had left a wife and three children for Mom, and although they lived with their mother, on weekends Trussoni Court hosted a Brady Bunch mix of six children, three girls and three boys. To make matters worse, Kelly, Matt, and I were very different from Andy's children. They were docile and well-behaved, nothing like us wild smart-mouthed Trussoni kids.

Nonetheless, my mother loved him, and this made me even more angry. I told her that she and Andy had ruined my life, and—whether out of teenage dramatics or simple nastiness—I did my best to kill their happiness. Family dinners? I showed up late and wouldn't eat. Family vacations? I was the girl giving the camera the finger. If I was miserable, I thought, I would make her equally so. Only as an adult did I understand how scared I had been of Andy.

If he had the power to take my mother from my father, surely he had the power to take her from me.

"Your mom must have had a hard time," Patty said, looking concerned.

"She did," I said, sipping my drink. "She divorced my dad when I was twelve."

Jim, who had been listening closely to my story, stared at me for a bit too long, his eyes narrowed. "You know," he said finally, "people deal with things in their own way. You shouldn't be judgmental."

For a second I wondered if I had heard him correctly. "Judgmental?" I asked. "I don't think I'm judgmental."

"No," he said, lighting one of Patty's cigarettes, "you probably don't. But you wouldn't have come all this way if you weren't pissed as hell at someone."

FOR A LONG TIME—EVEN AFTER THE DIVORCE BECAME final—my father could not grasp that our life on Trussoni Court had ended. It was as if a grenade had gone off too close to his head, leaving an echo of the explosion in his ears. He would be fine and then, suddenly, he would remember my mother and look vacant, shell-shocked. Drinking was the only thing that snapped him out of his stupor. Sometimes even that didn't help.

The first Christmas after the divorce, we went to my uncle Gene's place. My oldest uncle was a successful contractor and owned a nice house off Cass Street, in the best part of La Crosse. His marriage was happy, and although our cousins (four girls and a boy) knew about the divorce, they could not imagine what Kelly and Matt and I were actually going through. On Christmas Eve, we sat around their tree, watching them open presents. Dad reclined on the couch, a drink in his hand and a chip on his shoulder. *I bet your mother is having a very merry goddamned Christmas. What do you think, kids? Should we give her a call?* I watched my aunt pass out gifts. Toni, the cousin closest to my age, opened a box containing a leather jacket. She slid into it and danced around the living room, singing "Lucky Star." She didn't notice how extraordinary her life was, how perfect, how much I envied her. Dad had bought us gifts too, and we sat quietly, each with a package on our laps, waiting for a sign from him that we could open them.

Gene had got to talking about old times, when the Trussoni boys would prowl the river road. He told about the time Dad got beat up at a bar in Stoddard, a few months before he got kicked out of high school. He had been beaten so badly he couldn't walk. Someone dropped him off on the farmhouse lawn, where he lay, bleeding. When my uncles found him, they got into a car and drove down to Stoddard, back to the bar, and tore the place apart. "That sure got their attention," Uncle Gene said, smiling. "Nobody who knew his what-for messed with us again after that."

Gene loaded all of us—his kids and Dad's kids—into a van and drove us through the streets of town to see Christmas lights. Dad sat in the front passenger seat, laughing as Gene cracked jokes. We had spent all our Christmases in the country and had never seen so many houses on fire with green and red bulbs. Gina (my oldest cousin, named, as I was, after her father) had snuck a beer along. As we drove down King Street, we saw a house covered in white lights. A giant sleigh rested on its roof, filled with presents and a fat stuffed Santa Claus. "Look!" Matt shouted, pointing to the roof. He still believed in Santa, and Kelly and I, disabused many years before, let him believe.

We drove away from Gene's house happy, as if this were any other Christmas. Dad cracked his window and lit a cigarette. As the freezing wind blew across us, Matt leaned his head against my arm and fell asleep. Kelly and I tried to count all the lights we had seen. Ahead, the highway forked. To the right branched the road that led to Dad's house on the North Side; to the left was the county highway going to Trussoni Court. Nobody noticed when Dad flicked the turn signal, the green arrow pulsing *left, left, left, left,* and nobody noticed as Dad turned off the highway toward Trussoni Court. We drove for a good mile before Dad realized his mistake. When the truth hit him, he slammed on the brakes and cut the engine, leaving the truck mid-road. Folding his arms over the steering wheel, he buried his head in his hands and sobbed. We kids looked from Dad to the long empty highway, scared. We had never seen our father cry before. Soon, anger replaced anguish. Dad ground the truck into reverse and peeled away.

Dad cried the whole drive back. After he parked, Kelly jumped out of the truck, taking Matt with her, and hid in our bedroom. "Are you okay, Dad?" I asked him, touching his arm.

"Get in the house," he mumbled. "Go on. I'm fine." I think it was then, as I walked over the icy sidewalk, leaving my father to cry in his truck, that I began to hate my mother.

"POTTY BREAK!" PATTY ANNOUNCED, STUBBING HER CIG-arette in a ceramic ashtray. "Care to join me?"

We pushed our chairs away and walked past the pool to the elevator. "Let's go to the room," Patty said, pushing the button for the ninth floor. "I left my lipstick down there."

When she came out of the bathroom, Patty pulled a bottle of champagne from the fridge, popped it open, and poured our glasses full. We sat by the terrace door, the night breeze sweeping the curtains away. "Expensive champagne has less bubbles," she informed me, as she held a flute filled with golden, effervescent liquid to the light. "But I'll tell you a secret: I prefer the kind with more."

I raised my glass and took a sip.

Patty said, "You know, Jim wasn't always so open to talking about the war. There were years after he came back that things were . . . difficult. For both of us."

"You knew him before he went?"

"Since high school. We graduated the same year."

"Did he change?" I asked. "I mean—was he very different when he came back?"

Patty looked at me as if I'd just asked the stupidest question she'd ever heard. "Of course he changed." As she poured herself another glass of champagne, her diamond ring caught the light and sparkled. "You think any man who goes to war stays the same? But I'll tell you one thing about Jim: He's worked on this. He has really faced this part of his life. I don't know about your dad, but I know that if Jim didn't look Vietnam square in the eye and deal with it—and by that I mean therapy—he'd be in sorry shape. I think"— she said, raising her glass—"he's doing pretty well."

"That's great," I said. "He's lucky."

"No such thing as luck, kiddo," she said. "Just hard work."

"It's weird," I said, feeling able to talk to Patty in a way I had never been able to talk to my parents. "I don't really know my father at all anymore. I feel like he's impossible to break through to. Our views about everything—politics, family, life—are different. He doesn't know who I've become, and he doesn't want to. I remember, when I was in college, I used to want him to understand where I was coming from. I'd give him books and try to talk to him about my feelings. But we can't even be in the same room together half of the time without fighting."

Patty sighed. "That's just how it is, growing up."

"But it shouldn't be that way," I said. "I wish it hadn't turned out that way." Hoping to change the subject, I looked at the digital clock. It was long past midnight. "Shouldn't we go back up? Jim might wonder where we are."

"That's okay," she said, smiling. "A little mystery is good for him." As she drank her champagne, she cocked her head and looked me over. "How old are you, anyway?"

"Twenty-four," I said. "Twenty-five in November. Why?"

"No reason, I guess," she said, twisting a ring around her finger. "It's just—Jim and I lost a baby in 'seventy-five. He would have been about your age."

Something about the way she turned from me as she said that, refusing to meet my eye, reminded me of my mother, when she was pale and sick in the weeks before her miscarriage. Feeling the same sense of helplessness I felt then, I said, "I'm sorry."

"Thank you," she said, pouring herself more champagne. "But there's nothing to be done. Sometimes you have no choice but to play the cards God gives you." She held the bottle out to me. "Another glass?"

twelve

When Patty decided to go to the rooftop to find Jim, I took the elevator down. The doorman lounged near a line of taxis outside of the hotel. I paused on the sidewalk and gazed up at the pristine marble façade to the ninth floor. Each window was dark and reflective. I couldn't help but think of Jim and Patty, drunk on rum, stumbling through the brass-finished hallways to their room, where they would drink champagne and watch satellite TV. They were the same age as my parents and still in love. How, I wondered, had they made it when so many others had not?

The doorman caught my eye and opened the door of a taxi with a grand sweep of his arm. But, as I was not far from Dong Khoi Street, I decided to walk. I shoved my hands in the pockets of my jeans, walked past the taxis, and retraced the route back, along Dai Lo Le Duan. The boulevard was all palm trees and luxury hotels and security guards, well lit and safe. I was in the Government District, where the Communist Party convened in an old French hotel modeled after the Hotel de Ville. I walked past the British Consulate, the French, and the American, clustered

211

together. Ho Chi Minh's narrow goateed face stared out from the front window of the Viet My bookshop. Ho Chi Minh was Vietnam's guardian deity, framed and hanging in nearly every building in the city. A large glassy-eyed portrait oversaw the Central Post Office, where I had gone one afternoon to buy postcards. He looked down on me as I licked my stamps and wrote out my cards.

There had even been a large oil portrait of Ho Chi Minh in the War Remnants Museum, which I had visited earlier in the week. It hung near a wall of photographs taken at My Lai, the famous ones printed in *Life* magazine in 1968. I had seen some of these pictures before, when I was in college, but they were more powerful, even more disturbing, in the museum. The photographs had been enlarged and framed. One showed a woman lying in the mud, facedown, with a baby—whose head seemed bigger than its mother's—dead next to her. There was another of men stacked one upon the other, all dead. There were small white captions below the photos: *Woman and child murdered by American bullets. Mass grave at My Lai hamlet.*

I stood, studying them. After some time, a Vietnamese woman had walked to my side. Quite young, she had perfectly straight glossy black hair and wore tiny embroidered slippers. She crossed her arms and squinted at the pictures, as if she needed eyeglasses. I wondered if, after seeing these pictures, she would ever look at a child without feeling a tinge of protectiveness. I wondered if she (or I or any woman who had stood here, looking) would ever gather the courage to have a baby of her own.

My father was a few hundred kilometers south of My Lai on March 16, 1968, when Task Force Barker swept the district of Son My. He always said he had not known what had happened at My Lai, that he hardly knew what was happening a mile away, let alone all the way up there. But he had heard rumors, he said, of search-and-destroy missions ending hard and sloppy. And he could see how it might happen, he said. He never knew who he was fighting; he was never sure which villagers were VC and which ones weren't. When I asked him what he would have done if he'd found himself under Lieutenant Calley's command, he shrugged. "It isn't a soldier's place to decide those things," he said. "When you're told to burn a village, you burn a village. Period."

Dad was always open about the fact that he had killed, not just once but many times, during his tour. "If I didn't get them," he would say, shaking he head ruefully, "they sure as hell were going to get me." After his PTSD diagnosis, when the cancer had spread from his throat to his lungs, he would tell me (matter-of-factly) about the men he had killed, spreading his war photos out and saying, *I got that one in a firefight*, and *I got that one outside a village*, and *I got that one after he threw a grenade in our perimeter*. I always wondered how my mother felt, loving a man who had killed other human beings, and I always wondered if my father still thought of those people he had been forced, by circumstances, to shoot. Once, when he was digging through his war things, pushing aside a canteen and his dog tags, trying to find the pictures of his kills, he said, "I know I had some pictures in here of bodies. I took them after the firefight that got me my Combat Infantry Badge. But they're not here. Where in the hell are they?"

I had seen those photos many times before, and I felt relief that he had lost them. "Maybe it's better," I said. "I don't think it's good for you to look at those anymore."

"Why?" he shot back, as if I'd accused him of being crazy. "Those bodies were all Vietcong. They don't bother me one bit."

I turned off Dai Lo Le Duan and onto Dong Khoi. It was after midnight, and save for the occasional homeless person the streets were deserted. There would be more nightlife in the streets surrounding my hotel, but it was so warm, and the night was so peaceful, I was content to stay in the quiet shadowy government zone.

Notre Dame Cathedral rose behind a high iron fence, its neo-Romanesque towers reaching for the sky. A statue of the Virgin Mary stood mid-square, illuminated by a small spotlight. I pushed open an iron gate and walked to her. She was large and serene, her marble arms open to the world, as if to embrace it. I sat at the base of the statue and leaned my head against her cold side. I was drawn to the peacefulness in her face, and I felt almost safe, touching her cool marble feet. Suddenly, a shadow passed through the grating, sending sepals of gray over the stonework square.

The shadow came closer and I saw it was a girl, dressed in a white *ao dai*. She had long hair that fell over her shoulders and hung loose to her waist. She held a woven conical hat in her hand, thrusting it forward as she walked, like a beggar's bowl. As she came closer, I saw she was not a girl at all but a small thin woman with high cheekbones and deep-set eyes. She came up to me and took my hand, her fingers cold as ice in my palm. There was something off about her expression, as if the edge of her reason had cracked. Her eyes were slightly crossed and her mouth slack. "Do you speak English?" I asked, but she said nothing at all. Instead, she shoved the hat at my chest, pushing it so that the brim bent in, collapsing upon the center.

As the hat pressed into my chest, I looked into her eyes. *Give, give, give,* they said. *Give, give, give.* I wanted to fill her hat with money or love or hope or happiness. I wanted to fill her hat with something I did not have. I tried to pull away from her, but she did not let go of my fingers. She placed my hand into the center of her hat, to touch the emptiness.

"Here," I said, pulling 30,000 *dong* from my pocket. For some reason, I thought of the story my father had told me, years before, about a prostitute and her mother. I pulled out another ten thousand *dong*. "Here," I said. "Take this."

The woman responded in rapid-fire Vietnamese. Perhaps she was whispering something about her life, maybe about her childhood in a nearby village or about her family in the years after the war. Surely she remembered a time when parents kept their children close, afraid of wayward bullets and napalm. Although I could not understand her language, I listened, careful to look her in the eye. The night inhaled her words, keeping them for itself. If I spoke Vietnamese I would have said, *Your father fought on one side and my father on the other, but we are not that different, you and I.*

When she saw I had nothing more to give, the woman

released my hand. She clutched the money in her fist, put her hat on her head, turned, and walked back to the street, a flat white image claimed by the night.

It was late, so I followed her out of the courtyard, walked past the church, and went out the rear gate onto a street of small shops. It must have been after two in the morning; everything was closed for the night. There was the Diamond Department Store, its windows filled with silk ties and summer jackets, and a darkened movie theater. A stray dog limped ahead of me. I followed him into an alleyway that smelled of fish. As it slinked behind a Vietcom bank, weak light shivered over its back and rested upon the packed red-dirt roads. The buildings were chipped and crumbling. Dim lights emanated from above, glowing behind window curtains. White sheets drooped from balcony clotheslines. I felt as if I had fallen into another city, into the Saigon of my father's stories.

The dog stopped to dig in a mound of trash. I walked past it, out onto an open empty boulevard.

As I walked in the direction of Dong Khoi, I could see a man at the end of the boulevard. Passing under a streetlamp, half a block in the distance, his shadow cast itself forward upon the street. He was tall and skinny, an Ichabod Crane in blue jeans. For a fraction of a second, I told myself this could not be the man I saw earlier but someone else, another foreigner foolish enough to walk alone after dark. A tourist, like me, seduced by the vaporous heat. When I saw he was not wearing a baseball cap or sunglasses, I felt a rush of relief. I told myself he was not tall enough or ragged enough or dark enough to be my man. But when he came closer and we faced each other at opposite ends of the street—one in darkness, the other in light—I saw his sunglasses, clipped to the front of his shirt, and knew I was in trouble.

When he started toward me, I turned on my heel and ran into the narrow nameless alleyway. But I heard him, running behind me. When I picked up speed, his footsteps became louder. After 150 feet the alley narrowed. If I were to stretch my arm out, my fingertips would have brushed a kumquat tree, a motor scooter, the white metal grating of a sealed storefront window. At the end of the street, there was a shop filled with packaged noodles and metal colanders and bags of rice. A clerk slept at the counter, his chin resting in his arms. He had left his bicycle near the road. I grabbed it by the rubber handlebars, pushed it off its kickstand, and threw my leg over. As I pedaled away, veering with the slim serpentine road, I listened: Was that him behind me? I rode as fast as I could through the dark until I saw, up ahead, the flash of neon. Back onto Dong Khoi, near the tourist village, there were illuminated storefronts, women in high heels, tourist-filled bars and nightclubs. I looked over my shoulder. The man was no longer there.

I PARKED THE BIKE NEAR THE ENTRANCE OF A CAFÉ AND walked across the terrace to the bathrooms. Locking myself inside a small dank room, I put the toilet seat down and sat upon the cover, drawing my knees to my chin and burying my face in the scruff of my blue jeans. I felt an overwhelming urge to change my plane ticket and return home on the first flight out. Was this how Dad felt in Vietnam—scared and alone in unfamiliar territory? The sense that with a single misguided step he would fall into enemy hands?

My hotel was just down the road, within sight of the café. I took a table on the terrace, so I could watch the street. If the man knew where I was staying, he might follow me there. The waiter brought my order—a double whiskey on the rocks—a pack of cigarettes, and an ashtray that said 333, the local beer. After my first drink, I almost felt calm. Lifting the match and inhaling the rich, poisonous smoke, my hands almost stopped shaking.

Just then the girl with the blond dreadlocks walked by, on Dong Khoi. Seeing me alone, she came to my table, bringing a boy wearing a Grateful Dead T-shirt with her. They both hauled large canvas backpacks. Looking them over, I was reminded that, for some people, Vietnam was just the backdrop for a cheap, sunny vacation. They joined me, and the waiter brought them a menu.

"I'd like some spring rolls," the girl said. "But wait. What kind of meat is in them?"

"Pork," the waiter replied.

"Well . . .," the girl said, thinking this over, "can you make the spring rolls with chicken?"

"I will ask," the waiter said, writing something on the pad.

"Actually, I'd feel better about eating this if there was no meat involved. Can you make *vegetarian* spring rolls?"

"You want chicken and vegetable spring rolls?" the waiter asked.

"No, vegetarian. Only vegetables. Wait a minute—are the spring rolls fried?"

The waiter was perplexed. He said, "Spring roll price?"

"Fried," the girl insisted.

"Five thousand *dong*."

"No," she said, enunciating each word. "*Are they fried?*"

The Grateful Dead guy came to the rescue. He said, "She wants to know: Are they fried? Like, Kentucky Fried Chicken fried? Hot oil. Sizzle, sizzle. *Fried* spring rolls?"

"Ah, yes," the waiter said, relieved. "*Fried*. The spring rolls are fried."

"Then I definitely don't want meat in them," the girl said. "Way too many calories. Just vegetables. No pork. No chicken. Tofu, if you've got it. But if not, whatever."

The waiter said, "You want fried vegetable spring roll no meat?"

"Exactly," the girl said, happy to have been understood.

When the waiter turned to me, I lifted my empty glass. "Another one of these," I said. "Lots of ice."

It was nearly three in the morning; the crowd on Dong Khoi Street had thinned. The three of us sat at the café, smoking. When I told my new friends what had happened and that I was too frightened to leave the café, the girl with the dreadlocks offered to let me sleep in their room, just down the street, but I refused. The man who had chased me was nowhere in sight. Maybe he was gone for good.

"I think I'll just lock myself in my room and get some sleep," I said. "If he knew where I was staying, he would have come here by now."

"I don't know if that's a good idea," the girl said, leaving some cash for her food on the table and hoisting her backpack over her shoulders. "I'd be totally freaked if I were you."

When the café was about to close for the night, the waiter collected my empty glass, wiped the table with a cloth, and presented me with the bill. I stacked the bright-colored *dong* on the plastic tabletop, weighting the money with the ashtray. All the hotels on Dong Khoi were required to lock their doors at 3 A.M., and when the neon sign in my hotel window flicked off I knew the door would soon be locked. I did not want to leave the safety of a public space. Suddenly, I wished I had taken the girl with the dreadlocks up on her offer, or that I were home, in the States, at a twenty-four-hour diner, drinking watery coffee clouded with nondairy creamer. But when I saw the receptionist locking the door, I left the café and hurried to the hotel. The receptionist, still wearing his Nike warm-up suit and flip-flops, handed me my room key and turned away, weary of tourists who kept him up all night.

FIVE MONTHS INTO HIS TOUR, DAD AND GOODMAN stumbled upon a tunnel complex during patrol. My father had been going down regularly, as many as three or four times a week, but this was different. Goodman taped his pant legs tight to his boots and slid his homemade kneepads over his fatigues. Making a wire loop on his belt, he dropped his flashlight through it. "We don't want to use the flash-lights too much this time," he said, and put the tape in his butt pack. "This one's warmer than usual, so be careful."

Goodman slid into the tunnel. My father followed

immediately, dropping into a wide cylindrical shaft, tall and horizontal, with a communication tunnel running out perpendicular. He sat on his haunches as fine dust rose and settled around him. There was no room to move, so he waited, letting his eyes adjust. Sunlight radiated from the entrance in half circles. He sat in the brightest ring, Goodman, just ahead in the darkest.

Goodman scraped a wall with his knife, checking for booby traps. My father imitated him, checking for roots and small fissures in the clay. His skin prickled and began to sting. Slowly, steadily, he inhaled the cool air. He knew there were hundreds of ways to die in a tunnel.

Goodman flipped his flashlight on and off, on and off, illuminating his face. Grinning, he turned and moved decisively away. Something was different about this tunnel. My father could feel it. Maybe it was the air, maybe the size. He realized, from the scratching of Goodman's hands and knees, that his friend was moving ahead fast, so he quickened his pace. If he lost Goodman, he would be trapped. He would never find his way out alone.

"Goodman?" he whispered. He couldn't hear him any longer. Goodman turned his flashlight on, then off, less than five feet ahead.

They crawled forward. The tunnel swung left and turned abruptly downward. Dad fell with its momentum, sliding, letting his knees scrape against the clay. Sweat soaked through his undershirt and fatigues; fine powdery silt stuck to his neck, mixing to sticky mud. He wished he'd made kneepads. He felt his .45 in his belt and wanted a lighter weapon, a .22 or .38 pistol, like Goodman's.

The darkness changed as the tunnel opened into a room. A small air hole in the ceiling let in a shaft of light that washed over Goodman, who was crouching against a wall. He ran his hands over the ground, checking for something, and then grabbed my father's arm and pulled him back. Dust particles spun, lit like a million moons.

Tunnels—two on the left and one on the right—opened from the wall. Goodman knelt before the entrances, checking them with his hands. He seemed agitated, tense, as he positioned my father near the communication tunnel. "What do you smell?" he asked. When my father didn't know, Goodman said, "You smell human shit," and pulled up a piece of thatch and exposed the rim of a buried clay pot. "They probably sleep in this room because of the fresh air."

Goodman ducked into the tunnel on the right. My father followed, trying to keep up. He crawled faster and faster, arms and legs burning, his neck cramped. The communication tunnel was much narrower than the others, but they pulled themselves along, inch by inch. When my father felt something move against his cheek, he brushed away a cobweb. Goodman kicked, hitting him in the head with his boot. "Backtrack," Goodman whispered, and so he scuffled backward. He heard the knife going at something, scratching at wood and metal. "Hold this," Goodman said, handing over his flashlight. The beam coned down, falling over the dirt. Goodman worked into the floor with his knife and heaved something up. Dust lifted, saturated the air, and a new convexity pulled at their ears, a new space revealed.

"Second-level tunnels," Goodman said. He pulled up an entrance cover—thick as an encyclopedia—made of crossed slabs of wood and pipe. "Come on," he said, as he stood over the hole, felt around its edges, and lowered himself down.

My father dropped the flashlight to Goodman and lowered himself too—until his body jammed in the space. The upper half of his body remained aboveground, as if stuck, but he scraped against the edges and worked himself in, twisting back and forth. His stomach pinched. He sucked it in, trying to redistribute his organs. Each twist allowed only an inch of movement. That's when they get you, Goodman had once told him, when you're vulnerable. They hide in the dark. They wait until you're halfway through a hole. Then they ram the punji stick in.

Finally, something gave way—his rib cage or a ball and socket—and gravity took Dad down. He fell, heavily, fully, onto the floor below. Goodman held out a hand and pulled him to his feet.

The room felt much larger and deeper than the first one. My father couldn't see much in the weak light, but he sensed that the space was cluttered with large, solid blocks. He turned his head and moved the flashlight around, attempting to discern the dimensions of the space. Goodman stood still, his .22 in his hand. Again, he asked Dad to use his senses: *What do you smell? What do you hear?* He said, "Listen to me. You don't take shortcuts down here. You get in a tunnel, you follow it all the way through. Don't cross a room until you're sure it's not rigged." Goodman backed up against the wall. He hadn't done any of this in the first tunnel, the cold one. He'd been almost careless. "They know we take shortcuts," Goodman said, and crawled on his stomach to the center of the room, where he lay listening,

223

watching. "She's empty," he said. He stood and scanned the room without hesitation, as if he'd developed a sort of sonar, a batlike ability to navigate the dark.

They set their flashlights vertically on a table. Their eyes began to focus as the light bloomed over the uneven arch of the ceiling.

"I've never been in a room like this," Goodman said, as he dug through the rucksack and found his camera. "I've been in lots of rooms, but this one—man, this is amazing." He snapped pictures, using the flashlight to illuminate the room's walls. "This complex must go down at least thirty feet."

The mass of clutter slowly took the shape of crates and plastic bottles. Fifty-five-gallon drums, the kind that stored herbicides, stood against a wall. The crates were filled variously with documents—the words blurred and uneven—and stacks of unused paper.

Goodman thought they'd stumbled upon a VC propaganda factory. Pacing from one end of the chamber to the other, he took more pictures, holding the flashlight above the camera. "VC communications, communist newsletters," Goodman said, excited. "Bet they got their own Cong *Stars and Stripes*." He picked up a stack of papers. "Pops is going to love these."

The tunnel passage swung left, arched, and Goodman followed its curvature. Indecisive, he slowed and accelerated, while my father—who copied his every move—crawled after him. They passed a number of holes that led off the communication tunnel, but Goodman kept going, as if looking for something. The tunnel dipped as they went deeper into the earth. The heat and lack of air didn't seem to bother Goodman at all; he kept going, his pace steady.

My father was tired. His wrists were tight and he could feel blood from his knees soaking through his fatigues. He knew there must be enemy, ahead or maybe behind, and he was as scared as he'd ever been. He wanted out of there, but Goodman kept going; he had no choice but to follow.

Suddenly, there was a thud. Then a click as an over-whelming brightness flooded into the tunnel. He laughed woozily, almost believing, for a second, he was free. He dragged himself to the tunnel's edge and there, six feet below, stood Goodman, his foot on the pedal of a massive gasoline generator.

Strings of bulbs had been tacked to the walls, and Dad saw, for the first time, the tunnels in full light. He didn't know what he'd expected, but the room was disappointing. The walls were dull brown and uneven; the ceiling was dull brown and uneven. He jumped down next to Goodman and walked across the room, stopping before a workbench. There were boxes of used shells and buckets of ball bearings. Tin cans had been stacked neatly next to a box of old detonators. Everything—reams of wire, pairs of metal scissors—was clean and neatly arranged. A box of fully assembled hand grenades sat on the far end of the workbench and, next to them, an assembled machine gun, probably Chinese, prop-ped up as a model. Goodman found his camera and took some pictures.

Dad made for the communication tunnel; Goodman followed. They crawled uphill, the tunnel angling and rising. He couldn't remember where he was. Entrances and forked paths and a hundred different hidden exits moved before his imagination. He stopped and Goodman, who wasn't far behind, crawled into him.

"I don't know where I'm going."

"Just go up. We'll feel our way out."

There was movement up ahead. My father leaned close to the tunnel wall, terrified. Goodman pulled out his .22, pushed past him, and lay flat and still. Lowering himself onto his stomach, Dad listened: There was a scraping, a brushing, someone moving toward them. He closed his eyes. The breathing came closer. He felt his throat contract and a sort of electric haze went through him, announcing, in a language composed not of words, or even of thoughts, but of the finer instincts of the body: *You are going to die.*

The scratching diminished, then stopped altogether. Goodman rose to his hands and knees. He whispered, "He went into a chamber."

"Let's get the fuck out of here."

"Come on," Goodman said. He crawled to the tunnel mouth, swiveled into the room, and shot. My father entered the room just as an NVA soldier hit the floor and scurried into a tunnel, at the opposite end of the room. Goodman ran to the tunnel and crawled in after him.

Lights were strung on the wall and an oil lamp burned in a corner, making the air thick and smoky. A second man lay on a mat near the wall. Covered with sweat, he stared up at my father helplessly, his eyes bright and unfocused. The man was old, with streaks of gray in his hair. His shirt was unbuttoned—his chest and neck were wet—and he turned his head back and forth, as if looking for something. His eyes met my father's eyes and fear passed through them. Then, the old man smiled. His face became filled with a strange happiness, almost joy. He took my father's hand, as if they were buddies, and the old man began speaking in Vietnamese.

The chamber was some sort of hospital. A chart of the human body hung on the wall, marking muscles and veins with Chinese ideograms and *quac ngu*. Near the bed, shelves were filled with rolls of Red Cross gauze and bottles of penicillin and morphine, all labeled in English.

The man repeated the same words over and over and Dad felt, for some reason, that he should understand them. He tried to repeat the words, and the man must have thought he was responding: He squeezed my father's hand harder and spoke louder.

Goodman emerged from the tunnel, his hair and face drenched with sweat, pulling the NVA soldier into the room by the shirt. From his rucksack, he took duct tape and bound the prisoner's wrists behind his back. Then, he yanked the prisoner toward the communication tunnel, holding the .22 to his head. Goodman held him forward, for my father to see, as if he'd just caught a trophy fish. The prisoner, really just a boy, probably only sixteen, stood straight and still, looking at the sick man and then at my father. The boy's eyebrow twitched reflexively. He flared his nostrils, trying to control his fear.

Goodman knocked bottles from the shelves, opening and emptying First Aid boxes. Kneeling before a medical kit, he began tossing out scissors, bandages, and spools of thread. He was fast and sharp, as if he had done this sort of thing a hundred times before. He walked to a woven mat and turned it over. A hole had been dug under it. Goodman pulled out metal boxes, opened them, and shoved the papers in his rucksack. The man in the bed moaned. My father gripped his hand, uncertain of what to do. He said, "This one's pretty sick."

"Looks like they've got him full of morphine." Goodman picked up a small glass bottle and syringe near the bed. "He's probably got malaria. We'll need to get him up top too."

"I don't think he can walk."

"We'll have to make him walk."

When my father tried to pull the old guy to his feet, he slumped into the bed. "Doesn't look like this one's moving."

Goodman wrapped more tape around the boy's head, making a harness. "You take this kid. I'll catch up."

Anybody could see the old guy was dying. He didn't even twitch or turn his head as Goodman placed the barrel of his gun between his eyes, connecting the fringes of his eyebrows with its tip. Goodman raised his weapon, aimed, and fired into the tunnel wall. The sound was sharp and loud and made a tinny echo. The man didn't move. My father tried to remember the sounds the man had made, but couldn't. Vietnamese was hard to memorize; he could never say even the shortest sentences. Goodman positioned the gun and fired again, into the man's head. Blood spread over the cot and dripped onto the floor.

Goodman took the prisoner by the harness. My father followed them into the tunnel. They moved slowly, even slower than before. Goodman pulled the boy and my father pushed from behind. The boy fell, face forward, into the dirt and lay still, recalcitrant, thoroughly against movement, so Goodman pulled him to his knees, prodding him with the gun. In this manner their strange caravan moved forward. My father said he would have never made it out of the tunnel complex without Goodman to navigate.

Soon, the quality of the air changed, became richer, easier to breathe. They steered the boy through holes and tunnels until they could see the pale light of a sleeping chamber. When they were almost to the surface, my father paused in the darkness, as if held back by a kind of gravity. Years later, in the dim light of Roscoe's, he would tell me that he felt a pain he hadn't felt before, the pain of something inside himself dying. He knew he had lost part of himself underground that day. What remained climbed up to the sunlight, and to the rest of his life.

thirteen

Police Officer No. 1, a white middle-aged man with a mustache, emerged from a squad car with LA CROSSE POLICE DEPT stenciled on the door. "Calm down, girls," he said. "Calm down and try to tell me: Where are your parents? We need to call them. The hospital will need their permission to treat your brother."

Kelly's face was blotched red. She stifled a sob and turned her blue eyes, which always became green when she cried, to the police officer. She appeared to be baffled by the question. "Parents?" she said.

Police Officer No. 2, a woman in her mid-twenties, hovered over her. "Yes, honey. We need to speak with your parents. There's an ambulance on the way, but we have to know which hospital your parents would want your brother to go to."

"Our parents are out of town for the weekend," I said, feeling so scared, so sick to my stomach at the sight of my brother, I thought I might throw up.

"Can you give me a telephone number where they can be reached?" she asked.

"We don't have one."

"Then who the heck," Police Officer No. 1 said, looking from Kelly to me, "is in charge of you kids?"

Laura, our cousin, had been busy keeping Amy and Jose away from the road. As she stepped to our side, she looked more scared than authoritative. She said, "I'm in charge. I'm babysitting."

Police Officer No. 1 asked Laura which hospital we normally used, and when she didn't know he asked us what religion we were. "There are priests at one hospital and ministers at the other," he said, looking down at my brother's twisted, bloody body. "Sometimes it makes a difference. For the family."

THE AMBULANCE ARRIVED AND THE MEDICS HOISTED Matt onto a board—*one, two, three: lift*—as if they were moving a sack of grain that might spill. All the damaged parts of his body were straightened and strapped down. They pressed him flat and dressed him in white gauze. His neck was clamped in a plastic splint. If the blood had not bloomed out the gauze, we would have thought Matt was a child mummy, a boy pharaoh, all still and wrapped and regal. He had not opened his eyes. Occasionally, however, he threw up. The medic opened his throat and cleared it, so he would not choke.

I told the police officers I wanted to ride in the ambulance with my brother. They consulted the medics and informed Kelly and me that we would be riding in the back of Police Officer No. 2's squad car. As the ambulance doors shut, swallowing our brother, Kelly and I huddled in the backseat of the police car, behind the metal grating. There were no door handles, only a beige wall of quilted vinyl. The locks clicked when Police Officer No. 2 shut her door.

I couldn't help but feel nervous being around the police. Most of the time, we were trying to stay clear of them. We believed the police to be another species from us. My uncle Albert, whom my father had been feuding with for fifteen years, was a state trooper, the only Trussoni in history on the right side of the law. When Dad saw a cop car, he'd tap the brake and turn onto the first road he saw, saying, "Another goddamned pig who's got nothing better to do than drive around with his head up his ass."

The ambulance lights ignited and flared. Kelly leaned her head against the window, steaming the glass with her breath, and I sat very still, too numb to cry, too numb to speak. We followed the ambulance through the streets. Cars pulled aside as we drove, and I felt—as people stared at us, girls in the back of a speeding cop car—as if I were a criminal, caught.

When we arrived at the ER, we were met by a swarm of doctors. Our brother was whisked off, while a nurse asked us questions.

"What is your brother's full name?"

"Matthew Jacob Trussoni."

"How old is he?"

"Seven."

"Is he allergic to any medications?"

"I don't know."

"Was he conscious after the accident?"

"Yes, maybe for a minute, but then no."

"How can we reach your parents?"

Kelly and I shrugged. We had no idea.

The ER waiting room was clean and shiny. Police Officer No. 2 bought us a cup of hot chocolate from a vending machine, asked us more questions, and wrote another report, putting everything down on a pink form. When she had finished with the questions, she placed the notebook on her lap and plucked a square of tissue from a box. She wiped Kelly's face, cleaning her cheeks of dirt and snot and dried-up tears. The police officer's face became maternal, as if, with one gesture, she had gone off duty. She said, "I can't leave you two here unattended. I need to call someone. Are your grandparents here in town?"

Police Officer No. 2 used the courtesy phone to search for our parents. After an hour, she told us that Mom's friend Sherry had located our mother. Mom and Andy were going to drive back from the other side of the state, but it would be hours before they arrived. Every ten minutes, I walked to the phone and tried to reach Dad. I looked through the yellow pages and called all the North Side bars, but he was not at any of them. He was not at home, either, and the mobile phone in his truck had been switched off. I left messages with bartenders, with his friends, on his answering machine. We needed him to come and get us, I said, at the hospital.

A nurse walked into the waiting room, toward us. "Are you Matthew's sisters?" she asked. When she saw our worry, she said, "You should know that your brother has woken up and we're moving him from ICU to the pediatrics floor. You can come to his room as soon as he's there. Your brother got pretty banged up, but he's going to be just fine."

As dusk came, the waiting room filled with people in need of repair. A man with a gash in his head paced the room, waiting to be admitted. Blood dripped through his fingers and dropped in fat wet splotches upon the white floor. A middle-aged woman walked in with chest pains. Placing her hand over her heart, she whispered *oh my god oh my god oh my god*. She waited her turn, next to us, her breathing labored. I studied her panic, interested in the way it distorted her voice.

DAD ARRIVED JUST AFTER DARK, REEKING OF BEER. WHEN he found us in Matt's room in the pediatric ward, he put his arms around our shoulders and asked us to tell him what had happened. Standing by Matt's bed, he listened to our account of the accident, closing his eyes as if praying. He looked as close to penitent as I had ever seen him. "Dumb little shit," Dad said, shaking his head, "running around in traffic like that." Which, in Dad code, was a prayer of thanks that his child was going to be okay.

A plaster cast covered the lower part of Matt's body. He would be in traction for two months, a doctor told us. I didn't know what that meant, and neither did Matt. He smiled, weak and dreamy from pain medication, and asked for Jocko, his favorite stuffed animal. Dad promised to go home and get him. The concussion made speech difficult— his words came out jumbled. He tried to speak more clearly, but he threw up into a small silver bedpan. I wiped his mouth with the back of my sleeve.

When Mom finally arrived, she was disheveled and single-minded, her face heavy with exhaustion, as if she had run the two hundred miles back to us. She pushed past the nurse, past us, to Matt, and bowed her head to his chest, hugging him. When she released him, she looked at us, accusatory. Dad averted his eyes and, for a moment, I thought that he would take Mom by the hand, lead her into the hall, and try to comfort her. I found myself hoping that Matt's accident would bring them back together.

But my father didn't try to comfort Mom. He said, "I'm planning to speak to a lawyer tomorrow. The police report says the guy who hit Matt was speeding. I'm going to start action, maybe get Matt some money out of this."

Mom narrowed her eyes. "I don't give a damn about that right now," she said.

"I'll take the girls for the night," he offered. "Give you some time, if you plan to stay here."

"No," she said, resting her hands upon my brother's forehead, as if taking his temperature. "No, you go home. They're staying with me."

After Dad left, Mom walked to the nurses' station to get a cup of water for my brother. Holding the straw to his lips, she said, "There you go, take a big drink, there you go," but no sooner had the water gone down than Matt threw it up again.

I stood by, watching my mother stroke Matt's hair. It had been a long time since I had seen her so tender. The warmth she had been capable of in my childhood had all but disappeared over the years. She was so icy, so resistant to affection, that she often recoiled if I touched her, moving away as if she'd been pinched. At best, she would peck me on the cheek when she wanted to show she loved me, and give a quick hug, tapping her hand on my back. But as Matt lay in his hospital bed, Mom seemed changed. We had been lucky. The worst had been avoided.

"Who was watching you kids?" she asked, turning to Kelly and me. When we told her, she said, "So your father left you with Laura while he was drinking at some beer tent? How could he? Has he no sense of responsibility whatsoever? I cannot trust that man to take care of you for one weekend!"

My mother never confronted Dad about the accident; she said he was volatile and she was too scared to talk to him about simple things, let alone something of such importance. But she promised herself that we would spend less time at my father's house. "That is it," Mom informed us, as she straightened the blankets over Matt's cast. Joint Custody was about to end.

MATT SPENT EIGHT WEEKS IN THE HOSPITAL, IN TRACtion, and then the entire summer in a cast that reached his hips. Hobbling around on tiny crutches, he would chase after Kelly and me, trying to catch us. When the cast came off, Matt's left leg was shriveled and scarred. He spent many months rebuilding his strength, and by the fall of the next year he walked normally again, without a limp.

As Mom had promised, Kelly and Matt spent less time at Dad's house. When Dad went out drinking, Mom would not let them come over. I, on the other hand, lived with Dad during those years. When he went out at night, I had the house to myself. Serenity and Tony Dimantilo (with whom I had begun to spend more and more time) came over, and we would pour drinks from the bottles of tequila, brandy, vodka, and rum Dad kept under the sink. On summer nights of the year I turned fifteen, we smoked cigarettes and sat on the back steps facing the alley, listening to music.

One Saturday that summer, Serenity decided to stay the night. She brought a duffel bag full of clothes and a plastic jug of orange juice mixed with Smirnoff vodka.

"Here," Serenity said, holding forth two tabs of acid, wrapped in the plastic of a cigarette package. The squares were white, with pink mushrooms printed over their surface. She lifted one tab by its edge. I stuck out my tongue and took it.

Earlier that afternoon, after school, we had worked the lock on the gun cabinet and taken two crisp twenties, to pay for the acid. I had only taken gun-cabinet money once before, the previous winter, to buy a new ski jacket. I had taken four twenties that time. When Mom saw my coat and asked where I'd gotten it, I told her Dad had bought it for me. She looked it over, saw that it was expensive, and said, "Columbia? Your dad must have been feeling generous."

The guy who sold us the acid said that Vitamin C would enhance our trip, and even though we suspected that this

237

was just an urban legend, we'd been drinking orange juice all afternoon, in preparation. We took turns swigging as we walked to the bus stop.

Although most people were averse to it, Serenity and I liked the bus. The Plexiglas shelters promised freedom to the carless kids of town. We would buy monthly passes and shuttle from one end of town to the other, riding until after midnight. The bus rumbled up, flipped open its door, and swallowed us into its cold chemical air. Sometimes, when I was alone, I took a seat next to a greasy-haired psycho killer in ripped polyester pants. I would strike up a conversation, flirting with death. The bus would drop me into the space odyssey of the icicle night. I wandered the holocaust streets, dodging wind-whipped newspapers. I would find myself alone in strange parts of town, a girl who liked to be lost.

The bus dropped Serenity and me downtown, at Riverside Park, a narrow strip of trees and benches skirting the Mississippi River. All of Tony Dimantilo's friends hung out there, mostly because the park was zoned for "roller skating and other sporting activities," and the police had to leave skateboarders (and the girls who hung out watching skateboarders) alone. Serenity and I went there after school and on weekends. With nobody keeping track, I went wherever I wanted. Nobody noticed my grades, my drinking, my many Saturdays spent in detention. I did whatever I chose.

Down by the water's edge, there was a pack of punk girls. I'd known these girls for the past few years, ever since Tony introduced me to his crowd. One of the girls said, "Yo, Dani! What's up? Looking for Tony?"

"None of your beeswax," I said, pulling Serenity by the

elbow to a park bench, next to the river. We sat down just as the world began to drain away. Serenity's face jittered before me, all electric skips. The Mississippi River was roiling, boiling lava. If I turned around, the park leaped into a burst of firework colors, hundreds of ribbons curling up.

This was the first time Serenity had taken acid. She looked confused. I had only done it once before myself, but to her I was an expert. She said, "Why is everything so . . . *colorful?*"

"I think the acid is kicking in," I said, holding on to the park bench with both hands, as if it would roll away.

Our bench was within a stone's throw of a six-foot mini-ramp. Skateboarders, Tony Dimantilo among them, strutted and sauntered around the ramp, leaned on their boards, ollied and performed every variety of flip (heel flip, kick flip, nollie kick flip) that they could manage. Jump ramps radiated from the edge of the mini-ramp. Each truck grind, each skid, had a tangible sound, tinny and resonant. The boys posed for the girls magnetized at the periphery.

Tony did not see us, and I was sure, suddenly, that Serenity and I were spies hiding behind the curtains of the real world, girl 007s. I said, "Do you think they can see us?"

"Who?" Serenity asked, her voice spacey.

"Everyone. The skaters. Tony."

Serenity squinted, examining the cartoonish tableau before us. She said, "I don't think they can."

"But we're here, right?"

Serenity crinkled her nose. "If they don't see us?"

"Exactly."

"If they can't see us," Serenity said, becoming suddenly authoritative, "then no, we're not here. We don't exist."

I tapped a cigarette from my pack of Marlboro Reds and lit it. Serenity touched my fingers. I gave her the cigarette. We smoked and I thought of my father, who was probably just getting done with work. Looking over my shoulder, I watched for his truck, wishing I were not here with Serenity but driving to Roscoe's with Dad. Although I was too busy with my friends to go to happy hour, it was a tradition I never got over. Every day at four-thirty, I felt an urge to be subsumed by smoke and darkness and stories of the war. Serenity suddenly said, "If we're not here, I wonder where we are."

"We're nowhere," I said, confident. "Nonexistence means nothing's here. Nada. Zilch."

"But we have to be somewhere." Serenity stuck out her arm. "Touch me. Do I feel like I'm here?"

I squeezed the key-teeth grooves of her wrist bone. "Feels like you're here to me."

We burst out laughing, fully aware of how ridiculous we sounded. Serenity covered my mouth with her hand, stifling my laugh, which only made me laugh harder. A boy with a T-shirt that read SKATE OR DIE rode by, leaving a sparkling elastic Wile E. Coyote trail behind him. I said, "That guy definitely turned his head in this direction. I think he saw us."

"Yikes! Yikes! Oh my God!" Serenity lifted her arm as if it were something she'd found on the street, a piece of wood or a lead pipe.

"What? What's going on?"

"I can see through my arm! Do you see this? My veins are on the outside! Oh my God! That is so freaky!"

I took her arm and stroked it, smoothing the veins into place. "There," I said. "You're fine. It's all skin now."

"Thanks," she said. "How the hell did that happen?"

The sky turned saffron yellow, as if the sun had been pricked and its essence sucked into the air, a color that contained greens and flecks of red, like a ripe peach. Looking across the park, at the road running along the river, I half expected to see my father, driving by in his truck, ready to take me to Roscoe's.

"If you're upset that your veins are changing places with your epidermis," I said, unwilling to give up on existence so easily, "then you must, in some sense, exist."

Serenity lit another cigarette. After a few seconds, she said, "You know, you're right. You're absolutely right. If I didn't exist, I wouldn't care if my veins were squiggling around on the sidewalk. This is solid proof."

Just then, as if in response to Serenity's empirical evidence of our existence, a pressure rose in my bladder. "Emergency," I said, crossing my legs tight.

"Emergency?"

"I have to pee. Really, really bad."

"How can you pee on this bench?"

"Duh. I can't."

Serenity said, "Here is a second instance of proof: If you didn't exist, you wouldn't have to pee. Or you could pee here and it wouldn't make any difference."

"If I didn't exist, I wouldn't have drunk so much fucking orange juice." I squeezed my legs tighter together, and for a moment I couldn't tell if I had a body at all. After a few minutes, however, I realized that I really needed to go.

Serenity pointed to a squat brick building in the park. She said, "There's a bathroom over there."

"But I don't know if I've got to go or not."

"Either you have to go. Or you don't have to go. One or the other."

"What I mean is, this is kind of a Big Question."

Serenity raised an eyebrow. "Is there something I don't know about peeing?"

"If I've really got to go it's settled: We exist. If I don't, and I've just made it up, we don't exist."

Serenity was all appreciation. "Good one," she said.

She shoved me onto the sidewalk, into the wavy, rain-bowing, off-the-bench universe. I walked quick, dodging the metallic stares of the skateboarders, stumbling over a patch of grass and onto a billowing sidewalk. My knees Jell-Oed. The punk girls, each one a different color (one purple, another green, a third a brilliant shade of blue), turned their Martian eyes on me, their gazes indicating my path: *It's right there, the answer to your existential questions!*

I grabbed the bathroom door, all of existence hanging upon the result of my task, and rushed inside, where I yanked up my skirt and squatted over a muddy broken-seated toilet. Two minutes later, I emerged from potty in the park, triumphant. "We're real!" I called, waving my hands at Serenity's small pink head, hovering like a balloon above the park bench. She waved back, ecstatic that we did, in fact, exist.

*

THE HOUSE WAS DARK WHEN WE RETURNED. WE FLIPPED on the kitchen light, went to the fridge, and loaded our arms with cans of Mountain Dew, sour cream and onion dip, and a bag of Doritos. We were on our way to my bedroom when Dad's truck pulled in front of the house. Serenity and I closed the door to my room and wiggled out of our jeans and into oversized T-shirts and sweatpants. We drank the Mountain Dew in bed, talking about boys and school and movies.

Dad and Debbie made themselves drinks and went to Dad's bedroom, where they had slow, screeching, raucous sex. There was only a plastic accordion door separating Dad's room from the rest of the house, so we heard every swish of the waterbed, every change of position, every moan. Dad didn't make much noise, but Debbie's high-pitched screaming went on for what seemed like forever. There was crashing and bumping and grunting. Serenity's eyes widened when the noise began, and she laughed in disbelief as we timed them (ten minutes, fifteen, thirty, forty-five). The effects of our afternoon acid trip hadn't worn off, and the sex sounds seemed magnified. They arced and boomeranged through the house, leaving a hard tinny resonance behind. It was two in the morning. The way it was going, we'd be up all night.

We cracked the window near my bed and lit a cigarette.

"Do they do this often?" Serenity asked.

"Every time they come back from Roscoe's," I said, rolling my eyes and taking a sip of Mountain Dew. "Which is practically every night."

"Wow," she said. "Sex education begins at home."

243

"Ewww," I said, swatting her leg. "That is so yucky."

But Serenity was right. Everything I knew about sex, I'd learned from Dad. I knew about condoms because Kelly found a used one in her bed, after one of Dad's after-bar parties. Suzie carried a vibrator in her purse. Once, she had shown it to me, turned it on, and said, "Get yourself one of these, kiddo, and you won't be disappointed." I knew about vasectomies and miscarriages and the willy-nilly nature of creation from Dad's tirades about illegitimate children. I told Serenity that Dad kept a jar of Vaseline next to the bed, one of the value-size tubs. Serenity said, "You should really tell him to use K-Y Jelly. That's what my parents use."

We sat Indian style on my bed, the cans of soda balanced on our knees, speculating about just how they were able to make so much noise. How, we wondered as we passed the cigarette back and forth, were they able to go at it for so long?

BY FOUR IN THE MORNING, SERENITY HAD FALLEN ASLEEP. The house had been silent for a long time, at least an hour. I closed the window in my bedroom, cleared Mountain Dew cans (filled with ashes and cigarette butts), and tiptoed to the kitchen, where I buried them in the trash. Although both Dad and Deb smoked, I would get in trouble if they knew that I did. *Do as I say and not as I do* was the unspoken rule of our upbringing. As I tiptoed back through the dark house, I heard a movement behind me. I turned and caught my breath. Dad was sitting in the living room, in the dark.

"Dad?" I said, stepping closer. A sliver of light fell across his terry-cloth robe and pooled on his bare feet.

"What are you doing up this late?" he asked, but I could tell by his voice that he was not really interested in knowing.

"I couldn't sleep," I said.

"That's good," he said. There was something both calm and scary in the way he spoke. I recognized the same suspension of emotion in his voice that he got before a bar fight or an argument with Mom. "It's good that you're awake, because I have something I want to ask you. Why don't you come in here a minute and have a seat?"

I sat across from Dad, my hands folded in my lap. There were two stacks of money on the coffee table. I looked over the cash and my heart sank. I knew exactly what he wanted to talk about.

Dad took his cigarettes from the pocket of his robe and lit one. There was a full ashtray on the coffee table, nearby. His voice was tense as he said, "It has come to my attention that someone in this house has been stealing money from the gun cabinet. Do you know anything about that?"

This was it. He knew. He knew that I took money last winter; he knew that I took money today. He knew that Kelly had been taking five bucks every weekend for the last year. A thrilling, dizzying, choking sensation began in my stomach and worked up to my throat. I felt, for a moment, as if I would throw up. I was really in for it this time, I thought. I'd been caught. "No," I said, weak with terror. "No, I don't know anything about money in the gun cabinet."

"I might not have noticed," Dad said, "but Debbie counted forty dollars missing this afternoon. That's a lot of money to just disappear."

"I haven't seen it. I didn't even know Debbie had money here."

Dad looked at me, his eyes intense. "Look at me," he said. "Look me in the eye and tell me that again."

It wasn't in our character to back down from a challenge. I looked into his dark, steady eyes. Dad did not tolerate dishonesty. Lying, in my family, was considered not only a sign of a rotten character but an act of treason. I knew I should face up to my crime, but if there was one thing I'd learned from Dad, it was the art of self-preservation. If I told the truth, I would be forever degraded in his eyes. I would no longer be special. I would be merely average. I lied to my father again. Only this time it was unforgivable.

"It wasn't me," I said. "I didn't take anything."

The tension in Dad's voice broke. It was easy for him to believe; he wanted to trust me. He sighed and touched my knee, taking me back. "I knew you wouldn't do that," he said, pride in his voice, warm and proprietary and heartbreaking. "You're not that kind of girl. Maybe Kelly, but not you."

I stood and went back to my room, leaving him to believe that Kelly was the only thief in his house.

fourteen

Although it was the middle of the night, the heat was overbearing. The wall-unit air conditioner in my hotel room didn't work, so I pushed away the curtains and opened the window near my bed. It was iron-barred; when I slid the frame up, I could see the concrete floor and metal balustrade of the hotel's outdoor hallway. Each room on the fifth floor opened off this communal passage. If it had been earlier in the evening, I would have seen people walking past my window, to their rooms. A group of American tourists (all men) were just down the hall from me. I'd met them at the Internet café on the first floor, checking e-mail. Later, they lounged on plastic chairs in front of the hotel, drinking Bacardi from the bottle. They laughed and joked and called the States from a cell phone, and it was clear they had come to Vietnam for pleasure, to relax in the sun.

As I sat on the bed, I saw that all the rooms were dark except mine. I'd left the bathroom light on, and mosquitoes buzzed around it, banging themselves against the bulb. Although I'd been at the hotel for days, I had not felt comfortable enough to unpack. All my belongings (a Lonely

Planet guidebook, clothes, shampoo) were stored in my backpack, at the foot of my bed. I kept it packed and zipped, as if I expected to have to grab my stuff and run. I didn't trust that I would be safe. I climbed off the bed, opened the door, and checked the corridor for the third time. Then, I turned the lock and propped a chair under the doorknob. The man with the sunglasses had rattled me. Shaken, so paranoid I was afraid to turn my light off and go to sleep, I promised myself I would change hotels the next day.

Jet lag had thrown off my sense of time. In the afternoon, when the sun was searing, I felt sleepy. At night, when it was a few degrees cooler, I was wide awake. I picked up a remote control, turned on the TV, and flipped through the stations, stopping to watch a black-and-white film, a Vietnamese war movie set during the fifties, during the battle of Dien Bien Phu. There were no Western soldiers in the film, only a huge French flag that was eventually captured as the Vietnamese closed in. A group of Vietnamese peasant women sang and held hands as their men—injured but victorious—stumbled home to their village.

For the Vietnamese, the wounds of the war were still fresh. In the War Remnants Museum, I had seen a display of articles and books about Robert McNamara. There were captions in Vietnamese and English claiming that McNamara's book, *In Retrospect*, which outlined mistakes he felt the United States had made during the war, proved that we had been wrong and the war was a miscalculation. As I looked down at the display, I remembered a night my father and I went out for drinks, when I was in college. I had just turned twenty-one, and although my age had never mattered much at Roscoe's, I was proud to be legal. I presented the bartender with my driver's license as I ordered. She rolled her eyes. "Put your plastic away," she said. "Your dad's got you covered."

I carried the drinks through the bar, to the back room. My father had recently read Robert McNamara's book. Dad was never much of a reader; although he was quick-witted and intelligent, he had a hard time staying with a book. That one, however, got his attention. I don't know if he finished it or not, but the parts he had read were memorized. He would rattle off sentences between sips of his drink, quoting McNamara's admissions of his miscalculations in Vietnam. I tried to understand exactly what made Dad so angry, but after a while he went silent and would answer my questions tersely. Finally, he turned to me and said, "Do you know what this book means? Do you know what this guy is saying?"

I didn't know anything about Robert McNamara back then. I had never even heard his name before. At that point in my life—before I studied the war—Vietnam was not a historical event. It was just something that happened to my family.

My father shook his head, disgusted. "McNamara's saying they didn't know what the hell they were doing over there. We were wrong from the goddamned beginning."

When I saw him stare at his weathered hands, so defeated he couldn't look me in the eye, I felt the same sense of sadness I had felt as a girl, when I watched Dad turn away from us, numb and distant. As a girl, I believed the war had taken him from us. It was an amorphous monster that would grab hold and pull us into it, kicking and screaming. Vietnam claimed Dad's past, his future, his health, his dreams. It was never satisfied. It came to live in our house, eat dinner at our table, sleep in our beds. It trailed me home from school; it lapped at my heels as I walked to Roscoe's. It was an elusive yet inescapable thing skulking through my life, a Jack-the-Ripper presence that hid in alleyways and in the sewers, waiting to get me alone. We could ignore it, but it would not go away. If we managed to shake it, it would track us down, hungry for more. Although there was no way for me, as a child, to understand this presence, I knew, when I saw my father's sadness, that he had never really left Vietnam.

After Dad made it clear he could not go, I decided to take the trip on my own. When I bought my plane ticket to Ho Chi Minh City, the travel agent suggested that I go with a tour group. He said women sometimes had a hard time traveling alone in Southeast Asia, and American tourists were sometimes met with suspicion by the Vietnamese and sometimes even followed by the police. He said I might want to travel with a male friend or relative. But I wouldn't consider this. I wanted to go to Vietnam on my own terms.

My visa application took months to process. I was asked to submit an itinerary of my stay in Vietnam, as well as a detailed reason for coming, and although I told the truth— that I wanted to go to the places my father had been during the war—I felt uneasy. Now, as I looked out the window, too scared to fall asleep, I realized that my travel agent had been right. It hadn't been a good idea to come to Vietnam alone.

It was daytime in the United States. I imagined Dad sitting in front of the TV, on his fat brown leather recliner, the remote control in his hand, flipping past the History Channel, past CNN, and pausing at the local sports news. I tried to call him. The phone was an ancient rotary, with a base as heavy as a bowling ball. After a series of whirls and clicks, I connected. Kelly's voice (she had recorded the message on Dad's answering machine) said, *I'm sorry, nobody is here to take your call. Please leave your name and number, and we'll return your call as soon as possible.*

I calculated the time difference and decided that my father was probably at the doctor's office. Since he got sick, he'd had regular exams at the Mayo Clinic, in Rochester, Minnesota. I knew the whole routine. When Dad came home from treatment, he would make himself a stiff drink. If we were on speaking terms, which was becoming less and less often, he would call me. Even after his chemotherapy, when it hurt him to speak, he would call. His voice was rough and whispery; I strained to hear him. "I'm going to fight this," he would say. "You better believe it. I'm going to beat this son-of-a-bitch." And from everything I'd seen of my father, I believed him. I knew the kind of battles this man had fought.

For Dad, being tough always mattered more than being right. He had been proud of his health, defining himself by his quickness and his workhorse strength. He was contemptuous of anyone he considered fat, lazy, slow-witted, or poor. If he saw someone begging in the street, he would say, *Get a job. I had to.* When Dad was in his late forties, when I still lived with him on the North Side, he worked the night shift at the train station. During the day, he worked construction; at night, he loaded boxes onto freight cars. He would come home late in the evening, so tired he could hardly stand, and crack open a beer. "I worked sixteen hours today," he would tell me, pride in his voice. "Working double-time is the only way you'll get ahead in this world. Work like you're two people, my girl, and you just might make it."

Work gave my father his edge and left him with little time to think about all the things he didn't want to remember. It also kept him in shape. One thing I knew for sure: My father would have starved rather than gain a pound of paunch. He didn't like sitting still and didn't allow himself much time to rest. The only criticism I'd ever heard him make of Andy was that he was overweight. Fat was a sign of laziness, something my father could not tolerate.

When I was in high school, I struggled to stay at 115 pounds. When my weight jumped to 125, I told myself I had to be more disciplined. Although I never liked jogging, I joined track and cross-country. Terrified of slipping into a category of derision, I became a vegetarian for a year, checking out health food cookbooks from the library. When I was still heavier than I wanted to be, I took diet pills and made myself vomit, a habit that stopped one day when my mother walked into the bathroom and caught me. I did not hear her come in, and she stood silently behind me, watching me gag. When I registered her presence, I turned. When our eyes met, she shook her head slightly—*no, this cannot be what I'm seeing*—and left. She never mentioned the incident to me, but there was no need; the look of disapproval and sadness I saw were enough. I never made myself throw up again.

In college, when I spent the extra money I had on coffee and books, I weighed 110 pounds. But in the months after college, when I began to take birth control pills, my weight rocketed. I gained 25 pounds in two months, putting the scale at 135, the most I had ever weighed. I began dieting again, and went to a doctor and a nutritionist, both of whom told me that 135 pounds was absolutely normal for a woman my age and height.

"I'm trying so hard," I said, "but the weight just stays."

They did not understand my concern. They suggested that I get some exercise and accept my body as it was. "You really shouldn't worry so much about your looks," the doctor said. "Many young women feel the same as you. They are afraid to leave the body they had as girls and become women."

You don't understand, I wanted to tell them. This curvy woman is not *me*. How could I make them understand that I had been raised to be tough, without a hint of softness? How could I make them understand that my father mistreated women and despised them for what he considered their weaknesses? How could I convey to these doctors why I felt so uncomfortable with my body, when I—who had not yet learned to see past the world I had grown up in—did not understand myself?

Not long after this, Kelly got pregnant. She was twenty-one, unmarried, and still living on the North Side, where she hung out in the same bars Dad had taken us as kids. Kelly bartended at Track II, the bar just down the street from Dad's house, mixing drinks for regulars. She'd had a lot of jobs—she'd worked as an electrician's apprentice and an assistant at a home for juvenile delinquents—but she loved working the taps at the Track (as she called it) best. She was good at it. She knew all the regulars and their families. The Track felt like home, and in many ways it was: She had spent her childhood in the North Side bars, and many of Track II's regulars were the children of Roscoe's regulars. Sometimes Dad went to the Track, and Kelly bought him drinks. She told me once that she secretly liked getting him drunk. "The only time I see him showing any emotion is when he's got a few too many brandies in him."

As we grew to be women, Kelly and I switched places. She was no longer the shy girl who bit her nails until they bled, and I was the one who cried when Dad raised his voice. Time tempered and strengthened her, while it stripped me of my hard protective coating. I had grown more vulnerable, and it was getting harder and harder for me to be near him. But when Kelly spoke to Dad, she was loud and crude and aloof to his feelings in a way I could no longer manage. She put her hands on her hips and told him where to go. They fought regularly, ignored each other for a few weeks, and then took up where they left off. Kelly was the strong one. She had learned how to survive Dad.

But Kelly was also hard on herself. She would start her days with a Bloody Mary and work her way into the harder stuff. She dated bikers and men twenty years older than her, guys who had just gotten out of prison. Giggling, she would tell me about doing cocaine on the back of a Harley David-son. One boyfriend (who was put back in the state penitentiary after beating his ex-wife) wrote her love letters on lined paper that Kelly would read to me, rolling her eyes as she pointed out the spelling errors. Although this guy was bad news, she liked his attention. "Nice men" (who were, by Mom's definition, anyone who had not spent time in jail) had asked Kelly out many times—one even bought her an engagement ring—but she wasn't interested. "I only like these fuckers who are mean to me," she would say, dragging on a cigarette. "Thank you very much, Dad."

Kelly's pregnancy resulted from a one-night stand with a man she met in a bar. Needless to say, Dad was furious. One afternoon, when I went to Dad's house for a visit, I found Kelly in the bathroom crying, something I didn't see very often. Dad had announced that Kelly should be ashamed of herself for getting pregnant, and that she didn't deserve to have the baby shower we were all planning. I listened as Dad sat in the kitchen, complaining about Kelly's lack of morals. Although my father had been married three times, had all but abandoned Phil Trussoni, and had denied Rita Trussoni completely, he was angry at my sister for planning to raise his grandson as a single parent. "I just wasn't raised that way," he said, chewing a toothpick. "My upbringing and my religion are against going around having babies out of wedlock."

Matt and I were ready to ignore our father, but Kelly wouldn't let Dad get away with this. She stormed out of the bathroom, her eyes puffy from tears, and said, "At least I didn't have an abortion!" This had the desired effect: Dad was horrified. He could not believe a child of his would say such a thing in his presence.

"No, you didn't," he said, pointing his toothpick in her direction. "That's one good thing you've done. But still. You were raised a Christian. I don't agree with your free and easy behavior, and I'm going to tell you so." Dad looked around the room, his eyes glossy, slightly unfocused, as if he expected us all to forget the past and join in on this new-and-improved version of our upbringing.

Turning my back on Dad, I took Kelly by the hand. "You are having a baby shower," I said.

"Of course I am," Kelly said, wiping her eyes with her sleeve. "What does he expect me to do, hide away in shame?"

After the birth I went to Wisconsin, to see my nephew. Kelly and I rented a room at the Holiday Inn, where all of us swam and drank margaritas and sat in the hot tub. Kelly carried her new son—whose middle name was Daniel and family name was Trussoni—with her in a hard-shelled baby carrier. Dad and Debbie sat drinking brandy and Coke at a poolside table.

I pulled up a chair and listened as Dad complained about the police, who he still believed were out to get him. He told a story about the good old days when, after being picked up for drunken driving, the cops didn't arrest him and haul him away (as they do now), but said, "You just get back from Vietnam, Trussoni?" When my father answered yes, as a matter of fact he had, the officer would let him go with a warning. In the good old days, Dad said, being a veteran gave a man an advantage. Veterans walked around town like they owned it and, come to think of it, they did: They had fought for their country, had nearly died for it, and they were entitled to have a few drinks now and then, if they wanted to. People understood that, back then.

"Now," Dad said, "there is no respect at all. It's dog eat dog." The month before, my father had been arrested for driving haphazardly through a Hardie's drive-thru at three in morning. He was given a ticket for DUI and spent the night in jail.

"And you'll never guess what they did next," Dad said, taking a sip of his drink. "Those bastards started watching me." My father told us that the police had stationed one of their cruisers behind his house, for surveillance. Dad and Debbie would sneak out the back door at all hours to check if the cops had left.

"When I saw they weren't leaving, I decided to take matters into my own hands," Dad said. "I wrote their boss a letter. I told the chief of police that he better put a stop to this kind of harassment. Put a stop and good!" Dad shook his head and, finishing off his drink, said, "Don't these people have anything better to do than harass a hardworking, tax-paying veteran? What this country needs is another war. That will solve all of this bullshit. That will make people give veterans the respect they deserve."

Kelly brought Dad her son, and this seemed to calm him down. He held the baby with one arm while making drinks with his free hand. True to form, my father had not apologized to Kelly about how he had treated her during her pregnancy. But the baby melted him. After Dad held his grandson for the first time, all moralizing stopped.

I watched Dad play with the baby. I was still wearing my swimming suit, which felt too tight with the extra twenty-five pounds I'd gained. I wrapped a towel around my waist and crossed my arms over my stomach, to hide myself. Dad eyed my discomfort, a vicious smile growing upon his face. "Danielle," he said, wryly, "it looks like you're getting fat."

Although Dad was teasing me, I interpreted his comment as a judgment and a condemnation. This time, Dad's criticism hit me harder than usual. For the first time in my life, I felt mad enough to fight him. I squared myself, looked him in the eye, and told my father to fuck off. I had never said such a thing to anyone, let alone my father, but it worked. Dad was blindsided. He did not know how to respond. He stammered, full of indignation, and I was glad. I loved that I had shocked him. I loved that I had surprised him speechless. And, most of all, I loved being my father's daughter, quick with a sucker punch and cold-blooded. I wouldn't take an insult lying down.

Dad and I did not speak for months after that, which was not all that unusual. We had not seen eye to eye for many years. When we had an argument, we would not speak and then, when enough time had passed, we would both try to pretend that nothing had happened.

Once, when I was in college, I rented a room in a house in Madison. My landlord lived in the house, and although my apartment was detached from his—with a separate entrance and bathroom—we had a common phone line. The man was thirty years older than I, with a wife and a family, and I never thought the situation was at all unusual. One evening, my father called looking for me, and my landlord answered the phone. I was not home (I was a waitress in a sushi restaurant and worked the dinner shift), and he took a message. Dad called three more times before I got home. When I came in at ten o'clock, tired and smelling of soy sauce, my landlord handed me a stack of notes. Clearly worried, he said, "Your father seems to be quite upset. You better call him back right away."

The phone was in my landlord's kitchen. "What's going on?" I asked, when my father picked up the line. From the way he answered the phone, and the sound of ice tinkling in a tumbler, I knew it was a drinking night. Although I had not lived near him for years, I had spent many nights on the phone with Dad. He was always drunk when he called, and I was always ready to listen. "Is something wrong, Pop?"

"You found that one pretty quick, didn't you," Dad said, slurring his words.

My landlord and his family were in the next room, watching TV. I pulled a chair from the kitchen table and sat, drawing my knees to my chest. I said, "I'm not sure I know what you mean."

"You get rid of one," my father continued, "and already you're shacking up with another."

It took me a minute, but I realized that Dad thought I was having a relationship with my landlord. I laughed and said, "Dad, you don't understand."

"Oh, I understand. I wasn't born yesterday. You girls are just like your mother. Kelly doesn't live with them; she can't even get one to stay more than the night. But I know what you're up to."

"But Dad," I said, trying to explain.

"Don't 'but Dad' me. I've been around the block a time or two. Some kind of slut, I see. Probably got that man paying your rent and buying your drinks. Don't think I don't know what goes on. You women. Get some poor sucker to pay your way. Next thing you know, you'll be pregnant. If you aren't already."

"Dad." I was whispering, so my landlord wouldn't hear me. "You are totally wrong about this. I'm renting a room from that guy. He's married. With kids."

As Dad paused to consider this, I heard Debbie in the background, egging him on. *Those girls of yours! I never lived with a man until I was thirty years old!*

"My room has a separate entrance and everything. I just use his phone."

"Well," Dad said, trying to absorb this information. "What's that supposed to mean?"

"It means you don't know what you're talking about."

Rather than admit his mistake, Dad became angry. "Who in hell lives in a man's house like that?" he said. "What do you think his wife thinks about you, hanging around all the time? Nothing you'd do would surprise me anymore." And with that, my father hung up.

Crying, I called Mom. I was too upset to explain myself well, and for a few minutes I simply sobbed. When I finally told her what had happened, she said, "Your father is just drunk. Don't pay any attention to him. He doesn't even know what he's saying."

Maybe Dad didn't know what he was saying that night. Maybe he hadn't ever understood the effects that his tirades had on us. But I always took him seriously, trailing after his words as if I might understand him by the tracks he had left in the sand. When I hung up the phone, I saw my landlord standing at the kitchen door, watching me cry. I had never felt as vulnerable as I did then, crying before this stranger. He was a decent person, and what was I?

"Is everything okay?" he asked. "Is there a problem at home?"

"It's nothing," I said, as I left the kitchen to go back to my room. "This is just how my family works."

Again, months went by before Dad and I spoke. I was not the one to hold a grudge. Although he had made the mistake, Dad expected me to apologize to him. He told my sister that his father never apologized for anything, and this was how he expected it to be with us. But I didn't think that was fair. I wanted to be treated better. Clearly, my father didn't care to discuss our problems. He wanted me as I used to be—young, unformed, and voiceless. At twelve, I could be this girl, no questions asked. I didn't see myself as different from him; I saw with Dad's eyes, I spoke with Dad's voice. I was the dummy to his ventriloquist. But I was no longer that girl. I couldn't be her again.

During the months of silence, I missed Dad. Sometimes I tried to find him in the war, reading books and watching *Platoon* (the film Dad said reminded him most of his time in the jungles) and *Apocalypse Now*. My head would fill with tunnels, with war talk, with tanks and helicopters. At night, I dreamed war dreams, which I'd record in my notebook, always trying to capture my father's voice the way I remembered it from my childhood.

Eventually, I swallowed my pride and went to my father's house to apologize. We sat like zombies in front of the TV, both of us pretending that his drunken phone call had not happened. "Nope, nothing new here," he said, and crunched an empty can of Miller Light in his hand. "Nothing new here, either," I said, echoing him. After a few minutes of silence, my father picked up the remote control and flipped on the TV. The weather channel flashed temperatures from Helsinki, Tokyo, New York, Rome. We sat, staring at the screen. Dad shook his head and said, "This is goddamned terrible weather we're having this year." I looked over my shoulder, out the window, feigning interest. "Terrible weather, Pop," I said as I stood, went to his chair, and kissed the top of his head. When I hugged my father goodbye, I looked in his dark blue-ringed eyes, feeling miserable. We had nothing left to say to each other.

THE TROPICAL NIGHT WAS HOT AND HUMID, MY SKIN sticky with sweat. My jeans clung stiff to my legs, so I eased them off and threw them on the nightstand, near the bed. Wearing a long T-shirt and underpants, I stretched my bare legs in the moonlight as a breeze fell through the curtains. I was almost asleep when I heard a scraping in the hallway outside my room—*scratch, scratch, scratch*—as if someone were sweeping the steps. Lying very still, I listened. The noise approached. I wanted to believe it would pass by, but somehow I knew that it was coming for me.

Before I had a chance to get out of bed, a sharp pain stabbed through my shin. I rolled off the bed just in time to see a metal hook—attached to a broom handle as long as an arm—jutting from the window ledge. From the floor, I watched it rise and descend, swooping near the backpack I'd left at the foot of the bed. When I reached for the light switch, the intruder saw me and dropped the metal hook onto the cement. Rushing to the door, I flung it open. Moonlight caught upon the jeans of the man with aviator sunglasses as he crawled over a balcony and climbed down to the street. Shaking, I leaned against the rough stucco wall, trying to catch my breath.

My hands trembled as I picked the hook up off the floor, propped it against the wall near the bed, and locked the door.

There was a cut near the bone of my left shin, where the hook had caught me. It was only a scratch, but a streak of silt had lodged under a flap of skin. I went to the bathroom and cleaned the wound with a white bar of soap that soon turned pink, removing the dirt with my fingernails and splashing it with water. Rivulets of blood twisted around the drain. I pressed a towel against the cut, and after a few minutes the bleeding stopped.

If I had been scared before, I was now terrified. I picked up the phone and dialed the front desk. The receptionist, who was asleep, answered. I asked him to come up to my room. When he protested—it was four-thirty in the morning, after all—I told him it was an emergency; I needed him immediately. He sighed and hung up.

When he stood in my room, I held the hook before him. "This," I said, pointing from the hook to my wounded shin. "Did this."

The receptionist looked me up and down, clearly surprised; I'd been so upset I'd forgotten to put on my jeans. Feeling beyond modesty, I grabbed the jeans from the night table and slipped into them then and there, as he examined the hook. It had been tied with rope to the broom handle, a layer of masking tape winding down the base for strength. The receptionist turned it before him, examining the craftsmanship. He was not surprised that someone would attempt this kind of theft, he said, but he found it incredible that the burglar would use such a poorly made tool. He said, "This was not made by a Vietnamese. Some foreigner made this."

I leaned against the wall, hugging my arms over my chest. Although it was at least 90 degrees Fahrenheit, I felt cold. My hands shook, and I had to swallow every few seconds, to keep my throat from closing. It was as if some wayward malaria-infested mosquito had gotten into my room, landed on a throbbing vein, and begun to feast.

The receptionist put the hook outside, leaning it against the balustrade, and turned to me. "You," he said, looking me over, "are not well. If you want, I will call a doctor."

I didn't want a doctor. I wanted to shut the windows, lock the door, take off my clothes, and crawl into the bathtub. I wanted to turn the tap marked HOT all the way to the right, so that the water sprayed over my feet and knees and filled the basin of the tub, inch by inch.

"I'm okay," I said, as I led the receptionist to the door. "But I want to call the police. I saw who tried to break in. There is a man who has been following me all week." When I described the man (his jeans and T-shirt and sunglasses), the receptionist seemed to recognize him.

"Is the man very tall?" the receptionist asked. "Does he have a nose like a foreigner?"

When I told him yes, the man was taller than most Vietnamese men, the receptionist said, "Yes, I know him.

That man lives on this street. His mother owns a dress shop near the market. His father was here in one of the wars—he was French or American, I don't know. I see him every day. He has no father and no identity card. He cannot work legally."

"Do you know his name," I asked, "or why he would be following me?"

The receptionist shook his head and walked toward the door.

"If you know where he lives, will you call the police and have them talk to him?" I said. "I don't want him following me anymore."

"The police will come tomorrow," the receptionist promised. "But now it is too late."

Although I knew the man had crawled down the balcony, I touched the receptionist's arm on his way out, stopping him. "Please check the hallways," I said, "in case he's out there."

When the receptionist had gone, I turned off the light and sat in the dark, waiting for the intruder to return. I was still shaking. Trying to relax, I closed my eyes. An image of a door filled my mind. I opened the door, and another door sprang up behind it. I opened this second door, and another smaller door appeared. This smaller door gave way, and another even smaller door opened, and then another and another and another, until one final tiny door unlatched. I crawled through this door and into a room. My knees sank into wet dirt; my vision slipped through the oily-black darkness. My fingers spidered and groped for a light switch. I sat in the dark, empty, waiting. I was not finished with

Vietnam. Or perhaps it was not finished with me. I threw my backpack over my shoulder, unbolted the door, and left.

THE SUN WAS RISING AS I WALKED DOWN THE STAIRS AND into the hotel lobby. The receptionist, asleep on a fold-out cot, didn't hear me, so I let myself out the front door. Outside, the air was cool. I hoisted my backpack over my shoulder, feeling lucky to have escaped the hotel.

As I walked toward the rising sun, I tried to place myself. Where was I? Dong Khoi? Cholon? I wondered if my father had, years before I was born, walked this same road. He had not spent much time in Saigon during his tour, only a few nights, when he was given leave. On the day he and Goodman took their prisoner from the tunnel, they were given clearance to escort him to the ARVN base just south of Saigon. Scotty, who had come along, knew Saigon well. He had been stationed there on his first tour in '66. "I'll show you boys some real action," he said, as they loaded onto the back of a munitions truck. Scotty drank from a flask and gave it to Goodman. Goodman took a swig, raised his .22 in the air, and shot a bird. As the truck drove toward Saigon, my father wouldn't look back, toward the jungle. He didn't want to remember that he would have to return.

Highway One was muddy from the monsoon rains. The munitions truck slid and jerked as they hit washed-out tank tracks. Scotty pulled out his .45, showed it to the prisoner, and then bound a cloth over his eyes. Only the rapid-fire movement of an eyebrow twitching above the blindfold attested to the boy's terror. Scotty spun him around. "Find the piñata, compadre," he said, as the prisoner stumbled and fell onto a pile of replacement APC sheet metal. Scotty shot once, twice, into the air. The prisoner lay still on his back, his eyebrow going like mad.

The truck stopped before the ARVN base.

Scotty pulled the prisoner by his arm and told the others to wait by the river. Half an hour later, he met them at the ferry, a rickety sampan made of deep mahogany-colored wood, its sides darkened by water. A woven reed canopy arched over its middle, creating a band of purple shade over the slightly scooped interior. It sat lightly on the water, prow and stern arching like a wide canoe.

The Saigon River was dirt brown. A group of peasants stumbled as they climbed in: a woman carrying a half-naked baby, two teenage girls with long black braids, and an old woman. As they stepped over the sampan's side, an ARVN soldier gripped the plastic handle of the motor rope, lifted one foot onto the sampan's ledge, and pulled back until the engine thrummed. The boat moved out, toward the not-so-distant shore.

They walked through the Saigon streets as the sun went down. Men in civvies sat at open-air cafés, drinking glasses of rum and coconut milk with pretty Vietnamese women. A drunk GI, a Vietnamese woman on each arm, stumbled ahead, lost his balance, and fell, face-first, to the sidewalk. He turned on his back and laughed as the women tried to pull him up.

Scotty walked into the crowd, stopping at an open-air market. "Hey, Trussoni," he said, pointing to a small Colt .22 pistol on a vendor's table. "You need this. Your .45 is too big for tunnels."

Dad picked up the gun and turned it in his hand. "How much?" he asked the old lady selling it.

"Good deal for you," the old lady said, which meant she was ripping him off. She wrote a price on a piece of paper and gave it to him. Dad gave her the money and slid the gun in his belt.

They found some seats at a bar near the river, where they ordered drinks and took a load off. Dad once said he always felt scared up-country. Every minute was spent looking over his shoulder to check who was behind him or who might be. Saigon was a relief. He felt almost human as the waitress came to their table.

She strode up, smiling. "You boys want a drink?"

"Sure, give me what you got, sweet stuff," Scotty shouted over the music. "And I'd like to buy you a drink as well."

"I'll be back," she said, turning away.

"Now this," Scotty said, opening his arms to the tables of soldiers, "is a party."

"Better than dying in the fucking boonies," Goodman said.

Goodman told Dad about living in Tennessee, about his parents' business and the way he planned to run it when he got back from the war. During the months in the jungle, they had become friends. Dad knew all about Goodman's family—his father was a federal judge—and his girlfriend—who had broken up with him in a letter—and Goodman knew all about Dad's ex-wife and kid back home. They made each other a promise: If one of them got aced, the other would take his belongings back to the world. If they both made it back, they promised to keep in touch.

The waitress returned with a tray of drinks. "I bring you whiskey Coke. Two dollar. And for me, whiskey Coke. Two dollar." The waitress set a plastic cup in front of Scotty. "That five dollar, please."

Scotty gave her some money, and she sat on his lap.

"Hey, Scotty," Dad said. "How the hell are we getting back to the boonies?" They had lost their ride, and if they didn't find another one soon they would get their asses chewed by Pops, that was for sure. Not that they had much to lose. Nothing was worse than the boonies.

"We'll find our way," Scotty said, but he was too busy with the waitress to pay much attention.

"Trussoni, let's get out of here," Goodman said. Dad slammed his drink and followed Goodman out to the terrace.

They sat at a table outside, drinking from plastic cups and waiting for Scotty. An enormous Sky Crane Chinook came down fast nearby, shattering the music with its rhythm. When some ARVN guys joined them, Goodman bought them a round. They spoke English well enough to say they lived in the city, close by. When the crowd began to thin out, they invited them back to their place for a drink, so Goodman and my father followed them home, where they sat at a rickety wooden table drinking rice wine and playing cards.

NEXT MORNING, THEY WALKED BACK TOWARD THE RIVER, naming the streets as they walked: Tran Hung Dao, De Tham, Le Loi. They were exhausted, as if they'd been out on LP or ambush all night. It was a long way back to the jungle. My father gripped his gun and looked behind him—what if they were being watched? A guy couldn't ask for a more perfect target. A mandatory curfew was in effect, but where were the Saigon police? Where were the ARVN? Although the streets seemed deserted, paranoia transformed every tree and fence post into the enemy. Goodman walked ahead, oblivious to danger. After an hour they stopped to share a cigarette. It seemed, as they stood in the street, unsure of which way to go, that they had hundreds of miles before them.

Soon, they found their way to District One, where they hired a taxi to take them to the ferry. As they drove through District Five, past the Seventeenth Field Hospital, a triad of camouflaged jeeps sped by. Floodlights lit up the Field Dispensary Building, shining over the cement courtyard. The taxi took them out to the bleak torn-up shanties at the edge of Saigon.

The driver pulled off onto a dirt road and parked the taxi near some trees.

"*Beaucoup VC. Beaucoup,*"the taxi driver whispered. He motioned with his hands: They are here. They are everywhere. When my father stepped out of the taxi, he heard voices in the distance. In the weak light, he saw shacks full of people. Chickens moved through the shadows. The heavy smell of food and burning wood filled the air. The taxi drove off, leaving them in a nest of Vietcong.

A group of men sat in front of a shack, guns in their hands. My father stepped forward, to get a better look, and kicked a rusted can lying in the road. All noise and movement in the yard stopped. One of the men faced them, his hand on his weapon.

Goodman grabbed his arm. "Stand up straight and walk," he said. "Put your hands at your side and don't move them."

My father walked toward the river, scanning the narrow road, as if intent on memorizing every stone and root. He did not look up, sure that eye contact, even the slightest hint of confrontation, would be deadly. When someone shot off a round, Goodman said not to worry. "They would have shot us earlier if they wanted us."

The dock was beyond a bend in the road. They walked for fifty yards, through scraggly trees that cast shadows in their path. The air was wet and new, morning air not yet singed by heat. At the river, the rising sun reflected upon the water's surface. They walked to the dock and sat. The ferry was not there. They were stuck.

Goodman took out a cigarette and smoked, defeated. Mosquitoes hovered, and soon a bead of blood rose on Goodman's cheek. The men on the porch talked; my father wished to God he understood Vietnamese. "What do you suppose we do?" he asked.

"First things first. We've got to get across the river," Goodman said. He scanned the banks, looking for a narrow place, somewhere to cross. My father saw, on the opposite bank, the ARVN base, full of activity. Maybe it was the river, with its dead, mossy smell, but he suddenly longed for home in a way he hadn't since he had first stepped off the plane, at Tan Son Nhut. The smell was a Mississippi River smell, an August smell with a summer's worth of fish in it.

He wanted to be back home, free to do as he pleased. This is war, he realized. Terror. Paranoia. Being stranded on the wrong side of the river.

"We'll have to swim it," Goodman said, taking off his shirt. The situation wasn't all that serious, he said. If they could just get to the other side, they'd make it to the ARVN base and get a lift to the boonies on an early supply truck. The river wasn't wide; it was just a channel. Goodman emptied his pockets, wrapped the contents in his shirt, and stuffed them in his pack. Mud slurped around his boots as he waded in.

My father didn't move. He watched Goodman walk into the river.

"What's wrong, Trussoni?" Goodman asked. "You think they're going to shoot us?"

The men in the shacks laughed and talked. It was obvious that they had chosen to ignore them.

My father looked at Goodman and smiled, weakly. He said, "I've got something to tell you, Tommy. Something that you probably don't know about me." He took one last drag on his cigarette, flicked it into the black water, and said, "I can't swim."

DAD AND GOODMAN MADE IT BACK TO THE PLATOON early the next morning. The Saigon River hadn't been deep at all; they'd held their weapons over their heads and walked the whole way. A supply truck took them to the base and a chopper dropped them with their platoon before lunch. Pops took one look at them and shook his head. He kicked his boots aside and stretched his legs before him, sprinkling antifungal powder between his toes.

"No more of the bullshit you pulled last night, boys," Pops said. "Anymore of that, and I'll have your ass."

"Yes, sir," Goodman said. They acted sorry, but they weren't. Everybody knew Pops couldn't do much to hurt them. They were already in the worst of the war. Anywhere Pops could send them would be better than the boonies.

"And I know you didn't get lost in Saigon. I've been in Saigon enough to know."

"Yes, sir," Goodman said.

"Probably got yourself drunk and laid."

"Yes, sir," my father said.

"Probably got some women and didn't know what to do with them." Pops laughed and wiggled his toes.

"You're speaking from experience?" Goodman asked, grinning.

"I got a wife and two little girls," he said. "You think I'm speaking from experience?"

"Must be rough," Goodman said. "I mean, missing them."

Pops dropped the foot powder. He looked at his greenish yellow feet. "It's rough all around, Goodman."

They set up camp in the remains of a rubber plantation. Shots sounded on and off all night. The next morning, the rubber trees seemed to dissolve in the sunrise. They heard a commotion at the perimeter: The two guards had been found dead. Both had been shot in the head and their bodies pulled into the concertina wire. Everybody ate breakfast and smoked and pretended not to notice as the medics zipped the dead guards into body bags. The morning mail chopper lifted them away. The mechanized infantrymen respooled the concertina wire, dumped sand from bags, and loaded their APCs.

Their platoon left the combed orderly rows of rubber trees and entered tangled jungle. They tramped over hills and onto flat fields charred black by bombs. The whole area was suspect, Pops said, and not only because of the two dead guards that morning. The Ho Bo woods covered miles and miles of tunnel complexes. He said, "If the Ho Chi Minh trail funnels supplies from north to south, we're the bucket catching the runoff." The tunnels siphoned and distributed the supplies through the Iron Triangle all the way to Saigon.

They trekked north, toward An Nhon Tay. Goodman was ahead, on point; my father patrolled the rear. The jungle was quiet. The air seemed weighted with imminent rain. Scotty shot a spider monkey off a tree branch. The report echoed.

Scotty said, "The Michelin plantation is still operating up near Tay Ninh. Must be some money in it."

"Bombs or no bombs," Pops said. "It's business as usual."

A new GI, Rudy's replacement, asked my father if he'd been down the tunnels. "I heard you and Goodman are tunnel rats," the kid said. "What's down there?"

"I'm not a guidebook to 'Nam, Cherry," my father said.

GOODMAN AND MY FATHER TOOK TURNS. THEY WOULD find an entrance—usually one or two every couple of miles—and then Goodman would blow it or my father would blow it. The smoke would clear. They'd move on. They went on like this, tossing frags and CS gas grenades. They walked for miles, all morning. By early afternoon, they had left their platoon far behind. For a while, they thought the tunnels were cold: no sweet potatoes or cassava growing, no abnormal smells, not even any rigged bamboo.

"This whole stretch is cold as Alaska," my father said.

Goodman walked ahead, slow and relaxed, as if he liked blowing the tunnels. He said, half teasing, "Sure, Trussoni. Cold as Alaska."

On mornings like that, when they walked through the sunlit jungle, my father realized how beautiful Vietnam was, lush and green where they hadn't bombed it. The heat was overwhelming, but the shade created pockets of cool air.

Then they found signs of activity—broken foliage and fresh human shit—and they knew there were VC close by. Goodman lifted a clump of leaves with his weapon, revealing an entrance. The earth was sliced clean, but the hole cap didn't fit; a black ridge, fine as a scar, outlined the tunnel entrance. It was Goodman's turn to blow it, so my father backed up, crouching behind a hill. Goodman lowered himself down to the entrance, a grenade in one hand, his weapon in the other. He pried the entrance up and stuck his M-16 down the tunnel. "Fire in the hole," he said. The grenade rolled off his fingers. He jogged back behind the hill and squatted. The explosion was like a car backfiring, loud and solid, muffled by the earth. The ground rose slightly, throwing chunks of vegetation and clouds of dust into the air.

"Another entrance," Goodman said, tossing a burned-down cigarette.

It was my father's turn, so he moved toward the tunnel entrance, but Goodman stopped him. "I'm right here," he said, walking to the hole. "I got it."

Dad turned, to take cover. Goodman bent over the hole and lifted a clump of brush away from the entrance with his hand, too fast, too careless. Suddenly, my father heard an AK-47. He hit the ground just in time to see Goodman jolt back, as if he'd been punched, and fall heavily to the ground not two feet from his smoldering cigarette. The VC slipped back down in the hole.

Goodman had been hit square between the eyes, and the back of his head had been blown off. Blood mixed into the red dirt, making a black stain round as a halo beneath his head. My father looked down at Goodman, stunned, unable to fully understand what had happened. Tommy had just been there, in front of him. He threw a grenade down the tunnel entrance, hoping to get the VC before he crawled off, into the complex. It exploded, sending up gray smoke.

Dad picked up Goodman's burned-down cigarette and took a deep drag. He told me this story many times over the years, and every time he said the same thing: "That bullet had my name written all over it. It was my turn, and Goodman took it." Sometimes I would say, "Somebody must have wanted you around for a while," and my father would look dismayed. "Something I always felt bad about," he said, "was what I did after Tommy died. He had a canteen full of water, and I took it. He was dead, lying right there at my feet, and I unscrewed the cap and drank every drop of his water. We never had enough water—or ammunition, for that matter—and seeing Goodman like that made me thirsty."

My father hoisted Goodman up over his shoulder and carried him back to the others. Goodman was bigger than Dad, and heavier, and yet he didn't feel his weight. Blood ran over his neck and slithered warm upon his chest.

My father heard the platoon in the distance, talking and laughing.

"You see anything interesting, Trussoni?" Scotty shouted, but when he saw Goodman's body, his expression changed.

Pops walked to my father. He didn't say anything, just looked at the body with a sad, defeated stare, as if he himself had squandered something precious. He said, "Shit, Trussoni, how'd this happen?" but he knew how. Tunneling was dangerous. It was bound to happen to one of them. Pops called in the dust-off and limped into the bush.

Scotty knelt down at Goodman's side. He ran his fingers over the side of the face still intact, as if to remember the chiseled bones of the cheek and the big goofy ears. After a minute, he ruffled his blood-soaked hair and pushed his body over, unzipped his butt pack, and began to go through it. He took out two packs of Kools and a roll of purple MPC, at least a couple hundred dollars' worth. "Sorry, buddy," Scotty said, as he stuffed the money and cigarettes in his pack, "but you don't need this no more." The other guys smoked and tried not to look as Scotty went through Goodman's ruck. He took out a small metal camera and gave it to my father. "I believe this," Scotty said, "belongs to you."

My father leaned his head against a tree, waiting for the

dust-off. As the Huey landed and they loaded Goodman on, my father was numb. Even then he was still unsure of what had happened.

"You want to show me where?" Pops asked, and my father led them back, through the jungle, to the tunnel entrance. Occasionally he saw a splotch of blood in the dirt and knew he was not lost. Soon the platoon stood over the tunnel, staring down at the circle of black blood near the entrance.

Dad threw his rucksack to the ground, pulled out his new .22, and felt the edge of the tunnel. Using a stick, he tapped inside, feeling for traps. Then, he lowered himself down. The darkness swept over him and he felt a kind of recognition, a return, as if the tunnels had worked themselves into his senses, into his body. Now, after months of going down, he could taste the dark. He was going to do this one fast. Go in and get out, quick as possible.

The tunnel mouth narrowed and forced him to his knees. His gun thumped against the clay. He tried to remember what Goodman had told him. First thing: Go in slow. He felt the walls and tunnel ceiling. The clay was chalky under his fingers, smooth and without roots. He listened for noise and then crawled ahead, out of the communication tunnel and into a pocket of air where the tunnel forked. There was a wide central tunnel ahead, and a smaller narrow one that veered off to the left. He sat on his heels and flipped on the flashlight. A fork in the tunnel presented him with a choice, and for a moment this seemed like a bad thing. He considered turning back. He could tell Pops anything. He could say, "Nothing down there but a dead end."

He crawled into the left passage. The right tunnel's possibilities, rejected, melted behind. He had made such decisions—stepping one way rather than another, taking a different path—a hundred times in the past month. Goodman had made a seemingly inconsequential decision and died. Every action led to something. He could do nothing but choose.

He lowered himself onto his forearms and pulled himself through.

Within minutes he crawled out of the communication tunnel and into a long low-ceilinged room. Tiny shafts of light broke through pinprick holes in the ceiling. Squat tables and rows of potbellied crockery sat against a wall. The room smelled of smoke. Goodman had told him about the VC kitchens. They had started making them while fighting the French. Boxes of C-rations and tinned meat, all stolen from a U.S. base, were stacked neatly on a metal shelving unit. He moved his flashlight over boxes and crates and then lifted the cover off a ceramic pot. The terrible smell swelled and he dropped the lid. It banged like a gun. He lifted the other lids: rice, tea, cassava. He trained the light over a hollow space in the wall and then stuck his head in. The VC had dug the ovens in and up so that the chimneys sent the smoke into channels the size of reeds, where it funneled out gradually, leaking slowly into the elephant grass up top. They had fires below the earth, but nobody could see them.

There were two communication tunnels leading off the room. He looked from one to the other, knowing they had been built as an escape route. He crawled into one. As he moved inward, the tunnel narrowed, and he thought for a moment that he had, in fact, hit a dead end. But then, ahead, there appeared a coloration in the darkness. As he got closer, a terrible smell filled the air, as if a whole village's rice supply had gone to rot. He followed the stench into a low airless room. Light hazed through a thatched entrance above.

He lay very still, close to the ground, his heart pounding. As he steadied the flashlight and surveyed the room, he saw an ankle and then a shin. The body before him couldn't have been dead long—the skin was still intact—but the smell was awful. He could hardly breathe. He slanted the beam over the body and saw, beyond, more bodies spread across the floor, a tangle of corpses. He moved the light over a head, cocked sideways. This one had been dead longer than the first. The skin had shrunk and shriveled, and was completely gone in places.

There didn't seem to be movement above, so he pushed through the thatch and poked his head aboveground. He found himself peering into a hut. He blinked, trying to regain sight. Palm leaf baskets were clustered next to a primitive plow, and a different variety of stench filled the hut; the baskets were filled with fertilizer.

He had heard that the Vietcong hid the bodies of their dead to frustrate American body counts. When an American body disappeared, the VC were immediately suspected. Weeklong search missions, with platoons scouring villages and dredging rice paddies, often ended without a body. He wondered if any American bodies had been hidden below, or if they'd made a separate chamber. Maybe the villagers pulled the Vietnamese bodies up, eventually, and gave them a proper burial. Or maybe they simply filled the chamber to the top with bodies and sealed it.

He lowered himself back into the tunnel, ready to backtrack. When he got to the tunnel entrance, he would take the platoon to the bodies from up top, through the village. He sat in the darkness, feeling disorientated and dizzy, waiting until he could get his balance. He turned his flashlight to the tunnel and crawled out.

When he had made it back to his platoon, he told them to follow him around, to the village. He looked down on the dark halo of Goodman's blood as he walked away. It had already faded into the dirt.

fifteen

Forgive me, Father, for this time I have really, really sinned.

Can I help you, miss? The saleslady asked me. *Yes,* I said, leading her to the back of the store. *Where are the Mozart sonatas for piano and violin? Right this way, dear. We have a nice selection of Mozart. Do you enjoy classical music? No,* I said, *I'm buying my mom a birthday present. Aren't you a nice girl!* she said. *Yes,* I replied. *Yes, I'm a nice girl.* I paid ten bucks for the Mozart CD, and then slid five others up the sleeve of my trench coat. Serenity—who was shopping Jazz—got seven disks as well. As we walked through the mall, a man took us each by the arm. He said, *Will you girls please step back into the store? We would like to speak to you for a moment about some merchandise that you have forgotten to pay for.*

THE COURT CLERK TOOK MY NAME, LOOKED AT MY CITA-tion (offense: *Shoplifting.* FINE: *$125*), and gave me directions to the courtroom. I walked past her desk and into a large chamber filled with mahogany benches. Lawbreakers were everywhere: in the doorway, at the drinking fountain.

It was a great town hall meeting of transgressors, all the bad citizens of La Crosse, Wisconsin, waiting for judgment.

I sat on a bench, next to a middle-aged woman with a blond shag haircut. She leaned over and told me that she was being charged with a second-offense DUI. "I got kids and everything," she assured me. "It's not like I'm a real criminal."

I told her not to worry; my father had been through it many times himself. "My dad is raising me," I said, "and look how good I'm turning out." The blond woman looked me up and down, from my combat boots and black fishnet stockings to the leather dog collar around my neck, uncomfortable. She was not sure if I was joking. Neither was I.

I had managed to keep my parents in the dark about my troubles. If I had detention, I simply stayed after school and took the bus home. Upon receiving my report card (which presented a staggering C average), I tore it up and threw it away. When the notice of my shoplifting trial arrived in the mail, I intercepted it. Nobody noticed that I had lost interest in school and did little more than sleep and watch MTV on weekends. Dad was gone most of the time, and my mother was busy with her work in the finance department of a heating and air-conditioning company.

When my name was called, I walked to the front of the courtroom. The honorable Judge Jones scanned my file, pushing her glasses into her gray frizzy hair. "Miss Trussoni, I presume?" When I admitted to my identity, Judge Jones said, "First-offense shoplifting. Misdemeanor. How do you plead?"

"Guilty," I mumbled.

"Well, then," Judge Jones said, shuffling through my file. "It appears that this is not the first time you've been in trouble. You have had two citations for skateboarding on public walkways, one underage drinking ticket, and one curfew ticket. That is quite a record for a fifteen-year-old girl."

I agreed with her. It had been a remarkable year.

Judge Jones bit her lip and returned her pop-bottle-thick glasses to her nose. Her eyes magnified to watery brown amoebae. "I have two options in dealing with juveniles like you, Miss Trussoni. The first option: I can accept your plea of guilty and send you to the cashier, where you will pay your fine and be on your merry way. I usually opt for this choice. Most juveniles in your position would be happy to get off with a fine. But as I look over this file and observe you here before me, I don't think I will be able exercise that option. Your repeated delinquencies, and the seriousness of your shoplifting offense, call for option two, which is, if you read the back of your citation, Coda Four, Section B: Community Service. Where do you go to school?"

"Central," I said, wary of the sudden interest in my education.

"Beginning next week, you are to report to your guidance counselor at Central and receive your schedule. You will perform one hundred hours of community service. This means that for the next twelve and a half weeks your Saturdays belong to the community. Do you understand?"

I sighed, resigned. I understood perfectly.

Judge Jones continued. "Your program officer will keep me informed of your progress. Any questions?"

I rolled my eyes and shrugged, as if to say, *Nothing you can do is going to change me. I come from a long line of the irredeemable*.

Judge Jones was not pleased. She said, "And one more thing, Miss Trussoni. If I get a negative report about your behavior, you will be spending more time in our program. You had better get yourself a new attitude. And quick."

TO CELEBRATE MY NEW STATUS AS JUVENILE DELINQUENT, Tony met me outside city hall, where we drank from a bottle of vodka, washing it down with cranberry juice. We walked across the street, ate at Burger King, and then made our way to Riverside Park. When it got late, we took the bus back to Dad's house. Although I knew we'd have the place to ourselves—Dad and Debbie were at Roscoe's for the evening—I was a little worried. The month before, my father had come home after work while Tony and I were there. We weren't doing anything wrong—we were sitting on the couch watching TV and eating Wonder bread and lunch-meat sandwiches—but Dad stomped in the back door, set his HungryMan cooler on the counter, and promptly kicked Tony out. "What the hell do you think I am," he had shouted, as he pointed Tony to the door, "the neighborhood restaurant? Scram!"

At home, we went right to my bedroom, stripped, and closed the door. Tony smelled of vodka and something vaguely chemical, wheel wax or axle grease. When the room felt too hot, I opened a window, letting a cool breeze fall over us. Passing cars and the occasional police siren expanded beyond the window. Occasionally, I looked over at my alarm clock, aware that Tony should have left long ago, but I didn't have the heart to tell him to go. His Levi's were in a heap on the floor; his black leather motorcycle jacket kept its shape on a chair; his skateboard stayed against the wall, under the window. He was about to retrieve his clothing when the front door slammed.

I sat up and grabbed my T-shirt.

"Is that your dad?" Tony asked, terrified. My father had the ability to make the most composed of my boyfriends lose their cool.

"I can't believe he's back so early!" I said, rummaging through the dark, looking for my skirt. "Get in the closet!"

Tony slipped one leg, then the other, into his jeans.

"No, wait," I whispered, frantic. "Go out the window."

"Where the hell is my T-shirt?" Tony said, kicking a stuffed animal out of his way. I rifled the bed for my skirt, but couldn't find it. The floor was black, the corners were black, my skirt was black—one black thing had fallen into the next and disappeared. I heard footsteps and voices outside my bedroom door. For some reason, I thought of my father, opening his gun cabinet and running his hand over the polished barrel of a hunting rifle. Tony gave up on his T-shirt and slid into his leather jacket. His boxer shorts had disappeared. His socks had disappeared. He found his T-shirt and stuffed it into the back pocket of his jeans. He said, "Have you seen my shoes?"

I heard Debbie's voice, coming closer.

Tony was astride the window, about to make his escape, when I grabbed his arm. I couldn't help it. I said, "Kiss me goodbye."

I stood on tiptoe, holding Tony's head between my palms as I kissed him. My hair brushed the arch of my back. I was Rapunzel, or some other make-believe girl. Our kiss was soft and defiant, a slow tender kiss without a hint of panic, as if I believed the world would stop for it. And, for a moment, it did. It was the most perfect kiss I would ever give, the only one that contained every part of my heart in it. I did not care what existed beyond my bedroom door.

Then, my father came in.

"Danielle?" he said. Light cut across the room. As I turned to him, I could tell, by the way something in his face shifted, that he was taken off guard. He flicked the light switch. I squinted. A condom lay on the floor between us, for everyone to see.

"What the hell is going on here?" Dad said, angrier than I'd heard him in a long time.

"Where'd you say the tequila was, hon?" Debbie said, as she stepped into the room. ROSCOE'S VOGUE BAR was embroidered on the breast of her red satin jacket. She looked from the condom to Tony—who had one leg out the window—to skirtless red-faced me, and then back to the condom. She smiled—or, rather, she sneered—and I was suddenly ashamed. Debbie tried not to laugh, while Dad looked like he'd been socked in the stomach. And there was the condom, screeching out to everyone.

I threw Tony's boxers (which were lying near my feet) over it.

Debbie's makeup was bright: avocado eye shadow, watermelon blush. She sized Tony up and said, "Well, look who's got his hand in the cookie jar."

Tony lifted his leg back through the window.

Dad took me by the arm and led me to the kitchen. Tony followed.

Debbie was all business. "Where is that tequila?" she said, as she opened the cupboards.

"Behind the boxes of cereal," Dad said, straining to keep his temper under control. Usually, he would have just thrown Tony out, but tonight he seemed to have other plans for him.

I turned toward my bedroom, but Dad held my arm. "Where do you think you're going, young lady?"

"To put some jeans on!"

"Oh, no. You're dressed just fine. You look just perfect."

Dad yanked me backward, and my long hair shook. I pulled my arm free and stretched the hem of my Joy Division T-shirt to cover myself.

"Sit," Dad said, pulling back a chair and shoving me into it. "Your throne, missy."

"Dan!" Debbie said, her voice high-pitched, bird-screechy. "I can't find no shot glasses!"

Dad sized up Tony. He said, "You sit down too, Romeo."

Tony said, "I really have to get going."

"What?" Dad said, pretending to be offended. "Can't have a drink with your girlfriend's old man?"

I realized, by the sarcasm in Dad's voice, that he was even drunker than Debbie. "Let him go home," I pleaded, afraid of what he was going to do. I couldn't help but think of the lumberjack, bleeding all over the bar. "Please, Dad."

He gave me a look that shut me up. Tony sat down, next to me.

Debbie set a bottle of tequila on the table. "I sure would like to drive around for a while. Maybe we should all have a few and drive down to the river?"

I tucked my bare legs under my T-shirt and bent my head to my knees. My hair gushed around my shins and curled at my toes.

"I would start explaining," Dad said, "if I were you."

"You aren't me!" I said. "You're nothing like me."

Debbie patted my back and said, "There, there. Nothing to get worked up about. You just got caught is all. Happens to the best of us." She salted four shot glasses, poured out the tequila, and gave us all a wedge of lemon.

Dad was still sizing Tony up, as if he wanted to ask him to step outside. "How old are you, anyhow?" he said.

"Dad!" I said. "Leave him alone."

"What?" Dad said. "Isn't an introduction in order?"

Debbie opened a vinyl cigarette case and took out a Virginia Slim. As she poured the tequila, she said, "Why don't we get to know each other over another round?"

"This is Tony," I said. Tony's leather jacket gapped and revealed his smooth chest, his graceful neck.

"Tony what?" Dad wanted to know.

"Dimantilo," Tony said.

"You Chuck's boy?" Dad asked, his eyes narrowing. "From Stoddard?"

"That's the one," Tony said.

"I know your father," Dad said, and I wondered whether the Dimantilos were friend or foe. "I know him real well," he went on, his voice rising in anger. "So, Tony Dimantilo, what in the hell are you doing in my daughter's bedroom at two in the goddamned morning?"

Tony cleared his throat, unable to speak.

"He was visiting me," I said, coming to Tony's defense.

"We gathered that much, darling," Debbie said, sarcastic. She tipped the ash of her cigarette into an Old Style ashtray and downed a shot. "Drink up, lovebirds."

Dad noticed a small tattoo on Tony's chest, just above his nipple. "What's that for?" Dad asked.

"It's a skateboarding logo," I said. "Tony skateboards."

"Your boyfriend can speak for himself, I suppose?" Dad said.

"He doesn't want to talk to you," I said. "Who would?"

Debbie clucked her tongue. "Now, is that any way to speak to your daddy? If I talked like that my father would've smacked me to Sparta."

I was, by now, feeling nauseated. I gave Debbie a dirty look. "It's none of your business how I talk to my own father," I said.

"So you skateboard for a living?" Dad said.

"I'm seventeen," Tony said. "I don't need to earn a living yet."

"Phew," Dad replied, and downed a shot. "So you've got a lot of time on your hands. I bet that skateboarding is hard work."

The shot glass, once emptied, filled as if by magic.

"It is," Tony said. "I mean, it's pretty difficult, Mr. Trussoni."

Dad liked being called *mister*. His voice softened when he said, "Why don't you play a real sport, like football?"

"He doesn't *like* football," I said.

Tony picked up the shot glass, examined it, and emptied the tequila. Although Tony's father took him to Roscoe's now and then, doing shots with people over the age of sixteen was clearly a new experience. "I like football," he said.

"You do?" I said, astonished.

"Football is OK."

"I thought you said you *hate* football. You told me you hated it."

"I love football," Debbie said, looking at Tony. "I've got tickets for the Packers game next weekend, if anyone's interested."

Debbie unzipped her satin jacket and slipped out of it. Her T-shirt was green, tight, and said PACK ATTACK in yellow letters. Cigarette smoke twisted above the table and folded into the orange-and-yellow stained-glass-like plastic light fixture.

"I played football when I was your age," Dad said. "I was damn proud to play football. I was pretty good at it too. But I got kicked out of high school, and that stopped that."

I had heard the story of Dad's dismissal from high school many times. My grandparents had scraped money together to send their children to Aquinas, a Catholic high school in town, where the teachers were strict disciplinarians who used corporal punishment to keep their students in line.

My father had never been good with authority and one day, when he saw a male teacher beating his younger brother Albert, Dad overtook the man and punched him senseless. Albert was allowed to stay at Aquinas, but Dad was expelled. He graduated from a public school near Genoa.

Debbie touched Dad's arm. She said, "I bet you were great at football, baby."

"Football is for meatheads," I said, just to be contrary. I wanted one of Debbie's cigarettes, so I leaned across the table and took one. I no longer cared if Dad saw me smoke.

"Football is cool," Tony said, and this seemed to win Dad and Debbie over. Dad gave Tony's empty shot glass to Debbie. She refilled it. "But I've got a bum shoulder. I can't play contact sports."

I rubberbanded my hair into a ponytail. Dad lit my cigarette. I inhaled, exhaled, and downed a shot of tequila. Then I turned to Tony. "You never told me about your shoulder."

"I don't tell you everything."

I raised an eyebrow and smiled. I contemplated telling Tony that he didn't know everything about me, either. He still thought I was a virgin when we met. "Oh, really?" I said, sarcastic. "You know *all* my secrets."

Tony narrowed his eyes, wanting to know what I hadn't told him.

"How about some music, huh?" Debbie said. She jumped up, going for the radio. "I'm the jukebox girl!" she said. "You still got eight-tracks, Dan? My God, you're about as cool as a sauna in Key West."

Tony took Debbie's shot glass and drank her tequila.

When Dad poured us all another shot, Tony drank that one too. Then, he stood and followed Debbie to the living room. He must have felt me watching him; he touched Debbie's shoulder, leaning his lips to her ear, asking for something, probably a cigarette. He smoked as Debbie danced to the Oak Ridge Boys. I wanted to go and pull Tony away from the living room, to take him back into the bedroom and pretend that the night was still ours. But I couldn't move. My T-shirt barely covered me.

Dad looked me over, almost smiling. "Your boyfriend's a good kid," he said. "His old man's got a problem or two, but still. Nice family."

"Can I please go get dressed now?" I said, stubbing my cigarette out in the ashtray.

"You go on, sweetheart," he said. "Go to bed. I'll tell these drunks it's time to clear out."

I HAD PROGRAMMED PIZZA HUT'S NUMBER INTO THE speed dial system, number 6, sandwiched between Roscoe's (number 5) and Dad's truck (number 7). When Dad was out for the night and there was nothing in the house to eat, I ordered pizza. I hunted through the house, collecting change from under the couch and behind the bed, stacking it in piles on the coffee table. Then I took the phone from its cradle and placed my order.

When the pizza came, and I had to count out each coin for the delivery boy, I realized it would have been much easier to have written a check. I'd learned to copy my father's handwriting so exactly, with such precision, that even he didn't recognize the forgery. I had mastered my mother's hand by fourth grade, when I needed her signature on the back of my report card. Her signature was fat-lettered, with oblong loops, and came in handy for absentee notes and excuses for tardiness.

I hadn't needed Dad's signature until recently. It took me a long time to get it right. Dad wrote with his left hand, causing a dizzying Tower-of-Pisa slant to his script, so to create his signature exactly I would turn the page upside down and write each letter at a tilt. After I mastered it, however, I could order pizza anytime I wanted. I would find Dad's checkbook, scribble the date, the words *Pizza Hut*, and then perform his shingled arachnoid signature at the bottom. A perfect forgery. If Dad questioned the check (which he did only once), I would remind him of when he had written it. He would look over the stub, examine the signature, confused, and put the checkbook away.

I didn't forge his checks much anymore, however. I no longer needed Dad's money. One afternoon, Dad saw a HELP WANTED sign posted at the Ground Round, a North Side bar and grill, and turned his truck into the parking lot. He found the manager in the lobby, and they sat in a booth together, discussing the terms. I stood by the door, watching. Although I was fifteen and technically not legal to work, Dad promised I would do a good job. He offered to sign whatever papers needed to be signed, to make me eligible for labor. "Danielle is a hard worker," he told the manager. "This would really help us out." Dad was a good talker, and by Monday morning of the following week I had a job scrubbing dishes and busing tables for minimum wage.

Dad was right about one thing: I was a hard worker. I

spent the summer I was fifteen washing floors and windows and toilets at the Ground Round. I cleared tables of dishes, stacked them in a plastic tub, covered them with soiled napkins, and carried them to a steamy back room. I scraped the half-eaten food into a garbage bin and loaded the dishes on a rack. The waitresses sometimes gave me a dollar or two, as thanks, but mostly they ignored me. I was not old enough or beautiful enough to have the kinds of boyfriends that they had, the ones with muscle cars and mullets. I was not invited to gossip with them in the back room. I was the busboy. I was the dish girl. I was the hand that cleared and cleaned and collected its meager pay and disappeared.

When I finished a shift, the cook got me high. He rolled a joint after the kitchen had been sanitized, and we smoked it by the smooth reflective stainless-steel dish machine. Twenty-three and still pimply, he offered to sell me a bag of marijuana, the good stuff, no ditch weed. I would have bought everything he had and more if I didn't hate the woozy, sickening slackness of being high. I could not abide being slow-witted, if even for a few hours. After we smoked a joint, I swallowed NoDoz, washing the pills down with burnt brewed coffee, to dispel the numbness.

Then, I walked through the North Side. My fingers were pruned and my clothes smelled of detergent and grease. I was exhausted, but work had made me worth something. I felt almost valuable. And although I'd gradually lost my friends, my handle on school, my interest in TV and movies and books, I increased my hours at the Ground Round. Every Saturday, I fulfilled my community service duties. One Saturday, I hacked weeds from the side of the highway.

Another Saturday, I collected bags of litter from Riverside Park.

When I told Mom about my job at the Ground Round, she said, "Are you sure you want to spend all your free time working?" Of course I did, I told her, trying to sound convincing. Dad and I were struggling. We didn't have enough money even to buy food. We had to work and work and work, if we were going to make it. And besides, I had always felt awful, asking Dad for money. Every time I did, he made it seem like I was stealing from him.

Mom looked me over as if I'd been brainwashed. She raised an eyebrow and laughed. "Is that what your dad has been telling you?" she asked. "That he's *poor*? I kept his books for twelve years. I know how much money he makes."

Mom told me Dad had been stashing his cash for as long as she had known him. He spent as little as he could and stuffed the rest away. Although he had lost the Trussoni Court house in the divorce, he'd kept everything else: the business, the land, their savings. He bought the Trussoni farm in Genoa from his father—a piece of land that should have remained in the family—and sold it off at a profit. He had side jobs and property and investments. He never hired union and avoided providing his employees with benefits. Dad was, by our standards, rich.

I had never heard Mom complain about Dad's stinginess; she had a habit of remaining silent whenever his name was brought up. But I knew that when they had been married, his frugality had driven her to find her own job. She vowed to make her own money. After the divorce, when Dad ducked out of paying his fair share of child support—because of the joint custody agreement, he paid half of what he should have—Mom never took him to court for more. She worked overtime and went to night school. She went into debt until we were on our own.

Mom told me the only way she made it through her time with my father was to ignore the bad things—the fights over cash, the bitterness, the secrets—and keep moving forward. She suggested that I do the same. She said there was nothing to be done but ignore him and go my own way. "Your father wants you to think he's broke," Mom says. "But if there's one thing your dad knows how to do, it is earn money."

It no longer made a difference to me how much money Dad had; I paid my own way. I worked full-time during the summer and twenty-five hours a week when school started. Mom opened a savings account in my name, but I didn't use it. I would not save a penny. I spent every cent I had on junk, as if to spite them both.

I HADN'T SPOKEN TO TONY DIMANTILO FOR MONTHS, NOT since he quit working for Dad. My father gave Tony a job mixing cement over the summer, offering to pay him six dollars an hour under the table. After the first week, Tony called me and said, "Jesus Christ. Your dad is something else."

"Oh, yeah?" I said, feeling defensive, as if Tony were not talking about my father but about me.

"He's a maniac! He stands behind me while I'm mixing cement, screaming at the top of his lungs *Get busy you lazy-ass! I don't pay you sons-of-bitches to stand around and pick your nose!* We work from six in the morning without a break. The man is a slave driver."

I knew Tony was right; I'd heard it before. Dad was always hard on his employees. Instead of apologizing, I simply said, "He has high expectations."

"I've had other bosses," Tony said, "and your dad is the meanest son-of-a-bitch I've ever worked for."

Once, at the end of the summer, Tony came to visit me at the Ground Round. He sent a waitress into the dish room with a note that said *Meet me out back*. I wiped my hands on my uniform, checked myself in a small mirror at the condiment station, and went out the back door, into an alley. Tony stood near a Dumpster, his skateboard in his hand. His black hair was combed over one eye; his Vision Streetwear T-shirt was pristine-white. He said, "Hey, I haven't seen you in a while," which was true: I spent so much time at the Ground Round that I didn't see my friends at all. I had given myself over to work. Serenity had acquired a new best friend, one with an excess of free time.

Tony and I sat near the Dumpster, sharing a cigarette. He looked me over, as if he had never seen me before, and I imagined how I must look to him, with my hair tied back, and my polyester uniform stained with ketchup. It was clear I was the least cool girl on the entire North Side. We didn't say much, but I knew, by the way he put his arm around my shoulder and I tilted my head so it brushed the edge of his shoulder, that something I loved was ending. When the cigarette had burned down, he tossed it under the Dumpster. "See you around," he said. He stepped on his skateboard and glided away. I was not surprised to find, the next week, that he no longer returned my calls. When I found out he had a new girlfriend, I stayed in my bedroom for three days, refusing to eat or accept phone calls. One afternoon, Dad slipped a Hallmark card under the door. Inside, he had written, *I'm sorry you have to go through this, sweetheart, but remember: If it doesn't kill you, it will make you strong.*

ONE DAY AFTER SCHOOL, I ATE PIZZA HUT PIZZA ALONE in front of the TV, flipping channels. Around midnight, I turned out the lights. I swept aside the curtains and opened the window, propping it up with an empty beer bottle. Freezing air blew in on me. I sat on the couch and covered myself with a wool blanket. Through the small wood-framed window, street lamps frazzled the sky. Sleep washed over me as the room temperature dropped.

Dad came home after two o'clock. I woke startled by the rattle of the key in the lock. He stood in the doorway, holding his cowboy hat in his hand, as if being polite. "You hungry?" he asked. I collected myself from the couch and stumbled to my room to find my coat.

Dad and I walked down Caledonia Street, swift and silent, to a twenty-four-hour diner, a place of sputtering electricity and fellow drunks. Dad ordered coffee and eggs and bacon and toast. I ordered the All You Can Eat pancake special—four head-sized buttermilk pancakes and more on the way. "Your eyes are bigger than your stomach," Dad said, and this was true: I always ordered more than I could eat. My hunger was tremendous. I wanted to eat and eat and eat. I wanted to expand and grow and leave my too-small skin behind me.

The waitress emptied ashtrays and refilled coffee cups. I could tell, by the way she walked, her back slightly bowed, that she was exhausted. Our neighborhood was filled with women like this, single mothers trying to make ends meet. She probably worked the night shift at that diner before working the day shift at another diner down the road. When she delivered our food, Dad spoke to her as if she were a stray animal that had wandered in his path. Make me a vanilla malt, he said, and make it quick. Then he turned to his plate, eating quickly, soaking his toast with egg yolk. I dumped every kind of syrup in the place on my pancakes: the boysenberry, the maple, the strawberry, the blueberry.

As I ate, Dad told me he'd been picked up for drunk driving again and would lose his license. "It isn't like the good old days," he said, "when they treated you like a human being. They don't care where you've been or what you've done. Now, everyone is out to nail your ass."

The waitress brought Dad a tall fountain glass with his malt. He took a sip and his face soured. He waved the waitress back over.

"What in the hell is this?" he asked.

The waitress stared at Dad, unsure of how to respond. After a moment of silence, he pushed the glass to the edge of the table. "I'll tell you what this is, since you don't seem to know. This," he said, slamming his fist upon the Formica for emphasis, "is a shake. You made it with milk and ice cream." He tapped his fork against the fountain glass *clink*,

clink, clink, and continued. "It is not what I ordered. When you can make me a malt, let me know."

The waitress, who was not used to customers who dressed her down with such severity, looked as if she might cry. As she took the glass and turned away, Dad added, "And this better not be on my bill."

Every customer in the diner was staring at us. My cheeks tingled. If I had a mirror, I would have seen that my face had gone bright red. I cut my pancakes into triangles and ate them, hoping that Dad would forget about the mistake. But he didn't. He mumbled about how everyone was out to screw him over. He worked day and night, he said. He was a tired man. He deserved better service than that, for Christ's sake. Dad ate ferociously, banging his coffee cup in its saucer. *Goddamned vanilla shake.*

I propped my chin in my hand and looked at my father. At one time I would have tried to make him happy. I would have cracked a joke or offered him my orange juice. I would have apologized for him, if not to the waitress, then to myself. Once upon a time, I could not have seen my father as rude and mean-spirited and temperamental. I loved him too much, and was too much a part of him, to be critical. But this had begun to change. I began to study my feelings, all of them, no matter how contradictory. I saw that I was adoring and proud and embarrassed and repulsed by my father, all at once. I felt love and anger and loyalty. I knew I understood him better than I understood anyone else, and yet I didn't understand him at all. I tried to look at my father, without judgment, without apology.

Then, more important than this, I looked at myself. The

similarities between Dad and me were striking. Dad's personality had grown into me the way a strip of barbed wire grows into the bark of a tree. I had incorporated all his traits—his sharp temper, his unrealistic expectations, his self-absorption. For the first time, I realized I needed to untangle myself from him. Yes, I was just like him. But I wanted to be somebody else. If given the chance, I would have stood and walked away from my life. I would have left it and never come back.

Now, in that run-down diner, surrounded by neon lights and drunks, it occurred to me that I could do this. I could leave. Although I knew it would hurt us both, I could pack my things and move in with Mom. I could work more hours at the Ground Round and rent an apartment. Perhaps, I thought, Dad would be just fine without me. Perhaps Dad didn't need me after all. The Dad code that had gotten me through my childhood began to unravel. I wondered if my father had ever thought about understanding *me*. Had he ever tried?

Dad ate, his head lowered. It was as if I were not there at all. And there was some truth to this—part of me had wandered away. There was me, the sleepy-eyed girl twisting her hair around her finger, and then there was this other girl, the one who had begun to pack her bags. This girl was planning her escape. She was rehearsing an elaborate bust-out.

I watched Dad, my eyes narrowed. I felt as if a shutter were clicking in my mind, a reel of film going behind my retinas, taking the imprint of light upon it, exposing images of him. If I locked him in this infinitely reproducible medium, his actual self became irrelevant. If I remembered everything about him, I wouldn't need him so much. His face became lined with tiny fissures. The skin shivered into fine cracks that crisscrossed his forehead and cheeks. Piece by piece, he fell away. His nose, his left ear, the little freckle near his eyebrow—those features chipped until there was nothing left but the images I had captured. I wanted to memorize my father, to store him away in my imagination. It was my only recourse. Soon I would be gone.

I slid into my ski jacket and zipped it to my chin. "You ready?" I said. Dad looked up, surprised that I had spoken so abruptly. "Sure," he mumbled, and opened his wallet, leaving a ten-dollar bill on the table. "I need some sleep," I said. "I've got school tomorrow."

sixteen

I had been eating only fruit and candy bars since I got to Vietnam and, although still upset about the previous night, I was starving. My guidebook listed cafés in the tourist district that served breakfasts of brioches and croissants and cappuccino, but it was still early, only seven in the morning. Nothing was open, and I was wary of the Dong Khoi area anyway. I couldn't imagine that I had seen the last of the sunglasses man.

I found a vending machine near a bus station and inserted a handful of coins. A box of Dunhill cigarettes tumbled to my fingers. I had already finished the pack I bought the night before, at the café. Tapping it against my wrist, I pulled back the thin foil, broke the filter, repacked the tobacco, and lit a cigarette. Delicious, poisonous smoke filled my lungs. I walked and smoked, wandering from street to street, killing time.

As the sun rose higher, light filtered over the buildings. It must have rained in the hours I spent at the hotel; the streets were clean and wet. My father had told me that sunrise in the Iron Triangle was a kind of boundary: The days belonged to them; the nights belonged to the guerrillas. I was hoping that daylight would make me feel better about what had happened in my hotel room, but it didn't. My hands were still shaking; I still wanted to book a flight out.

The streets turned muddy as I walked away from the city center. A man with a conical straw hat sat on his haunches near a *pho* cart, sipping soup. I bought a bowl and fell into a wooden chair, ravenous. A yellow plastic Pokémon clock hung from the *pho* cart. Despite the hour, many people were already awake and on the street. A girl swept steps with a homemade broom. An old woman, her back bent and curved like a camel's, lumbered past with baskets of green bananas balanced on her shoulder. Lifting her head, she smiled as she passed me, her teeth stained black by betel. A motorbike swerved through the street, nicking a beggar whose wooden bowl fell to the sidewalk, spilling nothing.

DISTRICT THREE WAS THE FRENCH DISTRICT, WHERE THE colonial mansions were palatial, their green lawns funneling to wide verandas. Each mansion was surrounded by thick stone walls and locked iron gates. These houses were occupied in the sixties and seventies by American military, diplomatic, and relief organizations. I walked past them, trying to see into the wide linen-draped windows, imagining characters from a Graham Greene novel lounging on a veranda, drinking iced Vietnamese coffee and speaking in cryptic spy-novel sentences. What would it be like, I wondered, to lie in the shade of a colonial mansion, a slow squeaking fan spinning overhead?

The French had come to Vietnam in search of a paradise

of palm trees and sunshine. For centuries, many foreigners had come. There were all the usual guests—the Chinese, the Khmers, the French—as well as the more unusual ones, such as the Hindu Kingdom of Champa, who built Gaudi-esque temples in central Vietnam. But the Vietnamese had never been polite hosts, receiving foreigners with steely suspicion. When the Chinese (who taught the proto-Vietnamese to grow rice) tried to reorganize Vietnamese society along Chinese lines, they resisted, just as they resisted contact with the West in A.D. 166, when the Romans arrived under Marcus Aurelius, and again in the sixteenth century, when Portugal sent its missionaries. They resisted the British, who came and left after an agent of the East India Company was murdered in Hanoi. The missionaries came; the natives killed them. The missionaries came; the natives killed them.

I walked through the afternoon heat, trying to stay in the shade of the palm trees. At the end of the district, I found myself at the mouth of a dirt road. Following it through a grove of trees, I came to a bright yellow building, half hidden by bushes, a wooden fence surrounding it. A curved rooftop swooped above. Painted dragons arched below the eaves, peering down the slanted corners like watchdogs. Glass tiles formed pictures on the dull yellow wall—a blue-and-white bird, a red dragon, a turtle—each one at a corner of the entrance. The bird's feathers spread geometrically, square by square, around the doorframe.

I banged my hand on a set of warm red-and-black lacquered doors. When there was no response, I pushed them open and walked into a large room with a peaked ceiling and a cement floor. Huge wooden doors, big as barn doors, stood ajar at the opposite end of the room, letting in sunlight. Incense rose in ringlets, filling the air with layers of slim evanescent smoke. A very old bald monk stood near the doorway. When he saw me, he motioned for me to come closer. He was wrapped in long drapes of maroon cloth that twisted from his bare feet to a knot at his collarbone. He offered me a cigarette. He was missing most of his teeth.

"*Asseyez-vous!*" he said, pushing a chair at me. The table was nothing more than a wooden wheel balanced on an oil barrel. Teacups and saucers sat around a china teapot.

"*Quel âge avez-vous?*" the monk asked.

Although I had studied French in high school, I responded in English. "Twenty-four," I said.

The monk clucked his tongue, as if he did not approve of youth. "*Très jeune,*" he said.

The monk did not seem to speak a word of English, and so when he told me (in French) that he had been at the monastery for sixty years, from the late thirties, I thought I must not have understood him correctly. But the monk drew a six and a zero on my palm, confirming that he had moved into the pagoda thirty-five years before I was born.

He poured me tea, and I looked around the temple. There were tiny shrines cut into the walls, each one painted gold and crimson. Hundreds of plaques (embossed with prayers) stood next to black-and-white photographs. Incense and butter lamps burned below them.

When the monk wanted to speak to me again, he waved over a group of younger monks, Vietnamese men who were my age or slightly older. The old monk opened my hand, pressed down my fingers, and stroked my palm, as if he might read my fortune. He said something in slow, ambling Vietnamese, and one of the young monks translated it into perfect English. He said, "Our master welcomes you to our pagoda. He is sorry that he doesn't speak your language. He learned French very well, many years ago. But he never learned English."

The head monk waddled away, slow as a goose, and the younger monk led me by the arm. "He would like to show you our pagoda, yes?"

I had not been inside a church for over ten years, and I'd never seen a Buddhist temple before. The statues and funeral tablets were so strange that I wanted to take a picture. But, when I dug for my camera, the young monk said, "Please. It is not allowed to take photographs here. It is not good luck."

We followed the head monk through the cavernous temple. He took us to a row of bodhisattvas, a group of semihuman figures lounging against a wall with demons and dragons and all sorts of strange animals twisting around them. He led me to the Quan The Am Bo Tat, the Goddess of Mercy, a white statue of a woman armed like an octopus. She had eyes where eyes shouldn't be—in her forehead and cheeks—each eye looking a different direction. The monk showed me A Di Da, the Buddha of the Past, and Di Lac, the Buddha of the Future, two fat golden statues high on a dais. A pyramid of smaller statues surrounded the Buddhas. Incense rose from clay pots below them, releasing wisps of smoke through the room. An elderly woman lay prostrate on yellow satin cushions, her long thin arms stretched out before her.

The young monk asked me if I was a Christian. I told

him I was raised Catholic, but had no idea of what I believed any longer. He studied me, pity in his eyes, and said, "You must discover this. It is important to know who you are."

Perhaps the monk could sense how uncomfortable I was in the temple. After Father Rossitor had been shot and killed, I felt uneasy with God. I couldn't understand the inner workings of a force that could allow something like the shooting at my school to happen, so I kept my distance. It was the same way with men. I became suspicious of love after Tony Dimantilo broke my heart.

I remember going to a high school party after a football game, to a parentless house in the suburbs, where we drank shots of peppermint schnapps with Kahlúa chasers. A keg of beer iced in the bathtub. The pom-pom girls giggled and sang fight songs; the football players talked shop. I'd just moved from middle school to a big public high school, and I didn't know many people yet. I walked through the party, tipsy and insecure. When I saw a boy look at me in a certain way (part interest, part terror), I slammed a shot of schnapps—the way I'd seen Roscoe's regulars do a shot before they took their cue to the eight ball—and sauntered over to him. I led him by the hand to a back bedroom, where I told him to do whatever he wanted but do it fast. It was over in less than three minutes. I had heard that it would hurt, and had braced myself to suffer, but it was no more painful than twisting a rubber band around my wrist until the fingers went bloodless. When it was over, I stood, got dressed, and walked out. I didn't even get the boy's name.

As a young woman, I was more particular than this. I

was attracted to men who nurtured addictions, whose chemicals were unsyncopated, off-wire, jazzed. I wanted the ones who needed me to balance them out. My lovers were artists, hustlers, musicians, drifters. They would come into my life, shake things up, and disappear. One lover—a trumpet player—died of a heroin overdose. Another left me on a park bench in a strange southern city and drove off into the sunset, his 1954 hollow-body Gretch in the backseat. But most men did not exit my life so dramatically. I was the one to run. I was terrified of gentle words said sober in the glare of morning. I did not understand tenderness; I did not like to be touched. I felt at ease with men who offered nothing but booze and a good story. I would drink and listen. Then I would move on.

I was a month out of college when I met a man at a bar. He had a rough way of talking and tattoos on his arms. We had known each other five minutes, and he was so drunk he could not stand, when he lifted his sleeve and showed me slash marks where he had cut himself to the bone. Scars striated his biceps like a rope ladder. When I asked him why he had done such a thing, he said he had wanted to know what it felt like, such pure pain. I thought I understood a certain look, a certain desperation that said, *I dare you to resurrect someone like me.* I thought I was capable of this. And for a little while, I was.

He would drink a bottle of Jim Beam in the evening, fall into our bed after midnight, and tell me he needed me more than anything in the world. I loved his smell of stale cigarettes and the sourness of his breath; I loved that, in the spill of a whiskey binge, it was me he wanted; and I loved how essential he made me feel. During the four years we were together, I struggled to create a state of equilibrium between us. When that balance never came and I could no longer support his seductive hopelessness, I packed my things and left. I could not stay. I had my own darkness to escape.

The praying woman began to chant. Her voice rose to a high-pitched moan.

"This is a very old pagoda," the young monk said. "I have been here since I was seven. It is a sanctuary for us."

The old woman's prayer—half song, half groan—made me nervous. I was just about to excuse myself and leave when the old monk put three joss sticks in my hand. He pointed to the Buddha statues and said something in French.

The young monk translated. "He says you must pray."

"Pray for what?" I asked, as he lit the incense with a plastic lighter.

"You will know," he said, guiding me to the altar, "when you begin."

I had not knelt in prayer in so long that my knees felt rigid as I bent next to the old woman. Up close, I could see that she had a weathered face and was much older and more battered than I had originally thought. The sadness in her face made her voice less abrasive. I blew on the joss sticks, and the ends fired orange. The rich, sharp smoke blanketed the base of the altar. I felt clumsy as I leaned forward, over the wooden steps that led up to the Buddhas, and stuck the sticks of incense into the sand of a clay pot, all three at once. They stayed for a moment, wobbled, and then fell over. When I tried to extricate them from the mess of smoke—so many sticks of incense burning with prayers—I singed my knuckles. Trying again, I pushed one stick in at a time. This time, they stayed.

Through the haze of the smoke and the chanting, images of my childhood filled my mind. I remembered the reels of eight-millimeter film shot during the years I was growing up. When we lived on Trussoni Court, we used to watch them on the wall of the living room, all of us kids in our pajamas. We had forgotten those tapes after our parents broke up, but for some reason Dad had recently decided to transfer the film to video. My father always said that the best years of his life were those spent with my mother, raising us, so it must have taken a lot of strength for him to sort through the hours and hours of this forever-lost past, watching each reel. But he went through them all, selecting the best scenes and preserving them.

Dad gave me the tape when I was in graduate school. I watched it one evening, the lights turned low, as I drank a glass of pinot noir. The video cut across ten years and presented me with a father I had long forgotten. I saw my father at Matt's christening, holding my brother as if he were the thinnest, most delicate Christmas ornament. I saw him planting a tree in the front yard of the house, just after Matt was born. In another shot, I saw myself, at two years old, dressed in OshKosh overalls, my hair drawn in pigtails: an apple-cheeked girl with big black eyes gazing up at my father, adoring.

My favorite part of the tape was a clip of my father helping me learn to ride a bike. I didn't know it at the time, but my mother had stood in the lawn and taped the whole thing. Dad wore jeans and no shoes. A cigarette dangled from his lips as he walked alongside the banana-seat bicycle I shared with my sister, holding it steady. The camera followed me down the driveway, as I looked over my shoulder, checking that my father was there, and began to pedal. Dad stayed alongside the bike, holding the bar of the seat so that I gained balance and momentum. With Dad next to me, I was confident. I pushed the pedals harder until I was riding down the driveway and onto Trussoni Court. I remembered that when I looked back and saw Dad far behind, I wavered and lost my balance, sending the bicycle crashing to the blacktop, scraping my knee on the stony pavement. But in the edited video I never hit the pavement. I keep my feet stiff on the pedals. I grip the plastic handlebars, sure that Dad will save me if I tip.

I was grateful that my father had made the videotape. It was a record of my childhood free of the distortions of memory. The tape helped me to see that many of my recollections had been colored by love and anger; I had often made my father in the image of my emotions. I saw that my memory had wrapped itself around the battle scenes of my life, ignoring the moments of tranquillity. There were many things about those years I had forgotten—the tenderness my father was capable of when he wasn't sad or drinking or lost in remembering. He had been pushed to the limit by the war; he looked defeated and worn out in every shot. The tape forced me to see that, more than anything, my father had been defeated by Vietnam. He had lost his war, his pride. Nothing would change that.

I folded my hands, as I had been taught to do in grade

school, and asked for my father's illness to disappear. I prayed that all the terrible things that had happened in Vietnam—to Americans and Vietnamese alike—would never happen again. I prayed for the one thing my father and I had never shared: peace. Then I stood and walked away from the altar. On my way out of the temple, I dropped a bundle of *dong* notes into a box for donations. My eyes had filled with tears. I could hardly see by the time I pushed past the doors. Outside, the afternoon had become hot and bright and overwhelming. I leaned my head against the sun-warmed door, letting the heat soothe me.

AS I WALKED BACK TOWARD MY HOTEL THROUGH DIS-trict three, I searched for a pay phone, to call my sister. As we had grown older, I'd become more and more dependent upon her. I called her often, especially when I wanted to talk about our father. I was also sure that Kelly would want to hear all the details about my stalker, with his iron hook. When I found a phone (in the lobby of a post office), I punched in the numbers of my phone card and then my sister's home phone number. After her answering machine picked up, I realized that she was probably at work. I dug through my backpack for my address book, hoping I had the number for Track II.

Track II was open twenty-four hours a day and did a steady business, with a perfectly calibrated rate of turnover: Night-owl drinkers were replaced by night-shift drinkers, who were, in turn, replaced by the lunch crowd. There were regulars like Skip, who lived in the alley behind the bar. Skip sold his house, bought a van, and parked it near the back entrance. Skip, Kelly once told me, was an efficient and reliable drinker. He drank and passed out, drank and passed out, drank and passed out by the clock, creating a schedule of inebriation that my sister could set her watch by. When Kelly came to work, Skip would be drinking; when she took a break, Skip would be drinking; when she finished her shift, Skip would still be drinking. Skip didn't have a job or a family, but he had a fulfilling social life. He gave out the telephone number at Track II and—if nobody called—he would drink and dial, leaving messages on answering machines all over the city. Whenever Skip passed out, Kelly would run his phone messages out to the alley and clip them under a windshield wiper of his van.

I used to go to see Kelly during her shifts. She would make me a drink and turn the TV down while I put money in the jukebox, choosing all the songs that felt right: old sad country songs. Some Johnny Cash and some Hank Williams Jr. Songs made for crying in your beer. One night, as Kelly and I drank Jack and Cokes, she told me that she had met Rita Trussoni, the Denied Daughter of our father's first marriage, the week before. Kelly and Matt had gone to Marge's, a North Side diner on Rose Street, for breakfast. As they looked over their menus, they saw, across the room, a woman wearing a jacket with Dad's construction company logo printed across the back. "Who is that?" Matt asked, pointing at Rita, and Kelly (looking the woman over and thinking she looked familiar) said, "No clue. Maybe she works for Dad."

"She doesn't work for Dad," Matt said, and he would know. Dad had been grooming Matt to take over his business. From the time Matt was fourteen, Dad gave him summer work laying bricks. Matt was a willing apprentice, and he learned everything Dad had to teach. (When brick-work wasn't enough and Matt wanted to know more about construction, he would go on to get a degree in engineering from the Milwaukee School of Engineering and then a master's degree in architecture.) There had been some talk of Matt taking over Dad's construction company, but my brother had bigger ambitions than building chimneys and fixing sidewalks. Matt would put himself through college and struggle to get into graduate school. Dad took the same attitude with Matt as he had with me—he was unsupportive financially, at one point refusing to surrender his tax returns so Matt could get federal aid.

Kelly and Matt waved the woman over. "Hi, there," Matt said. "We were just admiring your jacket."

"Thanks," the woman replied. "It's my dad's construction company."

"*Your* dad's construction company?" Matt said. "Who is your dad?"

"Dan Trussoni," the woman said, raising an eyebrow, as if daring my brother to say different.

"You better take a seat," Kelly said, making room for Rita in the booth. "We've got some things to talk about."

Although Rita Trussoni was raised by her mother and stepfather, she had not given up hope that Dad would one day want to know her. She called him every now and again, attempting to create a relationship, but Dad treated her with the same even-toned coldness with which he spoke to telemarketers. When Rita asked him to do a DNA test to prove once and for all whose daughter she was, he agreed. In private, he said he should have had a blood test years ago, to avoid all this bullshit. "After all these years," he said, confident of himself, "I will finally be proven right."

When the tests came back a positive match, it was official: Rita was a Trussoni and our sister, but the result did not matter to Dad. He didn't treat Rita any differently than he ever had. He didn't attempt to make up for his mistake. He didn't want to get to know her. And although he never said so, it seemed to us that he didn't believe the test. He grumbled and guffawed when I asked him about Rita. He had denied this girl so often, and with so much self-right-eousness, that he had come to believe his version of the story regardless. The test must be wrong; it had been rigged to make him look like a fool; the world was conspiring against him. He'd always thought of Rita as somebody else's problem, and he still did. She had never been a Trussoni, and she never would be.

THE YEAR MATT WAS BORN, I HAD A RECURRING NIGHT-mare. I would wake in the middle of the night and run to my parents' bedroom, where I would crawl into their bed, careful not to wake them. Once there, I would not fall asleep but would stare wide-eyed into the blackness. The electric clock would sear numbers upon my eye. The trees outside the window would sway in the windy night. In the dark, everything sounded louder. I would listen to the rustling of desiccated leaves below the window. I would listen to my parents breathe, all the while turning over the fragile world I had left behind ten minutes before, in the mysterious space of sleep.

In my dream, Kelly and Mom and I walked through the fields near Trussoni Court. A rusty railroad track stretched out before us, winding over the hills. We wore gingham and bonnets. When a train clamored by, Kelly fell in its path. Her body twisted around a great iron wheel, not broken but stretched. I stood at the tracks, screaming her name, as Mom and the conductor (who was my father dressed in blue-jean overalls) took each other by the arm and began to dance. They were happy she had died. They were free.

I remembered this dream as vividly as an adult as I had as a child. I once told my mother about it, sure that it said something about our family. Why, I asked her, would I feel such an intense fear of being abandoned at five years old? "I think everybody has those kinds of anxiety dreams," she said. As an example, she told me that she used to have a nightmare that Matt had fallen into the snake pit near our house. Only it wasn't the snake pit but a huge hole that went on forever. Mom was holding Matt's hand, and somehow he slipped from her grasp and tumbled into the abyss. She wanted to go in after him, but she knew if she tried to save him she would fall. She eased into the snake pit, ready to jump. "Every time I had this dream," she said, "I would wake up, so thankful it was not real."

I had recently discovered that there was an element of truth in both dreams. Not long before my trip to Vietnam, Mom picked me up in her car. "I have something to tell you," she said, as I climbed into her Toyota Celica.

"Something *important* to tell me," I said, emphasizing the words, "or just something you'd like me to be aware of in general?"

"Something *important* to tell you," she said, imitating my sarcasm, and I knew, by the tone of her voice (which was simultaneously lighthearted and yet full of self-reproach) that I should shut up and listen to what she had to say.

As she put the Celica in reverse and backed out of my driveway, she said, "Now I want you to know, before I tell you this, that this is hard for me to say." She shifted into second and turned onto Main Street. "I didn't expect that I would ever have to explain it. But then I didn't think anything would work out like it did. I guess there is no other way to say it, so here goes: You and Kelly and Matt have an older sister."

"I know," I said. "Rita Trussoni."

"Not Rita Trussoni."

"Not Rita Trussoni?"

"No. Your father and I had a daughter before we had you." Mom waited a moment, to let this information sink in. The last time Mom had made a similar important announcement—about the divorce—she had also been careful. Only then I had been ready for it.

"Excuse me?" I said, floored by her announcement. "You did what?"

"I was so stupid back then. I didn't know what to do when I got pregnant. Things just weren't as *open* as they are now. I can't believe how naïve I was. I thought I could put the baby up for adoption, and everything would be fine. But

319

of course it wasn't. Danielle, your older sister called me last week."

As I stared at my mother, too surprised to speak, Mom told me she had become pregnant on her eighteenth birthday and put the baby up for adoption three years before I was born. "I was so young," she said, shaking her head. "I didn't know how to handle someone like your father."

Mom met Dad when she was a seventeen-year-old senior in high school and traded in her homecoming-court boyfriend for a divorced, newly repatriated Vietnam veteran with two kids from his first marriage, one accepted, one denied. My father worked construction, had extra money, and showed his under-age girlfriend a good time. She got a fake ID, and he took her to the bars downtown. He lived with a brother, my uncle Albert—who my father would one day sue over a piece of property—in an apartment on the South Side. My father had big parties and a lot of friends and a human skull sitting on the TV set.

When my mother got pregnant, my father denied that he was responsible for the pregnancy. He said the baby belonged to my mother's ex-boyfriend, and he wanted nothing more to do with it. Then he disappeared, leaving my mother to fend for herself. Mom graduated from high school in her second trimester. Her parents refused to let her stay in their house, so she took a bus to a home for unwed mothers in Green Bay, where she gave birth to a baby girl in the fall of 1970. She nursed the baby for five days before giving her to an adoption counselor and boarding a bus for home, alone.

My mother did not see my father for two years after the

baby's birth, but when she did she fell in love with him all over again. I've always thought of this as the miracle of their marriage—that once upon a time they loved each other enough that everything bad could be forgiven. Mom forgave my father for abandoning her and trusted that he wouldn't do it again. He put aside his disappointing first marriage and decided to try again. They married on his birthday. I was conceived the same month.

As we drove past cornfields and barns, Mom looked over at me, anxious for my reaction. "Any more surprises?" I asked.

"There is nothing else," Mom said, and for a second she looked as if she would break into laughter, as if the situation was as difficult for her to believe as it was for me. Then, turning serious, she said, "I promise. You know everything now. The whole story."

"Well," I said, trying to adjust to the idea of having an older sister, "have you met her? Who does she look like? What's her name?"

"Tracy," Mom said firmly, as if trying to convince herself. "Her adoptive parents named her Tracy. And you know, I was surprised by how she looks. I always believed that she would look like you. But she doesn't. She looks exactly like your father."

Tracy had long sandy-blond hair and deep-set brown eyes, and was built small and strong, like a Trussoni. She had called Mom on Mother's Day, at work. After years of night school, Mom had earned an MBA and was working her way up in the finance department of a local corporation, promotion by promotion. "Happy Mother's Day, Mom!" the voice on the line said, and my mother—who had given this child up for adoption over twenty-five years before and believed she would never hear from her again—knew exactly who was calling. She put her head in her hands and cried.

They met the following week. Mom said that seeing Tracy was like being in the presence of my father as a young man. Wiry and tan and charismatic and unstoppably energetic, Tracy was exactly like my father. Although Tracy had never met him, she walked like Dad, had the same gestures, and spoke like him. Naturally charming, she even smiled like him, with a slight inflection to her upper lip, a kind of ironic, cocky smirk. As Tracy told my mother about her life (two kids, job as a waitress, so-so childhood with her adoptive parents), the hard tight ball of pain that my mother had carried around so long suddenly, like a blister that has caught a pin, burst.

My older sister had grown up in a small town north of Chicago. When she decided that she wanted to find her birth parents, she spent a year doing detective work, digging through adoption records, birth certificates, release forms, and mandatory parental biographies. She combed the texts (many of which were blacked out with a marker) until she found clues to her mother's identity: French and English and Norwegian heritage; black hair; five feet two inches tall; Betty Crocker Cooking Award 1969; Homecoming Court, 1969. My older sister drove her car through the rural Wisconsin highways, stopping at high schools to look at old yearbooks. At each school, she looked for a girl with black hair elected to a homecoming court in 1969, writing down all the names that matched Mom's profile.

"I thought about that baby all the time," Mom said. "Every single day I wondered where she was and if she was being taken care of properly. I couldn't hear about an accident involving a little girl without wondering: Was that her? Could that be my girl?"

"No wonder you left Dad," I said, feeling for the first time the pain Mom had gone through in her years of marriage to my father. "Weren't you angry with him? How could you live with that? Did you talk about it?"

"Never," she said, taking a sip of Diet Coke. "Not once. Your father was incapable of showing any emotion other than anger. He just pretended it never happened."

"Jesus," I said. "You shouldn't have gotten back together with him after Tracy was born."

Although Mom knew that I was right, she almost never openly criticized my father, remaining, despite everything, sympathetic. "I'm sure he had a lot of problems back then," she said. "He had just gotten back from Vietnam. He wasn't well. He was in no condition to be a father. I think he was just . . . incapable."

"I don't care what problems he had," I said, furious. "He shouldn't have treated you like that. You were only eighteen. He took advantage of you." I cracked the window of the Celica and lit a cigarette, something Mom normally would not tolerate. "I didn't understand at the time, Mom, but now I am so glad you divorced him."

NOT LONG AFTER THIS I WENT TO MY FATHER'S HOUSE. He had not been diagnosed with cancer yet, and he was brusque and healthy as we sat at his table.

Debbie had made pan-fried hamburgers and mashed potatoes. She had developed the habit of watching family gatherings from the sidelines; she walked around the table, poured milk into Dad's glass, and then receded into the background, lighting a cigarette and standing in the kitchen, her shoulders hunched, watching Dad eat quickly, ravenously, without tasting or chewing his food.

He was halfway through his hamburger when I said, "I called my older sister this afternoon. She would really like to meet you."

Dad paused, his hamburger in his hand. He swallowed what was in his mouth and said, his voice full of confusion, "You talked to Rita?"

I pushed my plate aside, put my elbows on the table, and looked squarely at my father. I said, "I'm talking about the baby you and Mom had before I was born. Her name is Tracy. She was given up for adoption in 1970."

My father looked as if he might choke. His face paled. He set his hamburger on his plate and clasped his hands together.

As I related everything Mom had told me, I watched him, waiting for a reaction. When I'd finished, nobody spoke. Finally, I said, "How could you have done that to Mom? How could you have let her go through that alone?"

Debbie, who was never prepared for our family—neither the loyalties nor the treasons we are capable of—had a terrified look in her eyes. "Dan?" she said. "What's this about?"

Dad did not answer her. He appeared confused, as if he himself did not know what was happening. He pushed his chair away from the table, ready to ignore what I had said. But then, in a moment of resignation, he put his head in his hands. His voice cracked, and I thought I heard the beginning of a sob. "I guess I wasn't very nice back then," he said.

A shot of panic moved through Debbie's features. She had never seen my father break in this fashion. She rushed to him and brought his head to her chest. "It's OK, Dan," she said, comforting him.

She held his head to her but she glared at me, her blue eyes frozen with warning. *Listen to me, little girl*, this icy look implied. *Do not bring your dirty past into my house.*

"It's OK, Dan," Debbie said again. "All this happened a long time ago. It's over."

But, of course, it was not over. Tracy wanted to meet our father. She called him, asking if they could arrange a meeting. By that time, Dad had recovered from the surprise. He had pulled himself back into the hard spiral shell he had lived in for so many years, and thus re-armored he went on as he always had. When Tracy called him, Dad said, "If you're looking for your father, you've got the wrong man. I know you probably want some answers, but I can't give them to you. I didn't have anything to do with this."

Dad stuck by his story. He denied his role in Tracy's creation so strongly, with such a sense of indignation, that nobody knew whom to believe. When one of my uncles invited Tracy to dinner at his house—my father did not come, but I was there—he could not help but see the obvious: Tracy looked more like our father, and more like the Trussoni family, than any of Dad's acknowledged children.

After months of denial, Dad agreed to go in for DNA testing. He and Tracy drove to the hospital together. Perhaps the lab techs recognized him from the time he came in with Rita. After the blood samples were analyzed and it was proven that he was Tracy's father (just as it had been proven that he was Rita's father), Dad was still reluctant to change his story. "What does she want from me?" he would ask, looking around, as if we, the recipients of legitimacy, could tell him. "I can't give her anything. I'm not a rich man. I don't have a thing she could want."

KELLY HAD JUST RUN A PHONE MESSAGE TO THE ALLEY for skip when I came into Track II. She took a break, asking the owner to cover for her, and she and I went to the back room to shoot a game of pool. As Kelly unloaded the parts of her pool cue from a small leather bag and screwed them together, I began racking the balls. I had not played pool much as an adult. I was better at it as a kid, when I spent my Sundays studying the techniques of Roscoe's pool sharks. But Kelly belonged to the North Side pool league, shooting every Wednesday night. She could beat me with her eyes closed. Once, when Kelly was eight months pregnant, she whipped a boyfriend of mine, nailing the eight ball before he could get in a shot. When he demanded a rematch, she beat him again. He was so embarrassed he sat at the bar the rest of the night, drinking Jim Beam, as Kelly and I laughed at him.

I leaned against my pool cue, watching Kelly sink the striped balls, one by one. After she'd won, she took her beer, raised an eyebrow, and said, "You are never going to believe what happened at Dad's house last night."

I knew that Tracy and Kelly had gone to Dad's place the night before, where the four of them—Dad and Debbie and Kelly and Tracy—drank cocktails and ate steaks. My father and I were not on speaking terms since I had confronted him about Tracy, and I had not been invited.

"It seemed to be going well," Kelly said. "Dad talked about the Trussoni Court years and Mom and the war. Debbie smoked like a chimney and got drunk and looked like she wanted to kill us. Same old shit. Different night." Kelly sipped her beer. "Except, of course, Tracy was there and had all sorts of questions for Dad. Which is understandable under the circumstances. She asked Dad why the adoption had taken place. I mean, Christ, of course she's going to want to know *why* they gave her up. I'm sure it's pretty weird for her, with you and me and Matt—her full-blooded brother and sisters—growing up together, while she got sent off somewhere. And what does Dad say?"

"What?" I asked, although I had a pretty good idea.

"He says, *I didn't have anything to do with it.* Simple as that. It was all Mom's decision. Can you believe that shit?"

Kelly said that when it got to be late, and it was clear that she and Tracy had drunk too much to drive home, they found some blankets and made up the couches in Dad's living room. After half an hour, the door to Dad and Debbie's bedroom flew open and Debbie stalked to the center of the living room, so drunk she could hardly stand. "I couldn't see her well at first," Kelly said. "It was dark, and

I didn't have my glasses on. She just sort of stood there, swaying back and forth. So I got up and turned on the light, and there she was, in the middle of the living room, skinny as a scarecrow and totally naked. I was trying hard not to laugh—I have to say, it was pretty hilarious—and Tracy actually giggled. This must have set Debbie off, because she ran at Tracy, pushed her up against a wall, and started screaming, "What do you want from us? You're not going to get a damn thing. Nothing. Not one cent!"

Kelly took a drag on her cigarette, an astounded look on her face, and continued. "Debbie really shouldn't drink—she can't handle her liquor at all. I couldn't do anything for a minute but stare at her. She was out of her mind. When I saw that Tracy was too scared to fight back, I grabbed Debbie from behind and pushed her away from Tracy. There's nothing to Debbie—she probably only weighs a hundred and ten pounds—so when I pushed her she fell against the wall, hard. That surprised her good. She stopped screaming. But then she pulled herself up and came after me! That was when I had had enough. I really let her have it. I picked her up and carried her kicking and screaming back to the bedroom. I opened the door—Dad was sound asleep, snoring through all of this—and threw her inside."

I started to laugh, and Kelly held up a finger. "No," she said. "Don't laugh. Our life has become an episode on *Jerry Springer*."

Kelly smiled and, despite herself, laughed at how absurd our family could be. I put my arm around her shoulder, wanting her to know then how lucky I felt, to have her.

Who else would understand the bittersweet nature of being our father's daughter?

"Poor Tracy," Kelly said, sipping her drink. "If she had known she was a Trussoni, she would never have come looking in the first place."

seventeen

Back at the hotel, the receptionist set his magazine on the counter. "You are looking better," he said.

After walking for hours without breakfast, I felt terrible. Nevertheless, I smiled and said, "You think so? I don't feel much better."

"Would you still like me to call the police?"

Leaning against the counter, I felt that all the weight of my trip hit me at once. Suddenly, I knew that I couldn't take another day of Saigon. Not the heat or the memories or this strange man who was on my trail. A stack of brochures for hotels on the South China Sea had been placed on the counter. Sorting through, I saw pictures of green water, tropical fish, white sand. Picking one up, I said, "This looks nice."

"That is Nha Trang," he said. "It is beautiful there. There are discos and beaches and boats for scuba diving."

"Sounds perfect. Maybe I'll learn to scuba dive," I said, folding the brochure and putting it in my back pocket.

"There is a Sinh Café bus that can take you there," he said, throwing his magazine below the counter. "Ten dollars, one way."

"Sounds great," I said, looking out the door at the sunny afternoon. "But I need to ask a favor. Can you leave the hotel for a few minutes?"

THE RECEPTIONIST WALKED AHEAD OF ME, DOWN DONG Khoi Street. It was two o'clock, the hottest time of the day, but it didn't seem to bother the throngs of tourists and street vendors. Masses of women carried bags of vegetables in the sun; schoolboys kicked soccer balls to one another, screaming and running in the alleys. But I couldn't take it any more. Exhausted, I walked close to the cafés and shops, in the shade.

"I don't think," the receptionist said, stopping with me as I bought a bottle of water, "that this is a very good idea. This man does not like Americans."

"But I thought you said his father was American."

"Or Australian. Or English. I am not sure exactly. His father was white and left Vietnam after the war. This is all I know," he said, sidestepping a moped as we crossed a busy street. "And I know he does not like Americans."

"But why?" I asked. "The war happened so long ago."

"Our memory is not so short here," the receptionist said quietly. "There are people in Vietnam who will always hate you for what happened."

He led me through an alley and onto a quiet narrow street with fenced-in dirt yards. As we walked, I realized that, although the tourist track was only a few blocks away, I had entered a different Vietnam. Away from the tourists and the vendors and all the trappings of Dong Khoi, I was no longer sightseeing. A baby cried from within one house;

the salty smell of cooking fish filled the air as we passed another. An old woman hung clothes on a plastic rack on a balcony. Young boys and girls in school uniforms were walking home for lunch.

"Here," the receptionist said, stopping before a two-story building. "He lives in an apartment here. With his mother, on the second floor. You will be careful, yes?"

I climbed the stairs, stepping up through a narrow dark hallway. On the first-floor landing, I stopped at a window overlooking the street. Rubbing the dust from the pane, I looked outside and saw that the road was empty. The receptionist had left.

Behind a door on the second floor, I heard an exchange of Vietnamese between a woman and a man. Assuming that I had found the sunglasses guy and his mother, I waited. I couldn't understand what they were saying, but their voices rose as if in an argument. Losing my courage, I began to walk back down the stairs when suddenly the door opened.

Although he must have been over thirty, in his black Iron Maiden T-shirt and ripped-up jeans, he appeared to be just a kid heading out. When he saw me on the landing, he paused. I was so scared I simply froze; I couldn't move or speak. Because of his sunglasses, I couldn't make out his reaction to me. I wanted to ask him what in the hell he was doing, following me around, but I didn't have a chance. He brushed past, as if he had never seen me before, and walked down the stairs, into the street. "Wait," I said, following him. He did not answer as he disappeared into the hot afternoon.

As I walked back to Dong Khoi, I took the brochure for

Nha Trang from my pocket. Some resort hotels had been listed on the back. I decided to pack my things and buy a bus ticket north. It was time to leave Saigon. I never discovered the identity of the man who had followed me, or exactly what he wanted. But I never forgot him. Sometimes, back home, in a store or on the street, I would feel someone behind me. I would turn expecting to find him there, watching.

AFTER I LEARNED ABOUT MY SISTER TRACY, I REALIZED that my parents' relationship had been more complicated than I had originally believed. Looking back over the years surrounding my parents' divorce, I saw that my mother had not been the only one at fault. I remembered how I had taken my father's side, always defending him. I had been so angry with my mother during those years that our relationship had never wholly recovered. In the light of Tracy's adoption and the real story behind my parents' troubled marriage, I understood that I had not been fair to my mother. I had not known the whole story.

One evening, after a particularly bad fight with my father (this time about money), I did something nobody in my family had ever dared—I wrote everything down. I composed a five-page letter to him, detailing my frustration with his drinking (which he had continued to do on a daily basis, despite his cancer diagnosis), my anger over the way he raised us, his treatment of my mother (especially in regard to Tracy), and even his treatment of Debbie, who had been a saint during Dad's cancer, giving up everything in her life—her job, her nightlife, even (briefly) her cigarettes—to nurse him back to health. I even told him I had stolen money from the gun cabinet, confessing to a crime I had committed ten years before. It was time, I wrote, to come clean.

I signed the letter and mailed it off.

I instantly regretted it. Perhaps I was being too hard on him. Sure, my father was a difficult man. Yes, we had our share of disagreements. And of course what happened with Tracy was wrong. But who was I to tell my father off? What right did I have to say, *You really fucked things up, didn't you?* Maybe I had judged him too harshly.

Then, Dad's cancer returned again, this time more serious than the last. Tests found tumors in his larynx, and he underwent immediate surgery to remove his voice box. The operation went well; the recovery did not. Years of chemotherapy had stressed the neck tissues and, after such an intrusive operation (the doctors had sliced vertically along the trachea, pulled the halves of the throat aside, and removed the voice box as if it were the pit of a peach), the wound would not heal. The muscles remained flaccid. The skin suppurated. The mass of stitches seeped infection and blackened. An emergency reconstructive surgery was undertaken, in which the doctors cut a flap of skin and muscle from my father's chest, flipped it up, and stapled it around his neck and the base of his jaw. The doctors predicted that it would take months before my father would be able to turn his head or eat properly. If he was lucky, they said, his appearance would not be affected too badly. My father would recover, they said, but he would never speak again.

I wasn't in town for Dad's operation, and I didn't get a

chance to see him for some time after the surgery. When I finally went to the house, he was still recovering. The muscles in his neck had healed lopsided. A small hole had been punctured in his throat. He had a device to help him speak, a voice machine that caught the vibrations on the roof of his mouth and created a mechanical robotic voice that sounded like Stephen Hawking or a Speak and Spell. The first time I heard this voice, I hurt in a way I had never imagined I could. My dad's voice was gone. I would never hear it again.

The day I went to visit, we sat down in his living room. My father has always been good at holding a grudge. Despite his sickness, he was fiery as ever. He brought the voice machine to his mouth. "Do you want to explain why in the hell you wrote that letter?" he asked, angry. The sound of his voice was tinny, shockingly cold. He continued. "How could you write such a disrespectful thing?"

Seeing him as he was—thin and weak and voiceless—I couldn't bring myself to argue anymore. I didn't have any fight left. I said, "I just wanted you to know how I felt."

Dad pulled a thick blanket up to his chest. He was cold, although the living room was almost too warm for comfort. He was only sixty, yet his face had become gaunt. He looked old and tired. Nevertheless, he was ready to go another round with me. "You have no right to say the things you said. Writing something like that was wrong."

"Did you want me to pretend I didn't feel that way?" I asked, keeping my voice conciliatory.

"My parents treated me three times worse than I ever treated you, and I would never have written them a letter like that."

335

"Well," I said, sighing. "Maybe you should have. You never felt close to your parents when they were alive. Maybe it would have helped if you had been honest with them."

"I would have never done that."

"Times change. Things are different now."

"I'm not different!" he said.

"I'm sorry, Dad," I said, "but I am."

Dad thought this over a minute, rolling the voice machine in his hand. Bringing it to his mouth, he said, "Well, are you sorry?"

"Sorry that I wrote it? No. I wanted you to know I was hurt by the way I grew up. I wanted you to know I was angry about Tracy and Rita. I wanted you to know how hard I've tried to get through to you, how much work it has been for me. I can't be sorry for telling you the truth."

This wasn't the answer he wanted to hear. "I want you to know," Dad said, "that I'm never going to forget that letter. I've still got it, if you want to read it again." He settled back in his chair, anger hardening his features. Lifting the voice machine to his mouth, he said, "I hope your children write a letter like that to you someday."

"That's right, Dad. Be mean. Be spiteful. I don't care. I'm over that by now."

"Disrespectful is what you are."

Exasperated, I said, "I'm sorry if what I wrote hurt you! And, by the way, if I have kids they won't write me that kind of letter because I'll encourage them to talk to me about our problems. Openly."

Dad thought this was so funny he almost choked, laughing.

"I mean it," I said. "I think we should have talked about all this a long time ago. Before the cancer."

"All that talking mumbo-jumbo is a load of horseshit," Dad said, fiddling with the selvage of his blanket. "I don't work that way." Becoming angry again, he went on. "Why don't you tell the truth? You've always looked down your nose at me because I'm uneducated."

"That is not true!"

"Yes," he said. "Yes, it is."

"Ask Kelly! I've always treated her exactly the same. Before college. After college. Ask Matt."

Dad looked at me the way he used to look at some poor sucker at Roscoe's who was about to lose his money at blackjack: smug, self-assured, right.

"You don't really believe that, do you?" I asked, my eyes full of tears. "Nobody has tried as hard as I have to understand you. At least I always loved you enough to try. I never gave up on you."

Dad shifted under his blanket. He pulled a leaf of Kleenex from a box and handed it to me. Lifting the device to his mouth, the mechanical voice said, "I know I'm not a perfect father. But can you show me a man who is?" He narrowed his eyes, daring me to give him an example, then continued. "I wasn't about to live my life for you or anybody else. I lived how I wanted to live. I did the best I could, under the circumstances."

"I know, Pop," I said, feeling terrible that I had written the letter at all, feeling as though our battles had gone too far. It was time to forget our differences, once and for all.

"I know I never showed you kids much affection. I always

337

loved you, but I was never able to show you," he said. "That's how I lost your mother."

He looked at me, gauging my reaction. In all these years, we had not talked about the divorce. Yet there it was, an open wound.

"You better start being nice to your old man," he said, the tiniest hint of a smile playing on his lips. "By the look of it, I'm not going to be strong again."

"You're going to get much better," I said, willing myself to sound cheerful. "You've been through the worst now. You're only feeling weak because you're getting older. It's natural, at your age, to get a little slower. I saw Slash Monti the other day, and he looks worse than you. Sure, you won't be as healthy as you were in your forties, but you're going to get strong again, I'm sure of it."

"Let me show you something," Dad said, and although the voice machine could not convey any of the old charm, I heard something of the man of my childhood and knew there was still a bond between us, despite everything. "I haven't shown this to anyone else yet," he said. "It's too ugly." He unbuttoned his shirt and opened it over his chest, showing me where they had cut the muscle away. Pulling away the bandage at his neck—exposing the scars that went from his collarbone up to his face—I saw how the chest muscle had been grafted. My father's body was lopsided, deformed.

"I'm having a hard time standing up straight, without the muscles in my chest," he said. "I can't keep my head up for very long. Hurts too damn much. And look at this," he said, showing me his nipple. "They moved my tit too far to the right. I told them they should have just stapled that to my forehead. At least then I could have made some money in the circus."

As Dad told me about the operation and his recovery, he was blunt and unsentimental, talking about his illness as if it belonged to another guy. He was never one to feel sorry for himself, and his biggest worry was not dying but that the cancer would take him slowly, with doctors removing a piece here, a piece there. The very idea of another operation scared him to death. As he talked, he became angry. He punched his fist in his hand, as if throwing a baseball into a mitt. Bringing the mechanical larynx to his mouth, he said, "I damn well know where this cancer came from. All my doctors know it too, although nobody's going to say so."

Dad had recently submitted a claim to the VA for compensation for his exposure to herbicides. The VA had processed his claim, classifying him as 280 percent disabled, a number that combined his PTSD, cancer, and ulcer. Although he had been awarded full benefits, nowhere did the VA state that Agent Orange had been a factor in his illness. "I saw that stuff all over the leaves, all over the place," Dad said. "We never had enough water—or anything else for that matter—so we had to drink from bomb craters. I know the stuff was in there too."

When I asked him if he could get some sort of test, to confirm his exposure to herbicides, he waved his hand at me, as if shooing off a fly. "I drank and smoked my whole life, and I'm sure that contributed to this as well. I'm not blaming all my problems on the war. But I would like someone to stand up and admit that this stuff poisoned us.

I'm sick of being given the runaround—file this paper and process that claim—just because nobody will admit that they made a mess out of things." There was a sparkle of defiance in his voice, a certain fierce pride that I recognized and loved. "Look at me, will you? How do I look?"

Loving him more than ever, I said, "You look like shit."

Dad thought this was funny, and although he couldn't laugh, I knew we were done fighting for good. "No matter how sick I get," he said, using the voice machine, "I'm going to fight all the way. I'm not throwing in the towel yet. I wasn't raised to be a quitter. And neither, Danielle-my-belle, were you."

It was then I knew I had to go to Vietnam.

eighteen

Six months before my sixteenth birthday, I got my learning permit. Mom took me driving all summer in her brand-new silver Celica. The car was a stick shift, and although it would have been easier to teach me on an automatic, she wanted me to give it a shot. "It's harder to learn this way," she said, "but you'll be glad you did."

The first time we went out driving, she backed the car down the drive-way and out onto Trussoni Court. It was a cool summer morning, the dandelions and black-eyed Susans all wet with dew. I remember being a little worried that I would crash Mom's new car, but I was even more afraid that she would know I was nervous. Looking at her then, as she pulled into a patch of sunlight and cut the engine, I felt a twinge of surprise. In the years that I had lived with Dad, when she and I had not spent much time together, Mom had changed. She had grown softer. Her cheeks were no longer angular, and her short hair fell around her ears, curling at her neck. The tiniest hint of sag had developed around her eyes. Her hands (wrapped tight around the steering wheel) were woven with blue veins, just visible under the skin.

Although I had spent an occasional weekend with her, it felt as if we hadn't spoken in years. During the rocky years after the divorce, I had simply withdrawn from her presence. At the time, she had let me go my own way—it was never her style to force me to do anything—but I could see she had missed me as much as I had missed her. I was growing up, and time was taking us farther and farther away from each other, a process I had not contemplated before. I wanted her back.

"What is it?" Mom asked, when she caught me looking at her. "You nervous?"

"About driving?" I asked. "No way."

Mom took the car out of gear, pulled the emergency brake, and switched places with me. Danielle, Kelly, and Matt—the three trees Dad had planted in the front lawn—had grown tall and healthy with green leaves and fruit. Trussoni Court had two new houses on it, not enough to mark it as a fashionable address but enough to dispel the sense of complete isolation I had felt there as a child. Development had torn up the pastures down the road from us as well, replacing them with housing divisions. The land was becoming valuable. Mom had recently hired a realtor to sell the house. She and Andy would be leaving Trussoni Court and moving to town as soon as it sold.

I fastened my seat belt and put on my sunglasses, ready to go.

"Push the clutch in with your left foot," Mom said. "As you ease off the clutch, push the gas slowly with the right foot." This maneuver seemed easy enough, but when I tried it the car lurched and died. Mom was not perturbed. After years of suffering Dad's perfectionism, Mom's easygoing approach was a relief. "You're letting the clutch out too fast. Try it again," she said. "It will take a few tries before you get it."

I started the car, pushed the gas, let up on the clutch. Again, the car stalled. After three attempts (with Mom wincing as I ground the gears) I had driven less than ten feet. I put the car in neutral and let the engine idle. She smiled and put her hand on the stick shift, covering mine.

"Do you remember," Mom said, "the time you ran away from home? You were five or six, and you and I had an argument about something. What was it?"

"I probably didn't want to clean my room," I said.

"Yes, it was something like that. You told me you were leaving, so I said, *Fine, be my guest*. You packed a bag full of your toys and went out the door."

I remembered hoisting the bag over my shoulder, walking outside, and stepping gingerly down the concrete steps of the porch, ready to take on the world by myself.

"You climbed that hill right there," Mom said, pointing to a slope covered with wildflowers that overlooked the house and garden. "I didn't stop you. I thought you'd be back in a few minutes, when you got hungry and figured out that running away wasn't much fun. But you were so stubborn. God, just like your father! You sat up there for four hours, without supper, until after dark."

"Weren't you worried?"

"No, I was watching you the whole time, from the window."

"You were?" I asked, surprised. I remembered sitting on

the hill, pulling daisies and scattering them over my legs as the sun fell behind the hills, but I had never suspected that Mom was keeping an eye on me.

"Yes, I was watching you," Mom said, smiling slightly as she turned to face the windshield. "Such a drama queen! You always thought you had to go somewhere to solve things. Just after dark, you came back, went straight to your room, and went to sleep." The smile faded and her expression became, once again, impassive, practical. "That was that. You were back."

I looked at the hill again, at the patches of yellow and lavender flowers, and wanted to stop everything around me—the car's engine, the sunny afternoon, time itself—and run back up there.

"You know," Mom said, rolling down her window so the smell of alfalfa filled the car, "when we buy the house in town, there will be a room for you. You're always welcome to stay. Any time you want."

"Maybe that's a good idea," I said. "Dad's place is kind of small."

"Come on," Mom said, tapping the dash with her fingers, suddenly impatient. "Let's get this show on the road."

I practiced driving all that summer and into the fall. After a few weeks, I got the hang of shifting and drove fast and reckless, going fifty over the country roads, burning rubber and sending clouds of dust into the air, as Mom (holding the dash for dear life) screamed, "Slow down, for God's sake! Slow down!"

My driving test was scheduled on my sixteenth birthday,

in November. Mom waited in the lobby of the DMV as I took the Celica through an obstacle course of tests. I lost a few points on parallel parking (a maneuver I could not practice much out in the country), but I did well enough on everything else to pass. As I drove out of the lot (Mom buckling her seat belt), my new license in my pocket, I felt as if my life had, in one instant, changed forever.

Or at least, it changed how much I saw either of my parents. When I had a car of my own (a beat-up gold Renault), I spent all my time away from home. Driving to work, driving to truck-stop diners on the highway, always driving farther and farther away.

After school one afternoon, I drove to Dad's house and let myself in through the back door. Looking around, I saw all the things my father had done to change the place over the years. The kitchen had been remodeled, he had put new carpeting in the living room, and he had spent over two thousand dollars to clear the termites out; the gun cabinet had been moved into his room and padlocked.

Nothing had changed much in my bedroom. It was still a mess of clothes and compact discs. I pulled an old Samsonite suitcase from under my bed and put my clothes inside and hauled it out to my car. I filled the trunk with books and the backseat with my stereo. When I had finished, I made my bed, pulled the shades down over the windows, and wrote a note, leaving it on the table for Dad. It was simple, without explanation. It read: *Dear Dad, I've decided to live with Mom.* It didn't occur to me to tell him more than that. Although there were many, many reasons I could have given him, I was not able to articulate them. At sixteen, nothing seemed clear to me. I only knew I wanted to crawl out of the life I was living and into another.

A couple of hours later, the phone rang at Mom's new house. She and Andy had bought a house on the South Side, close to her office. When I got on the line, Dad said, "What's this I see: You're moving in with your mom? Why would you do that? Aren't you happy here?"

I took a deep breath and said the first thing that came to my mind. "I really can't stand you and Debbie smoking all the time. It makes my clothes smell bad."

The line was quiet for what seemed like five minutes. Then Dad said, "That never bothered you before." His voice was soft. He had grown, since the divorce, to depend on me, and suddenly I was gone. He must have known his smoking could not be the real reason I had left.

"I didn't know the smoke bothered you so much," he said.

"Well," I said, "I never really told you."

"Do you want me to quit?"

Mom, who sat at the kitchen table, checking e-mail on her laptop, raised her eyebrows, asking if I needed her help. I shrugged, which she took to mean yes. "Danielle," she said, louder than she needed to, "I need to use the phone."

"Mom wants the phone," I said, relieved. "I've got to go, Dad. Look, can we talk about this later?"

"All right," Dad said, his voice weak. "Do what you want."

After I hung up the phone, I leaned against the counter, stunned by what I had done. It was as if I had accidentally stepped off the edge of a tall building. I could not step forward; I could not step back. Solid ground had been yanked out from below. I was free-falling, with nowhere to go but down.

Mom typed away on her laptop. Taking a sip of coffee, she said, "Well, that was easy enough." And although she was right—there had been no fighting and screaming, no anger at all—I could not forget something I had heard in my father's voice, something I had never heard before and I would never hear again: the gentle resignation of defeat.

afterword

A few years after my trip to Vietnam, I flew to Wisconsin to see my father. Dad wasn't a regular at Roscoe's anymore—age and sickness had made him reclusive—but every once in a while he'd go to the North Side to have a drink, for old time's sake. Roscoe's had a new owner and a new name and had been remodeled. The façade was hidden behind terracotta brown stucco; the interior suffered from an abundance of light. I didn't recognize anyone in the place. The crowd seemed younger and happier than I remembered.

I had a baby of my own by then, a boy whose eyes were so free of the past, so innocent, that I promised I would do everything I could to protect him. I tucked my son in a blanket and took him with me to the bar, where I climbed on a stool next to my father. It felt just like old times, only now I was the one with problems. I had recently left my son's father and was raising my baby alone. Although Kelly had done a great job of raising her son on her own—she had recently graduated from college, and was hoping to begin a career as a social worker—Dad was skeptical. He did not approve of my decision. He believed it was a sign of a weak character to walk away from a challenge. As Dad lectured me, I handed him my son and rested my head on the bar. The baby had been up all night, crying, and I was exhausted. I'd never expected that raising a child would be so much work. When I complained that I hadn't slept a full night in nearly a year, Dad's eyes sparkled. "Yes," he said, holding the voice machine to his lips. "Kids can be a real pain in the ass sometimes." He bounced his grandson on his lap, stroking his curly blond hair. I could see a slight resemblance between them, something in the eyes. "But then again, they can be pretty damn wonderful too."

Over drinks, Dad told me about a trip he and Debbie had recently made, to see Mrs. Goodman, in Knoxville. He had never forgotten the afternoon that Goodman died, and, as he had once told me, he had always felt somehow responsible for Goodman's death, as if Tommy had taken his bullet.

They packed the Cadillac and drove through small towns, sleeping in motels and Super 8s along the way. It was the first time Debbie had been south of Chicago, and they tried to see the trip as a vacation. Thomas Goodman's mother lived in a huge house surrounded by land. When they rang the bell, Mrs. Goodman was waiting. She led them inside, through vast empty rooms. Dad knew Tommy Goodman had come from money, but he never knew just how much until he saw the house. It looked exactly like he had always imagined a plantation house to look, with a columned porch and rooms that went on forever.

Mrs. Goodman was tall and thin, like her son had been.

Her husband, Thomas Goodman Sr., had died not long after Tom, and Mrs. Goodman had lived alone for many years. Dad thanked her for sending him Christmas cards every year. "It was nice of you to think of me," he said.

Mrs. Goodman led my father and Debbie into the sitting room, where she served them coffee in china cups. Pictures of Tommy were hung around the room. My father stood, to get a better look. He saw Tommy as a boy of four, sitting in his mother's lap, a happy-go-lucky grin on his face. He saw Tommy as a teenager, dressed for the prom, his arm around the girlfriend who had sent him a letter in Vietnam, breaking their engagement. He saw Tommy Goodman as he had not seen him before—not as a tunnel rat or even as a buddy but as somebody's son.

My father placed Tommy's camera on the coffee table. He said, "I've been keeping this, meaning to give it to you. I'm sorry it took me so long."

Mrs. Goodman took the camera in her hands, as if weighing it. "You know," she said, "Thomas volunteered for duty. His father thought it the right thing at the time; we both did. But one thing I've always wondered about. Nobody has ever been able to tell me how my son died. But you were there with him, weren't you?"

When my father said yes, he had been there with Tommy, Mrs. Goodman wanted him to tell her what had happened that day.

"Are you sure you want to know?" Dad asked her.

"Yes," she said firmly. "Please. I need to know."

After my father told her the story of Tommy's death—about the tunnels and the jungles and the terrible morning when Tommy had taken my father's bullet—Mrs. Goodman looked at him, tears running down her cheeks, and said, "You are a good man for coming down here like this. And a good friend to Tommy. God bless you for that. I never knew what happened to him. In all these years, I never knew for sure."

It was strange, listening to my father speak. His whole expression was full of sadness, yet his mechanical larynx made him sound robotic, unemotional. "You can't imagine how sad she was," he said. Resting his hand upon my son's arm, he continued, "You just can't imagine how great the loss, until you've got a child of your own."

I knew, as I sat with my father and my son, that Dad was right. Fifty-eight thousand American soldiers had died in Vietnam, and yet those numbers meant nothing to me until I walked in Washington alongside the dark mirror of the Vietnam Veterans Memorial wall and traced one name, THOMAS GOODMAN, with the tips of my fingers. Millions of Vietnamese had died in the war, but these deaths never touched me the way one Vietnamese soldier, whose picture I found in my childhood, had. And although twenty thousand American children were orphaned by the war, it was only when I looked at my own life that I saw the hole that Vietnam created, for all of us.

AFTER MY VISIT, DAD DROVE ME TO THE AIRPORT IN HIS new Chevy. It was an American-made gas guzzler, all silver and chrome, a truck unlike any he had driven when I was a kid. My son was buckled in his car seat, between us, but that didn't make Dad cautious; he drove over the speed limit, taking the back way to the airport, still running all these years later. As we drove alongside the Mississippi River, a white paddleboat floated into view. Dad veered over a viaduct and tapped the brake, slowing to twenty-five miles an hour. "The cops always sit right at the bottom," he said, holding his mechanical larynx between his fingers, like a cigarette. "I know their game by now."

At the airport, Dad insisted on unloading my suitcase from the bed of the truck and carrying it inside. Still weak, he couldn't carry it well. When I offered to help, he turned away, embarrassed, and struggled on. As we walked into the airport, a crowd of people stood by, holding signs that read WELCOME HOME with great yellow balloons and ribbons tied around the edges. Dad stopped dead in his tracks, set my suitcase down, and stared, as if he'd been punched in the gut. "I'll be damned," Dad said. "I know that family. They're from up around Romance. I wonder which of their boys is coming home." Dad walked over to the crowd and greeted them, shaking hands and slapping backs, one of the gang. He was too embarrassed to use his voice machine with anyone but family, so he wrote everything on an erasable whiteboard. Unable to go with my father, I stayed behind, holding my son.

"You know," Dad said, when he'd returned, "you've got a cousin in Iraq." Albert, the uncle my father had been feuding with for twenty-five years, had recently watched his son Nathan go off to fight. "I ought to give Al a call," Dad said, contemplating the terms of the truce, "and see how his boy is doing."

Dad picked up my suitcase and shuffled along to the

check-in desk. As I was getting my seat assignment, Dad watched the family from Romance. He couldn't seem to keep his eyes off them. "My older brother Gene picked me up from the airport when I got back," he said, using his mechanical larynx. "Nobody else came. Just Gene. He had a beauty of a car and he drove me straight into town for a beer. He told me, *Listen, Danny, you're free now. You've got to forget about what happened over there and get your life together.* And that's just what I tried to do."

As we walked toward the gates, a voice on a loudspeaker announced that my flight would be boarding in ten minutes.

"What Gene forgot to tell me," Dad said, "is that no matter how hard you try, it doesn't really end."

When it was time to go, Dad leaned and kissed my son gently on the cheek. He didn't speak to him—he didn't like to talk to the baby with his robot voice; he thought it would scare him—so he waved goodbye, making goofy faces, hoping to get my son to laugh. As we walked to the metal detectors, my son looked back at his grandpa, giggling, waving bye-bye to the silent old man with the silly grin on his face.

acknowledgments

A special thank you to my father, Dan Trussoni. Thanks also to my mother, stepfather, and Debbie Trussoni. Thank you Kelly, Matt, Phil, Rita, and Tracy. *Blagodaria* to Nikolai, Lachezar, Milena, and Ogniana, my Bulgarian family who provided patronage and Kamenitza as I wrote the first draft. Thanks also to Jesse Lee Kercheval, Ron Kuka, and Susan Bernstein at the University of Wisconsin. I am grateful to the James A. Michener/Copernicus Society of America, and to those at the Iowa Writers' Workshop—James Alan McPherson, Marilynne Robinson, Lan Samantha Chang, and Connie Brothers—who offered guidance. Above all, I owe thanks to Amy Williams and George Hodgman for believing in this book from the beginning.

Visit **www.picador.com** to read more about all our books and to buy them. You will also find features, author interviews and news of any author events, and you can sign up for e-newsletters so that you're always first to hear about our new releases.